Haskell Data Analysis Cookbook

Explore intuitive data analysis techniques and powerful machine learning methods using over 130 practical recipes

Nishant Shukla

BIRMINGHAM - MUMBAI

Haskell Data Analysis Cookbook

First published: June 2014

Production reference: 1180614

Published by Packt Publishing Ltd.
Livery Place
35 Livery Street
Birmingham B3 2PB, UK.

ISBN 978-1-78328-633-1

www.packtpub.com

Cover image by Jarek Blaminsky (milak6@wp.pl)

Credits

Author
Nishant Shukla

Reviewers
Lorenzo Bolla

James Church

Andreas Hammar

Marisa Reddy

Commissioning Editor
Akram Hussain

Acquisition Editor
Sam Wood

Content Development Editor
Shaon Basu

Technical Editors
Shruti Rawool

Nachiket Vartak

Copy Editors
Sarang Chari

Janbal Dharmaraj

Gladson Monteiro

Deepa Nambiar

Karuna Narayanan

Alfida Paiva

Project Coordinator
Mary Alex

Proofreaders
Paul Hindle

Jonathan Todd

Bernadette Watkins

Indexer
Hemangini Bari

Graphics
Sheetal Aute

Ronak Dhruv

Valentina Dsilva

Disha Haria

Production Coordinator
Arvindkumar Gupta

Cover Work
Arvindkumar Gupta

About the Author

Nishant Shukla is a computer scientist with a passion for mathematics. Throughout the years, he has worked for a handful of start-ups and large corporations including WillowTree Apps, Microsoft, Facebook, and Foursquare.

Stepping into the world of Haskell was his excuse for better understanding Category Theory at first, but eventually, he found himself immersed in the language. His semester-long introductory Haskell course in the engineering school at the University of Virginia (http://shuklan.com/haskell) has been accessed by individuals from over 154 countries around the world, gathering over 45,000 unique visitors.

Besides Haskell, he is a proponent of decentralized Internet and open source software. His academic research in the fields of Machine Learning, Neural Networks, and Computer Vision aim to supply a fundamental contribution to the world of computing.

Between discussing primes, paradoxes, and palindromes, it is my delight to invent the future with Marisa.

With appreciation beyond expression, but an expression nonetheless—thank you Mom (Suman), Dad (Umesh), and Natasha.

About the Reviewers

Lorenzo Bolla holds a PhD in Numerical Methods and works as a software engineer in London. His interests span from functional languages to high-performance computing to web applications. When he's not coding, he is either playing piano or basketball.

James Church completed his PhD in Engineering Science with a focus on computational geometry at the University of Mississippi in 2014 under the advice of Dr. Yixin Chen. While a graduate student at the University of Mississippi, he taught a number of courses for the Computer and Information Science's undergraduates, including a popular class on data analysis techniques. Following his graduation, he joined the faculty of the University of West Georgia's Department of Computer Science as an assistant professor. He is also a reviewer of *The Manga Guide To Regression Analysis*, written by *Shin Takahashi, Iroha Inoue, and Trend-Pro Co. Ltd.*, and published by *No Starch Press*.

> I would like to thank Dr. Conrad Cunningham for recommending me to Packt Publishing as a reviewer.

Andreas Hammar is a Computer Science student at Norwegian University of Science and Technology and a Haskell enthusiast. He started programming when he was 12, and over the years, he has programmed in many different languages. Around five years ago, he discovered functional programming, and since 2011, he has contributed over 700 answers in the Haskell tag on Stack Overflow, making him one of the top Haskell contributors on the site. He is currently working part time as a web developer at the Student Society in Trondheim, Norway.

Marisa Reddy is pursuing her B.A. in Computer Science and Economics at the University of Virginia. Her primary interests lie in computer vision and financial modeling, two areas in which functional programming is rife with possibilities.

I congratulate Nishant Shukla for the tremendous job he did in writing this superb book of recipes and thank him for the opportunity to be a part of the process.

www.PacktPub.com

Support files, eBooks, discount offers, and more

You might want to visit www.PacktPub.com for support files and downloads related to your book.

The accompanying source code is also available at https://github.com/BinRoot/Haskell-Data-Analysis-Cookbook.

Did you know that Packt offers eBook versions of every book published, with PDF and ePub files available? You can upgrade to the eBook version at www.PacktPub.com and as a print book customer, you are entitled to a discount on the eBook copy. Get in touch with us at service@packtpub.com for more details.

At www.PacktPub.com, you can also read a collection of free technical articles, sign up for a range of free newsletters and receive exclusive discounts and offers on Packt books and eBooks.

http://PacktLib.PacktPub.com

Do you need instant solutions to your IT questions? PacktLib is Packt's online digital book library. Here, you can access, read and search across Packt's entire library of books.

Why Subscribe?

- ▸ Fully searchable across every book published by Packt
- ▸ Copy and paste, print and bookmark content
- ▸ On demand and accessible via web browser

Free Access for Packt account holders

If you have an account with Packt at www.PacktPub.com, you can use this to access PacktLib today and view nine entirely free books. Simply use your login credentials for immediate access.

Table of Contents

Preface

Data analysis is something that many of us have done before, maybe even without knowing it. It is the essential art of gathering and examining pieces of information to suit a variety of purposes—from visual inspection to machine learning techniques. Through data analysis, we can harness the meaning from information littered all around the digital realm. It enables us to resolve the most peculiar inquiries, perhaps even summoning new ones in the process.

Haskell acts as our conduit for robust data analysis. For some, Haskell is a programming language reserved to the most elite researchers in academia and industry. Yet, we see it charming one of the fastest growing cultures of open source developers around the world. The growth of Haskell is a sign that people are uncovering its magnificent functional pureness, resilient type safety, and remarkable expressiveness. Flip the pages of this book to see it all in action.

Haskell Data Analysis Cookbook is more than just a fusion of two entrancing topics in computing. It is also a learning tool for the Haskell programming language and an introduction to simple data analysis practices. Use it as a Swiss Army Knife of algorithms and code snippets. Try a recipe a day, like a kata for your mind. Breeze through the book for creative inspiration from catalytic examples. Also, most importantly, dive deep into the province of data analysis in Haskell.

Of course, none of this would have been possible without a thorough feedback from the technical editors, brilliant chapter illustrations by Lonku (http://lonku.tumblr.com), and helpful layout and editing support by Packt Publishing.

What this book covers

Chapter 1, *The Hunt for Data*, identifies core approaches in reading data from various external sources such as CSV, JSON, XML, HTML, MongoDB, and SQLite.

Chapter 2, *Integrity and Inspection*, explains the importance of cleaning data through recipes about trimming whitespaces, lexing, and regular expression matching.

Chapter 3, The Science of Words, introduces common string manipulation algorithms, including base conversions, substring matching, and computing the edit distance.

Chapter 4, Data Hashing, covers essential hashing functions such as MD5, SHA256, GeoHashing, and perceptual hashing.

Chapter 5, The Dance with Trees, establishes an understanding of the tree data structure through examples that include tree traversals, balancing trees, and Huffman coding.

Chapter 6, Graph Fundamentals, manifests rudimentary algorithms for graphical networks such as graph traversals, visualization, and maximal clique detection.

Chapter 7, Statistics and Analysis, begins the investigation of important data analysis techniques that encompass regression algorithms, Bayesian networks, and neural networks.

Chapter 8, Clustering and Classification, involves quintessential analysis methods that involve k-means clustering, hierarchical clustering, constructing decision trees, and implementing the k-Nearest Neighbors classifier.

Chapter 9, Parallel and Concurrent Design, introduces advanced topics in Haskell such as forking I/O actions, mapping over lists in parallel, and benchmarking performance.

Chapter 10, Real-time Data, incorporates streamed data interactions from Twitter, Internet Relay Chat (IRC), and sockets.

Chapter 11, Visualizing Data, deals with sundry approaches to plotting graphs, including line charts, bar graphs, scatter plots, and `D3.js` visualizations.

Chapter 12, Exporting and Presenting, concludes the book with an enumeration of algorithms for exporting data to CSV, JSON, HTML, MongoDB, and SQLite.

What you need for this book

▶ First of all, you need an operating system that supports the Haskell Platform such as Linux, Windows, or Mac OS X.

▶ You must install the Glasgow Haskell Compiler 7.6 or above and Cabal, both of which can be obtained from the Haskell Platform from `http://www.haskell.org/platform`.

▶ You can obtain the accompanying source code for every recipe on GitHub at `https://github.com/BinRoot/Haskell-Data-Analysis-Cookbook`.

Who this book is for

► Those who have begun tinkering with Haskell but desire stimulating examples to kick-start a new project will find this book indispensable.

► Data analysts new to Haskell should use this as a reference for functional approaches to data-modeling problems.

► A dedicated beginner to both the Haskell language and data analysis is blessed with the maximal potential for learning new topics covered in this book.

Conventions

In this book, you will find a number of styles of text that distinguish between different kinds of information. Here are some examples of these styles, and an explanation of their meaning.

Code words in text, database table names, folder names, filenames, file extensions, pathnames, dummy URLs, user input, and Twitter handles are shown as follows: "Apply the `readString` function to the input, and get all date documents."

A block of code is set as follows:

```
main :: IO ()
main = do
  input <- readFile "input.txt"
  print input
```

When we wish to draw your attention to a particular part of a code block, the relevant lines or items are set in bold:

```
main :: IO ()
main = do
  input <- readFile "input.txt"
  print input
```

Any command-line input or output is written as follows:

```
$ runhaskell Main.hs
```

New terms and **important words** are shown in bold. Words that you see on the screen, in menus, or dialog boxes for example, appear in the text like this: "Under the **Downloads** section, download the cabal source package."

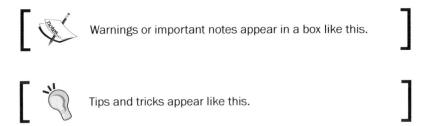

> Warnings or important notes appear in a box like this.

> Tips and tricks appear like this.

Reader feedback

Feedback from our readers is always welcome. Let us know what you think about this book— what you liked or may have disliked. Reader feedback is important for us to develop titles that you really get the most out of.

To send us general feedback, simply send an e-mail to feedback@packtpub.com, and mention the book title via the subject of your message.

If there is a topic that you have expertise in and you are interested in either writing or contributing to a book, see our author guide on www.packtpub.com/authors.

Customer support

Now that you are the proud owner of a Packt book, we have a number of things to help you to get the most from your purchase.

Downloading the example code

You can download the example code files for all Packt books you have purchased from your account at http://www.packtpub.com. If you purchased this book elsewhere, you can visit http://www.packtpub.com/support and register to have the files e-mailed directly to you. Also, we highly suggest obtaining all source code from GitHub available at https://github.com/BinRoot/Haskell-Data-Analysis-Cookbook.

Errata

Although we have taken every care to ensure the accuracy of our content, mistakes do happen. If you find a mistake in one of our books—maybe a mistake in the text or the code—we would be grateful if you would report this to us. By doing so, you can save other readers from frustration and help us improve subsequent versions of this book. If you find any errata, please report them by visiting `http://www.packtpub.com/submit-errata`, selecting your book, clicking on the **errata submission form** link, and entering the details of your errata. Once your errata are verified, your submission will be accepted and the errata will be uploaded on our website, or added to any list of existing errata, under the Errata section of that title. Any existing errata can be viewed by selecting your title from `http://www.packtpub.com/support`. Code revisions can also be made on the accompanying GitHub repository located at `https://github.com/BinRoot/Haskell-Data-Analysis-Cookbook`.

Piracy

Piracy of copyright material on the Internet is an ongoing problem across all media. At Packt, we take the protection of our copyright and licenses very seriously. If you come across any illegal copies of our works, in any form, on the Internet, please provide us with the location address or website name immediately so that we can pursue a remedy.

Please contact us at `copyright@packtpub.com` with a link to the suspected pirated material.

We appreciate your help in protecting our authors, and our ability to bring you valuable content.

Questions

You can contact us at `questions@packtpub.com` if you are having a problem with any aspect of the book, and we will do our best to address it.

1
The Hunt for Data

In this chapter, we will cover the following recipes:

- ▶ Harnessing data from various sources
- ▶ Accumulating text data from a file path
- ▶ Catching I/O code faults
- ▶ Keeping and representing data from a CSV file
- ▶ Examining a JSON file with the aeson package
- ▶ Reading an XML file using the HXT package
- ▶ Capturing table rows from an HTML page
- ▶ Understanding how to perform HTTP GET requests
- ▶ Learning how to perform HTTP POST requests
- ▶ Traversing online directories for data
- ▶ Using MongoDB queries in Haskell
- ▶ Reading from a remote MongoDB server
- ▶ Exploring data from a SQLite database

Introduction

Data is everywhere, logging is cheap, and analysis is inevitable. One of the most fundamental concepts of this chapter is based on gathering useful data. After building a large collection of usable text, which we call the corpus, we must learn to represent this content in code. The primary focus will be first on obtaining data and later on enumerating ways of representing it.

Gathering data is arguably as important as analyzing it to extrapolate results and form valid generalizable claims. It is a scientific pursuit; therefore, great care must and will be taken to ensure unbiased and representative sampling. We recommend following along closely in this chapter because the remainder of the book depends on having a source of data to work with. Without data, there isn't much to analyze, so we should carefully observe the techniques laid out to build our own formidable corpus.

The first recipe enumerates various sources to start gathering data online. The next few recipes deal with using local data of different file formats. We then learn how to download data from the Internet using our Haskell code. Finally, we finish this chapter with a couple of recipes on using databases in Haskell.

Harnessing data from various sources

Information can be described as structured, unstructured, or sometimes a mix of the two—semi-structured.

In a very general sense, structured data is anything that can be parsed by an algorithm. Common examples include JSON, CSV, and XML. If given structured data, we can design a piece of code to dissect the underlying format and easily produce useful results. As mining structured data is a deterministic process, it allows us to automate the parsing. This in effect lets us gather more input to feed our data analysis algorithms.

Unstructured data is everything else. It is data not defined in a specified manner. Written languages such as English are often regarded as unstructured because of the difficulty in parsing a data model out of a natural sentence.

In our search for good data, we will often find a mix of structured and unstructured text. This is called semi-structured text.

This recipe will primarily focus on obtaining structured and semi-structured data from the following sources.

 Unlike most recipes in this book, this recipe does not contain any code. The best way to read this book is by skipping around to the recipes that interest you.

How to do it...

We will browse through the links provided in the following sections to build up a list of sources to harness interesting data in usable formats. However, this list is not at all exhaustive.

Some of these sources have an **Application Programming Interface** (**API**) that allows more sophisticated access to interesting data. An API specifies the interactions and defines how data is communicated.

News

The New York Times has one of the most polished API documentation to access anything from real-estate data to article search results. This documentation can be found at `http://developer.nytimes.com`.

The Guardian also supports a massive datastore with over a million articles at `http://www.theguardian.com/data`.

USA TODAY provides some interesting resources on books, movies, and music reviews. The technical documentation can be found at `http://developer.usatoday.com`.

The BBC features some interesting API endpoints including information on BBC programs, and music located at `http://www.bbc.co.uk/developer/technology/apis.html`.

Private

Facebook, Twitter, Instagram, Foursquare, Tumblr, SoundCloud, Meetup, and many other social networking sites support APIs to access some degree of social information.

For specific APIs such as weather or sports, Mashape is a centralized search engine to narrow down the search to some lesser-known sources. Mashape is located at `https://www.mashape.com/`

Most data sources can be visualized using the Google Public Data search located at `http://www.google.com/publicdata`.

For a list of all countries with names in various data formats, refer to the repository located at `https://github.com/umpirsky/country-list`.

Academic

Some data sources are hosted openly by universities around the world for research purposes.

To analyze health care data, the University of Washington has published Institute for Health Metrics and Evaluation (IHME) to collect rigorous and comparable measurement of the world's most important health problems. Navigate to `http://www.healthdata.org` for more information.

The MNIST database of handwritten digits from NYU, Google Labs, and Microsoft Research is a training set of normalized and centered samples for handwritten digits. Download the data from `http://yann.lecun.com/exdb/mnist`.

Nonprofits

Human Development Reports publishes annual updates ranging from international data about adult literacy to the number of people owning personal computers. It describes itself as having a variety of public international sources and represents the most current statistics available for those indicators. More information is available at `http://hdr.undp.org/en/statistics`.

The World Bank is the source for poverty and world development data. It regards itself as a free source that enables open access to data about development in countries around the globe. Find more information at `http://data.worldbank.org/`.

The World Health Organization provides data and analyses for monitoring the global health situation. See more information at `http://www.who.int/research/en`.

UNICEF also releases interesting statistics, as the quote from their website suggests:

> *"The UNICEF database contains statistical tables for child mortality, diseases, water sanitation, and more vitals. UNICEF claims to play a central role in monitoring the situation of children and women—assisting countries in collecting and analyzing data, helping them develop methodologies and indicators, maintaining global databases, disseminating and publishing data. Find the resources at* `http://www.unicef.org/statistics`*."*

The United Nations hosts interesting publicly available political statistics at `http://www.un.org/en/databases`.

The United States government

If we crave the urge to discover patterns in the United States (U.S.) government like Nicholas Cage did in the feature film National Treasure (2004), then `http://www.data.gov/` is our go-to source. It's the U.S. government's active effort to provide useful data. It is described as a place to increase "public access to high-value, machine-readable datasets generated by the executive branch of the Federal Government". Find more information at `http://www.data.gov`.

The United States Census Bureau releases population counts, housing statistics, area measurements, and more. These can be found at `http://www.census.gov`.

Accumulating text data from a file path

One of the easiest ways to get started with processing input is by reading raw text from a local file. In this recipe, we will be extracting all the text from a specific file path. Furthermore, to do something interesting with the data, we will count the number of words per line.

 Haskell is a purely functional programming language, right? Sure, but obtaining input from outside the code introduces impurity. For elegance and reusability, we must carefully separate pure from impure code.

Getting ready

We will first create an `input.txt` text file with a couple of lines of text to be read by the program. We keep this file in an easy-to-access directory because it will be referenced later. For example, the text file we're dealing with contains a seven-line quote by Plato. Here's what our terminal prints when we issue the following command:

```
$ cat input.txt


And how will you inquire, Socrates,
into that which you know not?
What will you put forth as the subject of inquiry?
And if you find what you want,
how will you ever know that
this is what you did not know?
```

How to do it...

Create a new file to start coding. We call our file Main.hs.

1. As with all executable Haskell programs, start by defining and implementing the `main` function, as follows:

```
main :: IO ()

main = do
```

2. Use Haskell's `readFile :: FilePath -> IO String` function to extract data from an `input.txt` file path. Note that a file path is just a synonym for `String`. With the string in memory, pass it into a `countWords` function to count the number of words in each line, as shown in the following steps:

```
input <- readFile "input.txt"

print $ countWords input
```

3. Lastly, define our pure function, `countWords`, as follows:

```
countWords :: String -> [Int]

countWords input = map (length.words) (lines input)
```

4. The program will print out the number of words per line represented as a list of numbers as follows:

```
$ runhaskell Main.hs


[6,6,10,7,6,7]
```

How it works...

Haskell provides useful input and output (I/O) capabilities for reading input and writing output in different ways. In our case, we use `readFile` to specify a path of a file to be read. Using the `do` keyword in `main` suggests that we are joining several IO actions together. The output of `readFile` is an I/O string, which means it is an I/O action that returns a `String` type.

Now we're about to get a bit technical. Pay close attention. Alternatively, smile and nod. In Haskell, the I/O data type is an instance of something called a Monad. This allows us to use the `<-` notation to draw the string out of this I/O action. We then make use of the string by feeding it into our `countWords` function that counts the number of words in each line. Notice how we separated the `countWords` function apart from the impure `main` function.

Finally, we print the output of `countWords`. The `$` notation means we are using a function application to avoid excessive parenthesis in our code. Without it, the last line of `main` would look like `print (countWords input)`.

See also

For simplicity's sake, this code is easy to read but very fragile. If an `input.txt` file does not exist, then running the code will immediately crash the program. For example, the following command will generate the error message:

```
$ runhaskell Main.hs
```

```
Main.hs: input.txt: openFile: does not exist...
```

To make this code fault tolerant, refer to the *Catching I/O code faults* recipe.

Catching I/O code faults

Making sure our code doesn't crash in the process of data mining or analysis is a substantially genuine concern. Some computations may take hours, if not days. Haskell gifts us with type safety and strong checks to help ensure a program will not fail, but we must also take care to double-check edge cases where faults may occur.

For instance, a program may crash ungracefully if the local file path is not found. In the previous recipe, there was a strong dependency on the existence of `input.txt` in our code. If the program is unable to find the file, it will produce the following error:

```
mycode: input.txt: openFile: does not exist (No such file or directory)
```

Naturally, we should decouple the file path dependency by enabling the user to specify his/her file path as well as by not crashing in the event that the file is not found.

Consider the following revision of the source code.

How to do it...

Create a new file, name it `Main.hs`, and perform the following steps:

1. First, import a library to catch fatal errors as follows:

   ```
   import Control.Exception (catch, SomeException)
   ```

2. Next, import a library to get command-line arguments so that the file path is dynamic. We use the following line of code to do this:

   ```
   import System.Environment (getArgs)
   ```

3. Continuing as before, define and implement `main` as follows:

   ```
   main :: IO ()
   main = do
   ```

4. Define a `fileName` string depending on the user-provided argument, defaulting to `input.txt` if there is no argument. The argument is obtained by retrieving an array of strings from the library function, `getArgs :: IO [String]`, as shown in the following steps:

   ```
   args <- getArgs
     let filename = case args of
        (a:_) -> a
            _ -> "input.txt"
   ```

5. Now apply `readFile` on this path, but catch any errors using the library's `catch :: Exception e => IO a -> (e -> IO a) -> IO a` function. The first argument to catch is the computation to run, and the second argument is the handler to invoke if an exception is raised, as shown in the following commands:

   ```
   input <- catch (readFile fileName)
       $ \err -> print (err::SomeException) >> return ""
   ```

6. The `input` string will be empty if there were any errors reading the file. We can now use `input` for any purpose using the following command:

   ```
   print $ countWords input
   ```

7. Don't forget to define the `countWords` function as follows:

   ```
   countWords input = map (length.words) (lines input)
   ```

How it works...

This recipe demonstrates two ways to catch errors, listed as follows:

- Firstly, we use a case expression that pattern matches against any argument passed in. Therefore, if no arguments are passed, the `args` list is empty, and the last pattern, `"_"`, is caught, resulting in a default filename of `input.txt`.

- Secondly, we use the catch function to handle an error if something goes wrong. When having trouble reading a file, we allow the code to continue running by setting `input` to an empty string.

There's more...

Conveniently, Haskell also comes with a `doesFileExist :: FilePath -> IO Bool` function from the `System.Directory` module. We can simplify the preceding code by modifying the `input <- ...` line. It can be replaced with the following snippet of code:

```
exists <- doesFileExist filename
input <- if exists then readFile filename else return ""
```

In this case, the code reads the file as an input only if it exists. Do not forget to add the following `import` line at the top of the source code:

```
import System.Directory (doesFileExist)
```

Keeping and representing data from a CSV file

Comma Separated Value (**CSV**) is a format to represent a table of values in plain text. It's often used to interact with data from spreadsheets. The specifications for CSV are described in RFC 4180, available at `http://tools.ietf.org/html/rfc4180`.

In this recipe, we will read a local CSV file called `input.csv` consisting of various names and their corresponding ages. Then, to do something useful with the data, we will find the oldest person.

Getting ready

Prepare a simple CSV file with a list of names and their corresponding ages. This can be done using a text editor or by exporting from a spreadsheet, as shown in the following figure:

	A	B
1	**name**	**age**
2	Alex	22
3	Anish	22
4	Becca	23
5	Jasdev	22
6	John	21
7	Jonathon	21
8	Kelvin	22
9	Marisa	19
10	Shiv	22
11	Vinay	22

The raw `input.csv` file contains the following text:

```
$ cat input.csv

name,age
Alex,22
Anish,22
Becca,23
Jasdev,22
John,21
Jonathon,21
Kelvin,22
Marisa,19
Shiv,22
Vinay,22
```

The code also depends on the `csv` library. We may install the library through Cabal using the following command:

```
$ cabal install csv
```

How to do it...

1. Import the `csv` library using the following line of code:

```
import Text.CSV
```

2. Define and implement `main`, where we will read and parse the CSV file, as shown in the following code:

```
main :: IO ()
main = do
    let fileName = "input.csv"
    input <- readFile fileName
```

3. Apply `parseCSV` to the filename to obtain a list of rows, representing the tabulated data. The output of `parseCSV` is `Either ParseError CSV`, so ensure that we consider both the `Left` and `Right` cases:

```
    let csv = parseCSV fileName input
    either handleError doWork csv
handleError csv = putStrLn "error parsing"
doWork csv = (print.findOldest.tail) csv
```

4. Now we can work with the CSV data. In this example, we find and print the row containing the oldest person, as shown in the following code snippet:

```
findOldest :: [Record] -> Record
findOldest [] = []
findOldest xs = foldl1
            (\a x -> if age x > age a then x else a) xs

age [a,b] = toInt a

toInt :: String -> Int
toInt = read
```

5. After running `main`, the code should produce the following output:

$ runhaskell Main.hs

["Becca", "23"]

 We can also use the `parseCSVFromFile` function to directly get the CSV representation from a filename instead of using `readFile` followed `parseCSV`.

How it works...

The CSV data structure in Haskell is represented as a list of records. `Record` is merely a list of `Fields`, and `Field` is a type synonym for `String`. In other words, it is a collection of rows representing a table, as shown in the following figure:

The `parseCSV` library function returns an `Either` type, with the `Left` side being a `ParseError` and the `Right` side being the list of lists. The `Either l r` data type is very similar to the `Maybe a` type which has the `Just a` or `Nothing` constructor.

We use the `either` function to handle the `Left` and `Right` cases. The `Left` case handles the error, and the `Right` case handles the actual work to be done on the data. In this recipe, the `Right` side is a `Record`. The fields in `Record` are accessible through any list operations such as `head`, `last`, `!!`, and so on.

Examining a JSON file with the aeson package

JavaScript Object Notation (**JSON**) is a way to represent key-value pairs in plain text. The format is described extensively in RFC 4627 (http://www.ietf.org/rfc/rfc4627).

In this recipe, we will parse a JSON description about a person. We often encounter JSON in APIs from web applications.

Getting ready

Install the `aeson` library from hackage using Cabal.

Prepare an `input.json` file representing data about a mathematician, such as the one in the following code snippet:

```
$ cat input.json
```

```
{"name":"Gauss", "nationality":"German", "born":1777, "died":1855}
```

We will be parsing this JSON and representing it as a usable data type in Haskell.

How to do it...

1. Use the `OverloadedStrings` language extension to represent strings as `ByteString`, as shown in the following line of code:

    ```
    {-# LANGUAGE OverloadedStrings #-}
    ```

2. Import `aeson` as well as some helper functions as follows:

    ```
    import Data.Aeson
    import Control.Applicative
    import qualified Data.ByteString.Lazy as B
    ```

3. Create the data type corresponding to the JSON structure, as shown in the following code:

    ```
    data Mathematician = Mathematician
                    { name :: String
                    , nationality :: String
                    , born :: Int
                    , died :: Maybe Int
                    }
    ```

4. Provide an instance for the `parseJSON` function, as shown in the following code snippet:

    ```
    instance FromJSON Mathematician where
      parseJSON (Object v) = Mathematician
                            <$> (v .: "name")
                            <*> (v .: "nationality")
                            <*> (v .: "born")
                            <*> (v .:? "died")
    ```

5. Define and implement `main` as follows:

    ```
    main :: IO ()
    main = do
    ```

6. Read the input and decode the JSON, as shown in the following code snippet:

    ```
    input <- B.readFile "input.json"

    let mm = decode input :: Maybe Mathematician

    case mm of
      Nothing -> print "error parsing JSON"
      Just m -> (putStrLn.greet) m
    ```

7. Now we will do something interesting with the data as follows:

```
greet m = (show.name) m ++
              " was born in the year " ++
              (show.born) m
```

8. We can run the code to see the following output:

```
$ runhaskell Main.hs


"Gauss" was born in the year 1777
```

How it works...

Aeson takes care of the complications in representing JSON. It creates native usable data out of a structured text. In this recipe, we use the `.:` and `.:?` functions provided by the `Data.Aeson` module.

As the `Aeson` package uses `ByteStrings` instead of `Strings`, it is very helpful to tell the compiler that characters between quotation marks should be treated as the proper data type. This is done in the first line of the code which invokes the `OverloadedStrings` language extension.

 Language extensions such as `OverloadedStrings` are currently supported only by the **Glasgow Haskell Compiler** (**GHC**).

We use the `decode` function provided by Aeson to transform a string into a data type. It has the type `FromJSON a => B.ByteString -> Maybe a`. Our `Mathematician` data type must implement an instance of the `FromJSON` typeclass to properly use this function. Fortunately, the only required function for implementing `FromJSON` is `parseJSON`. The syntax used in this recipe for implementing `parseJSON` is a little strange, but this is because we're leveraging applicative functions and lenses, which are more advanced Haskell topics.

The `.:` function has two arguments, `Object` and `Text`, and returns a `Parser` a data type. As per the documentation, it retrieves the value associated with the given key of an object. This function is used if the key and the value exist in the JSON document. The `:?` function also retrieves the associated value from the given key of an object, but the existence of the key and value are not mandatory. So, we use `.:?` for optional key value pairs in a JSON document.

There's more...

If the implementation of the `FromJSON` typeclass is too involved, we can easily let GHC automatically fill it out using the `DeriveGeneric` language extension. The following is a simpler rewrite of the code:

```
{-# LANGUAGE OverloadedStrings #-}
{-# LANGUAGE DeriveGeneric #-}
import Data.Aeson
import qualified Data.ByteString.Lazy as B
import GHC.Generics

data Mathematician = Mathematician { name :: String
                                   , nationality :: String
                                   , born :: Int
                                   , died :: Maybe Int
                                   } deriving Generic

instance FromJSON Mathematician

main = do
  input <- B.readFile "input.json"
  let mm = decode input :: Maybe Mathematician
  case mm of
    Nothing -> print "error parsing JSON"
    Just m -> (putStrLn.greet) m

greet m = (show.name) m ++" was born in the year "++ (show.born) m
```

Although Aeson is powerful and generalizable, it may be an overkill for some simple JSON interactions. Alternatively, if we wish to use a very minimal JSON parser and printer, we can use Yocto, which can be downloaded from `http://hackage.haskell.org/package/yocto`.

Reading an XML file using the HXT package

Extensible Markup Language (**XML**) is an encoding of plain text to provide machine-readable annotations on a document. The standard is specified by W3C (`http://www.w3.org/TR/2008/REC-xml-20081126/`).

In this recipe, we will parse an XML document representing an e-mail conversation and extract all the dates.

Getting ready

We will first set up an XML file called `input.xml` with the following values, representing an e-mail thread between Databender and Princess on December 18, 2014 as follows:

```
$ cat input.xml

<thread>
    <email>
        <to>Databender</to>
        <from>Princess</from>
        <date>Thu Dec 18 15:03:23 EST 2014</date>
        <subject>Joke</subject>
        <body>Why did you divide sin by tan?</body>
    </email>
    <email>
        <to>Princess</to>
        <from>Databender</from>
        <date>Fri Dec 19 3:12:00 EST 2014</date>
        <subject>RE: Joke</subject>
        <body>Just cos.</body>
    </email>
</thread>
```

Using Cabal, install the HXT library which we use for manipulating XML documents:

```
$ cabal install hxt
```

How to do it...

1. We only need one import, which will be for parsing XML, using the following line of code:

   ```
   import Text.XML.HXT.Core
   ```

2. Define and implement `main` and specify the XML location. For this recipe, the file is retrieved from `input.xml`. Refer to the following code:

   ```
   main :: IO ()
   main = do
       input <- readFile "input.xml"
   ```

3. Apply the `readString` function to the input and extract all the date documents. We filter items with a specific name using the `hasName :: String -> a XmlTree XmlTree` function. Also, we extract the text using the `getText :: a XmlTree String` function, as shown in the following code snippet:

```
dates <- runX $ readString [withValidate no] input
    //> hasName "date"
    //> getText
```

4. We can now use the list of extracted dates as follows:

```
print dates
```

5. By running the code, we print the following output:

```
$ runhaskell Main.hs


["Thu Dec 18 15:03:23 EST 2014", "Fri Dec 19 3:12:00 EST 2014"]
```

How it works...

The library function, `runX`, takes in an **Arrow**. Think of an Arrow as a more powerful version of a Monad. Arrows allow for stateful global XML processing. Specifically, the `runX` function in this recipe takes in `IOSArrow XmlTree String` and returns an `IO` action of the `String` type. We generate this `IOSArrow` object using the `readString` function, which performs a series of operations to the XML data.

For a deep insight into the XML document, `//>` should be used whereas `/>` only looks at the current level. We use the `//>` function to look up the date attributes and display all the associated text.

As defined in the documentation, the `hasName` function tests whether a node has a specific name, and the `getText` function selects the text of a text node. Some other functions include the following:

▸ `isText`: This is used to test for text nodes

▸ `isAttr`: This is used to test for an attribute tree

▸ `hasAttr`: This is used to test whether an element node has an attribute node with a specific name

▸ `getElemName`: This is used to select the name of an element node

All the Arrow functions can be found on the `Text.XML.HXT.Arrow.XmlArrow` documentation at `http://hackage.haskell.org/package/hxt/docs/Text-XML-HXT-Arrow-XmlArrow.html`.

Capturing table rows from an HTML page

Mining **Hypertext Markup Language** (**HTML**) is often a feat of identifying and parsing only its structured segments. Not all text in an HTML file may be useful, so we find ourselves only focusing on a specific subset. For instance, HTML tables and lists provide a strong and commonly used structure to extract data whereas a paragraph in an article may be too unstructured and complicated to process.

In this recipe, we will find a table on a web page and gather all rows to be used in the program.

Getting ready

We will be extracting the values from an HTML table, so start by creating an `input.html` file containing a table as shown in the following figure:

Course Listing

Course	Time	Capacity
CS 1501	17:00	60
MATH 7600	14:00	25
PHIL 1000	9:30	120

The HTML behind this table is as follows:

```
$ cat input.html

<!DOCTYPE html>
<html>
    <body>
        <h1>Course Listing</h1>
        <table>
            <tr>
                <th>Course</th>
                <th>Time</th>
                <th>Capacity</th>
            </tr>
            <tr>
```

```
                <td>CS 1501</td>
                <td>17:00</td>
                <td>60</td>
            </tr>
            <tr>
                <td>MATH 7600</td>
                <td>14:00</td>
                <td>25</td>
            </tr>
            <tr>
                <td>PHIL 1000</td>
                <td>9:30</td>
                <td>120</td>
            </tr>
        </table>
    </body>
</html>
```

If not already installed, use Cabal to set up the HXT library and the split library, as shown in the following command lines:

```
$ cabal install hxt
$ cabal install split
```

How to do it...

1. We will need the `htx` package for XML manipulations and the `chunksOf` function from the split package, as presented in the following code snippet:

    ```
    import Text.XML.HXT.Core
    import Data.List.Split (chunksOf)
    ```

2. Define and implement `main` to read the `input.html` file.

    ```
    main :: IO ()
    main = do
      input <- readFile "input.html"
    ```

3. Feed the HTML data into `readString`, thereby setting `withParseHTML` to `yes` and optionally turning off warnings. Extract all the `td` tags and obtain the remaining text, as shown in the following code:

    ```
    texts <- runX $ readString
            [withParseHTML yes, withWarnings no] input
      //> hasName "td"
      //> getText
    ```

4. The data is now usable as a list of strings. It can be converted into a list of lists similar to how CSV was presented in the previous CSV recipe, as shown in the following code:

```
let rows = chunksOf 3 texts
print $ findBiggest rows
```

5. By folding through the data, identify the course with the largest capacity using the following code snippet:

```
findBiggest :: [[String]] -> [String]
findBiggest [] = []
findBiggest items = foldl1
                         (\a x -> if capacity x > capacity a
                                  then x else a) items

capacity [a,b,c] = toInt c
capacity _ = -1

toInt :: String -> Int
toInt = read
```

6. Running the code will display the class with the largest capacity as follows:

```
$ runhaskell Main.hs


{"PHIL 1000", "9:30", "120"}
```

How it works...

This is very similar to XML parsing, except we adjust the options of readString to [withParseHTML yes, withWarnings no].

Understanding how to perform HTTP GET requests

One of the most resourceful places to find good data is online. **GET requests** are common methods of communicating with an HTTP web server. In this recipe, we will grab all the links from a Wikipedia article and print them to the terminal. To easily grab all the links, we will use a helpful library called HandsomeSoup, which lets us easily manipulate and traverse a webpage through CSS selectors.

Getting ready

We will be collecting all links from a Wikipedia web page. Make sure to have an Internet connection before running this recipe.

Install the `HandsomeSoup` CSS selector package, and also install the HXT library if it is not already installed. To do this, use the following commands:

```
$ cabal install HandsomeSoup
$ cabal install hxt
```

How to do it...

1. This recipe requires `hxt` for parsing HTML and requires `HandsomeSoup` for the easy-to-use CSS selectors, as shown in the following code snippet:

    ```
    import Text.XML.HXT.Core
    import Text.HandsomeSoup
    ```

2. Define and implement `main` as follows:

    ```
    main :: IO ()
    main = do
    ```

3. Pass in the URL as a string to HandsomeSoup's `fromUrl` function:

    ```
        let doc = fromUrl "http://en.wikipedia.org/wiki/Narwhal"
    ```

4. Select all links within the `bodyContent` field of the Wikipedia page as follows:

    ```
        links <- runX $ doc >>> css "#bodyContent a" ! "href"
        print links
    ```

How it works...

The `HandsomeSoup` package allows easy CSS selectors. In this recipe, we run the `#bodyContent` a selector on a Wikipedia article web page. This finds all link tags that are descendants of an element with the `bodyContent` ID.

See also...

Another common way to obtain data online is through POST requests. To find out more, refer to the *Learning how to perform HTTP POST requests* recipe.

Learning how to perform HTTP POST requests

A **POST request** is another very common HTTP server request used by many APIs. We will be mining the University of Virginia directory search. When sending a POST request for a search query, the **Lightweight Directory Access Protocol** (**LDAP**) server replies with a web page of search results.

Getting ready

For this recipe, access to the Internet is necessary.

Install the `HandsomeSoup` CSS selector package, and also install the HXT library if it is not already installed:

```
$ cabal install HandsomeSoup
$ cabal install hxt
```

How to do it...

1. Import the following libraries:

   ```
   import Network.HTTP
   import Network.URI (parseURI)
   import Text.XML.HXT.Core
   import Text.HandsomeSoup
   import Data.Maybe (fromJust)
   ```

2. Define the POST request specified by the directory search website. Depending on the server, the following POST request details would be different. Refer to the following code snippet:

   ```
   myRequestURL = "http://www.virginia.edu/cgi-local/ldapweb"

   myRequest :: String -> Request_String
   myRequest query = Request {
       rqURI = fromJust $ parseURI myRequestURL
     , rqMethod = POST
     , rqHeaders = [ mkHeader HdrContentType "text/html"
                   , mkHeader HdrContentLength $ show $ length
                       body ]
     , rqBody = body
     }
   where body = "whitepages=" ++ query
   ```

3. Define and implement `main` to run the POST request on a query as follows:

```
main :: IO ()
main = do
  response <- simpleHTTP $ myRequest "poon"
```

4. Gather the HTML and parse it:

```
html <- getResponseBody response
let doc = readString [withParseHTML yes, withWarnings no]
  html
```

5. Find the table rows and print it out using the following:

```
rows <- runX $ doc >>> css "td" //> getText
print rows
```

Running the code will display all search results relating to `"poon"`, such as "Poonam" or "Witherspoon".

How it works...

A POST request needs the specified URI, headers, and body. By filling out a `Request` data type, it can be used to establish a server request.

See also

Refer to the *Understanding how to perform HTTP GET requests* recipe for details on how to perform a GET request instead.

Traversing online directories for data

A directory search typically provides names and contact information per query. By brute forcing many of these search queries, we can obtain all data stored in the directory listing database. This recipe runs thousands of search queries to obtain as much data as possible from a directory search. This recipe is provided only as a learning tool to see the power and simplicity of data gathering in Haskell.

Getting ready

Make sure to have a strong Internet connection.

Install the `hxt` and `HandsomeSoup` packages using Cabal:

```
$ cabal install hxt
$ cabal install HandsomeSoup
```

How to do it...

1. Set up the following dependencies:

```
import Network.HTTP
import Network.URI
import Text.XML.HXT.Core
import Text.HandsomeSoup
```

2. Define a `SearchResult` type, which may either fault in an error or result in a success, as presented in the following code:

```
type SearchResult = Either SearchResultErr [String]
data SearchResultErr = NoResultsErr
                     | TooManyResultsErr
                     | UnknownErr
                     deriving (Show, Eq)
```

3. Define the POST request specified by the directory search website. Depending on the server, the POST request will be different. Instead of rewriting code, we use the `myRequest` function defined in the previous recipe.

4. Write a helper function to obtain the document from a HTTP POST request, as shown in the following code:

```
getDoc query = do
    rsp <- simpleHTTP $ myRequest query
    html <- getResponseBody rsp
    return $ readString [withParseHTML yes, withWarnings
        no] html
```

5. Scan the HTML document and return whether there is an error or provide the resulting data. The code in this function is dependent on the error messages produced by the web page. In our case, the error messages are the following:

```
scanDoc doc = do
    errMsg <- runX $ doc >>> css "h3" //> getText

    case errMsg of
        [] -> do
            text <- runX $ doc >>> css "td" //> getText
            return $ Right text
        "Error: Sizelimit exceeded":_ ->
            return $ Left TooManyResultsErr
        "Too many matching entries were found":_ ->
```

```
          return $ Left TooManyResultsErr
    "No matching entries were found":_  ->
          return $ Left NoResultsErr
  _ -> return $ Left UnknownErr
```

6. Define and implement `main`. We will use a helper function, `main'`, as shown in the following code snippet, to recursively brute force the directory listing:

```
main :: IO ()
main = main' "a"
```

7. Run a search of the query and then recursively again on the next query:

```
main' query = do
    print query
    doc <- getDoc query
    searchResult <- scanDoc doc
    print searchResult
    case searchResult of
        Left TooManyResultsErr ->
            main' (nextDeepQuery query)
        _ -> if (nextQuery query) >= endQuery
            then print "done!" else main' (nextQuery
                query)
```

8. Write helper functions to define the next logical query as follows:

```
nextDeepQuery query = query ++ "a"

nextQuery "z" = endQuery
nextQuery query = if last query == 'z'
                   then nextQuery $ init query
                   else init query ++ [succ $ last query]
endQuery = [succ 'z']
```

How it works...

The code starts by searching for "a" in the directory lookup. This will most likely fault in an error as there are too many results. So, in the next iteration, the code will refine its search by querying for "aa", then "aaa", until there is no longer `TooManyResultsErr :: SearchResultErr`.

Then, it will enumerate to the next logical search query "aab", and if that produces no result, it will search for "aac", and so on. This brute force prefix search will obtain all items in the database. We can gather the mass of data, such as names and department types, to perform interesting clustering or analysis later on. The following figure shows how the program starts:

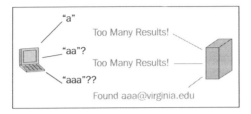

Using MongoDB queries in Haskell

MongoDB is a nonrelational schemaless database. In this recipe, we will obtain all data from MongoDB into Haskell.

Getting ready

We need to install MongoDB on our local machine and have a database instance running in the background while we run the code in this recipe.

MongoDB installation instructions are located at http://www.mongodb.org. On Debian-based operating systems, we can use apt-get to install MongoDB, using the following command line:

```
$ sudo apt-get install mongodb
```

Run the database daemon by specifying the database file path as follows:

```
$ mkdir ~/db
$ mongod --dbpath ~/db
```

Fill up a "people" collection with dummy data as follows:

```
$ mongo
> db.people.insert( {first: "Joe", last: "Shmoe"} )
```

Install the MongoDB package from Cabal using the following command:

```
$ cabal install mongoDB
```

How to do it...

1. Use the `OverloadedString` and `ExtendedDefaultRules` language extensions to make the MongoDB library easier to use:

    ```
    {-# LANGUAGE OverloadedStrings, ExtendedDefaultRules #-}
    import Database.MongoDB
    ```

2. Define and implement `main` to set up a connection to the locally hosted database. Run MongoDB queries defined in the `run` function as follows:

    ```
    main :: IO ()
    main = do
        let db = "test"
        pipe <- runIOE $ connect (host "127.0.0.1")
        e <- access pipe master db run
        close pipe
        print e
    ```

3. In `run`, we can combine multiple operations. For this recipe, `run` will only perform one task, that is, gather data from the `"people"` collection:

    ```
    run = getData

    getData = rest =<< find (select [] "people") {sort=[]}
    ```

How it works...

A pipe is established by the driver between the running program and the database. This allows running MongoDB operations to bridge the program with the database. The `find` function takes a query, which we construct by evoking the `select :: Selector -> Collection -> aQueryOrSelection` function.

Other functions can be found in the documentation at `http://hackage.haskell.org/package/mongoDB/docs/Database-MongoDB-Query.html`.

See also

If the MongoDB database is on a remote server, refer to the *Reading from a remote MongoDB server* recipe to set up a connection with remote databases.

Reading from a remote MongoDB server

In many cases, it may be more feasible to set up a MongoDB instance on a remote machine. This recipe will cover how to obtain data from a MongoDB hosted remotely.

Getting ready

We should create a remote database. MongoLab (`https://mongolab.com`) and MongoHQ (`http://www.mongohq.com`) offer MongoDB as a service and have free options to set up a small development database.

 These services will require us to accept their terms and conditions. For some of us, it may be best to host the database in our own remote server.

Install the MongoDB package from Cabal as follows:

```
$ cabal install mongoDB
```

Also, install the helper following helper libraries as follows:

```
$ cabal install split
$ cabal install uri
```

How to do it...

1. Use the `OverloadedString` and `ExtendedDefaultRules` language extensions required by the library. Import helper functions as follows:

   ```
   {-# LANGUAGE OverloadedStrings, ExtendedDefaultRules #-}
   import Database.MongoDB
   import Text.URI
   import Data.Maybe
   import qualified Data.Text as T
   import Data.List.Split
   ```

2. Specify the remote URI for the database connection as follows:

   ```
   mongoURI =
       "mongodb://user:pass@ds12345.mongolab.com:53788/mydb"
   ```

3. The username, password, hostname, port address number, and database name must be extracted from the URI, as presented in the following code snippet:

```
uri = fromJust $ parseURI mongoURI

getUser = head $ splitOn ":" $ fromJust $ uriUserInfo uri

getPass = last $ splitOn ":" $ fromJust $ uriUserInfo uri

getHost = fromJust $ uriRegName uri

getPort = case uriPort uri of
    Just port -> show port
    Nothing -> (last.words.show) defaultPort

getDb = T.pack $ tail $ uriPath uri
```

4. Create a database connection by reading the host port of the remote URI as follows:

```
main :: IO ()
main = do
    let hostport = getHost ++ ":" ++ getPort
    pipe <- runIOE $ connect (readHostPort hostport)
    e <- access pipe master getDb run
    close pipe
    print e
```

5. Optionally authenticate to the database and obtain data from the `"people"` collection as follows:

```
run = do
  auth (T.pack getUser) (T.pack getPass)
  getData

getData = rest =<< find (select [] "people") {sort=[]}
```

See also

If the database is on a local machine, refer to the *Using MongoDB queries in Haskell* recipe.

Exploring data from a SQLite database

SQLite is a relational database that enforces a strict schema. It is simply a file on a machine that we can interact with through **Structured Query Language** (**SQL**). There is an easy-to-use Haskell library to send these SQL commands to our database.

In this recipe, we will use such a library to extract all data from a SQLite database.

Getting ready

We need to install the SQLite database if it isn't already set up. It can be obtained from `http://www.sqlite.org`. On Debian systems, we can get it from `apt-get` using the following command:

```
$ sudo apt-get install sqlite3
```

Now create a simple database to test our code, using the following commands:

```
$ sqlite3 test.db "CREATE TABLE test \
(id INTEGER PRIMARY KEY, str text); \
INSERT INTO test (str) VALUES ('test string');"
```

We must also install the SQLite Haskell package from Cabal as follows:

```
$ cabal install sqlite-simple
```

This recipe will dissect the example code presented on the library's documentation page available at `http://hackage.haskell.org/package/sqlite-simple/docs/Database-SQLite-Simple.html`.

How to do it...

1. Use the `OverloadedStrings` language extension and import the relevant libraries, as shown in the following code:

    ```haskell
    {-# LANGUAGE OverloadedStrings #-}

    import Control.Applicative
    import Database.SQLite.Simple
    import Database.SQLite.Simple.FromRow
    ```

2. Define a data type for each SQLite table field. Provide it with an instance of the `FromRow` typeclass so that we may easily parse it from the table, as shown in the following code snippet:

```
data TestField = TestField Int String deriving (Show)

instance FromRow TestField where
  fromRow = TestField <$> field <*> field
```

3. And lastly, open the database to import everything as follows:

```
main :: IO ()
main = do
  conn <- open "test.db"
  r <- query_ conn "SELECT * from test" :: IO [TestField]
  mapM_ print r
  close conn
```

2
Integrity and Inspection

This chapter will cover the following recipes:

- ▶ Trimming excess whitespace
- ▶ Ignoring punctuation and specific characters
- ▶ Coping with unexpected or missing input
- ▶ Validating records by matching regular expressions
- ▶ Lexing and parsing an e-mail address
- ▶ Deduplication of nonconflicting data items
- ▶ Deduplication of conflicting data items
- ▶ Implementing a frequency table using Data.List
- ▶ Implementing a frequency table using Data.MultiSet
- ▶ Computing the Manhattan distance
- ▶ Computing the Euclidean distance
- ▶ Comparing scaled data using the Pearson correlation coefficient
- ▶ Comparing sparse data using cosine similarity

Introduction

The conclusions drawn from data analysis are only as robust as the quality of the data itself. After obtaining raw text, the next natural step is to validate and clean it carefully. Even the slightest bias may risk the integrity of the results. Therefore, we must take great precautionary measures, which involve thorough inspection, to ensure sanity checks are performed on our data before we begin to understand it. This section should be the starting point for cleaning data in Haskell.

Real-world data often has an impurity that needs to be addressed before it can be processed. For example, extraneous whitespaces or punctuation could clutter data, making it difficult to parse. Duplication and data conflicts are another area of unintended consequences of reading real-world data. Sometimes it's just reassuring to know that data makes sense by conducting sanity checks. Some examples of sanity checks include matching regular expressions as well as detecting outliers by establishing a measure of distance. In this chapter, we will cover each of these topics.

Trimming excess whitespace

The text obtained from sources may unintentionally include beginning or trailing whitespace characters. When parsing such an input, it is often wise to trim the text. For example, when Haskell source code contains trailing whitespace, the **GHC** compiler ignores it through a process called **lexing**. The lexer produces a sequence of tokens, effectively ignoring meaningless characters such as excess whitespace.

In this recipe, we will use built-in libraries to make our own `trim` function.

How to do it...

Create a new file, which we will call `Main.hs`, and perform the following steps:

1. Import the `isSpace :: Char -> Bool` function from the built-in `Data.Char` package:

   ```
   import Data.Char (isSpace)
   ```

2. Write a trim function that removes the beginning and trailing whitespace:

   ```
   trim :: String -> String
   trim = f . f
     where f = reverse . dropWhile isSpace
   ```

3. Test it out within `main`:

   ```
   main :: IO ()
   main = putStrLn $ trim " wahoowa! "
   ```

4. Running the code will result in the following trimmed string:

   ```
   $ runhaskell Main.hs


   wahoowa!
   ```

How it works...

Our `trim` function lazily strips the whitespace from the beginning and ending parts of the string. It starts by dropping whitespace letters from the beginning. Then, it reverses the string to apply the same function again. Finally, it reverses the string one last time to bring it back to the original form. Fortunately, the `isSpace` function from `Data.Char` handles any **Unicode** space character as well as the control characters \t, \n, \r, \f, and \v.

There's more...

Ready-made parser combinator libraries such as `parsec` or `uu-parsinglib` could be used to do this instead, rather than reinventing the wheel. By introducing a `Token` type and parsing to this type, we can elegantly ignore the whitespace. Alternatively, we can use the alex lexing library (package name, `alex`) for this task. These libraries are overkill for this simple task, but they allow us to perform a more generalized tokenizing of text.

Ignoring punctuation and specific characters

Usually in natural language processing, some uninformative words or characters, called **stop words**, can be filtered out for easier handling. When computing word frequencies or extracting sentiment data from a corpus, punctuation or special characters might need to be ignored. This recipe demonstrates how to remove these specific characters from the body of a text.

How to do it...

There are no imports necessary. Create a new file, which we will call `Main.hs`, and perform the following steps:

1. Implement `main` and define a string called `quote`. The back slashes (\) represent multiline strings:

```
main :: IO ()
main = do
  let quote = "Deep Blue plays very good chess-so what?\
    \Does that tell you something about how we play chess?\
    \No. Does it tell you about how Kasparov envisions,\
    \understands a chessboard? (Douglas Hofstadter)"
  putStrLn $ (removePunctuation.replaceSpecialSymbols) quote
```

2. Replace all punctuation marks with an empty string, and replace all special symbols with a space:

```
punctuations = [ '!', '"', '#', '$', '%'
               , '(', ')', '.', ',', '?']

removePunctuation = filter (`notElem` punctuations)

specialSymbols = ['/', '-']

replaceSpecialSymbols = map $
  (\c ->if c `elem` specialSymbols then ' ' else c)
```

3. By running the code, we will find that all special characters and punctuation are appropriately removed to facilitate dealing with the text's corpus:

```
$ runhaskell Main.hs
```

Deep Blue plays very good chess so what Does that tell you something about how we play chess No Does it tell you about how Kasparov envisions understands a chessboard Douglas Hofstadter

There's more...

For more powerful control, we can install `MissingH`, which is a very helpful utility we can use to deal with strings:

```
$ cabal install MissingH
```

It provides a `replace` function that takes three arguments and produces a result as follows:

```
Prelude> replace "hello" "goodbye" "hello world!"
```

```
"goodbye world!"
```

It replaces all occurrences of the first string with the second string in the third argument. We can also compose multiple `replace` functions:

```
Prelude> ((replace "," "").(replace "!" "")) "hello, world!"
```

```
"hello world"
```

By folding the composition (`.`) function over a list of these `replace` functions, we can generalize the `replace` function to an arbitrary list of tokens:

```
Prelude> (foldr (.) id $ map (flip replace "") [",", "!"]) "hello,
    world!"
```

```
"hello world"
```

The list of punctuation marks can now be arbitrarily long. We can modify our recipe to use our new and more generalized functions:

```
    removePunctuation = foldr (.) id $ map (flip replace "")
        ["!", "\"", "#", "$", "%", "(", ")", ".", ",", "?"]

    replaceSpecialSymbols = foldr (.) id $ map (flip replace " ")
        ["/", "-"]
```

Coping with unexpected or missing input

Data sources often contain incomplete and unexpected data. One common approach to parsing such data in Haskell is using the `Maybe` data type.

Imagine designing a function to find the nth element in a list of characters. A naïve implementation may have the type `Int -> [Char] -> Char`. However, if the function is trying to access an index out of bounds, we should try to indicate that an error has occurred.

A common way to deal with these errors is by encapsulating the output `Char` into a `Maybe` context. Having the type `Int -> [Char] -> Maybe Char` allows for some better error handling. The constructors for `Maybe` are `Just a` or `Nothing`, which will become apparent by running GHCi and testing out the following commands:

```
$ ghci
```

```
Prelude> :type Just 'c'
Just 'c' :: Maybe Char
```

```
Prelude> :type Nothing
Nothing :: Maybe a
```

We will set each field as a `Maybe` data type so that whenever a field cannot be parsed, it will simply be represented as `Nothing`. This recipe will demonstrate how to read the CSV data with faulty and missing info.

Getting ready

We create an input set of CSV files to read in. The first column will be for laptop brands, the next column will be for their models, and the third column will be for the base cost. We should leave some fields blank to simulate an incomplete input. We name the file `input.csv`:

Lenovo Thinkpad	T540p	832.15
Lenovo Thinkpad	X1 Carbon	
Lenovo IdeaPad		949

Also, we must install the csv library:

```
$ cabal install csv
```

How to do it...

Create a new file, which we will call `Main.hs`, and perform the following steps:

1. Import the CSV library:

   ```
   import Text.CSV
   ```

2. Create a data type corresponding to the CSV fields:

   ```
   data Laptop = Laptop { brand :: Maybe String
                        , model :: Maybe String
                        , cost  :: Maybe Float
                        } deriving Show
   ```

3. Define and implement `main` to read the CSV input and parse relevant info:

```
main :: IO ()
main = do
  let fileName = "input.csv"
  input <- readFile fileName
  let csv = parseCSV fileName input
  let laptops = parseLaptops csv
  print laptops
```

4. From a list of records, create a list of laptop data types:

```
parseLaptops (Left err) = []
parseLaptops (Right csv) =
  foldl (\a record -> if length record == 3
                      then (parseLaptop record):a
                      else a) [] csv


parseLaptop record = Laptop{ brand = getBrand $ record !! 0
                           , model = getModel $ record !! 1
                           , cost = getCost $ record !! 2 }
```

5. Parse each field, producing `Nothing` if there is an unexpected or missing item:

```
getBrand :: String -> Maybe String
getBrand str = if null str then Nothing else Just str

getModel :: String -> Maybe String
getModel str = if null str then Nothing else Just str

getCost :: String -> Maybe Float
getCost str = case reads str::[(Float,String)] of
  [(cost, "")] -> Just cost
  _ -> Nothing
```

How it works...

The `Maybe` monad allows you to have two states: `Just` something or `Nothing`. It provides a useful abstraction to produce an error state. Each field in these data types exists in a `Maybe` context. If a field doesn't exist, then we simply regard it as `Nothing` and move on.

There's more...

If a more descriptive error state is desired, the `Either` monad may be more useful. It also has two states, but they are more descriptive: `Left` something, or `Right` something. The `Left` state is often used to describe the error type, whereas the `Right` state holds the desired result. We can use the `Left` state to describe different types of errors instead of just one behemoth `Nothing`.

See also

To review CSV data input, see the *Keeping and representing data from a CSV file* recipe in *Chapter 1, The Hunt for Data*.

Validating records by matching regular expressions

A regular expression is a language for matching patterns in a string. Our Haskell code can process a regular expression to examine a text and tell us whether or not it matches the rules described by the expression. Regular expression matching can be used to validate or identify a pattern in the text.

In this recipe, we will read a corpus of English text to find possible candidates of full names in a sea of words. Full names usually consist of two words that start with a capital letter. We use this heuristic to extract all the names from an article.

Getting ready

Create an `input.txt` file with some text. In this example, we use a snippet from a New York Times article on dinosaurs (`http://www.nytimes.com/2013/12/17/science/earth/outsider-challenges-papers-on-growth-of-dinosaurs.html`)

> *Other co-authors of Dr. Erickson's include Mark Norell, chairman of paleontology at the American Museum of Natural History; Philip Currie, a professor of dinosaur paleobiology at the University of Alberta; and Peter Makovicky, associate curator of paleontology at the Field Museum in Chicago.*

How to do it...

Create a new file, which we will call `Main.hs`, and perform the following steps:

1. Import the regular expression library:

    ```
    import Text.Regex.Posix ((=~))
    ```

2. Match a string against a regular expression to detect words that look like names:

```
looksLikeName :: String -> Bool
looksLikeName str = str =~ "^[A-Z][a-z]{1,30}$" :: Bool
```

3. Create functions that remove unnecessary punctuation and special symbols. We will use the same functions defined in the previous recipe entitled *Ignoring punctuation and specific characters*:

```
punctuations = [ '!', '"', '#', '$', '%'
               , '(', ')', '.', ',', '?']
removePunctuation = filter (`notElem` punctuations)

specialSymbols = ['/', '-']
replaceSpecialSymbols = map $
                        (\c -> if c `elem` specialSymbols
                               then ' ' else c)
```

4. Pair adjacent words together and form a list of possible full names:

```
createTuples (x:y:xs) = (x ++ " " ++ y) :
                              createTuples (y:xs)
createTuples _ = []
```

5. Retrieve the input and find possible names from a corpus of text:

```
main :: IO ()
main = do

  input <- readFile "input.txt"
  let cleanInput =
    (removePunctuation.replaceSpecialSymbols) input

  let wordPairs = createTuples $ words cleanInput

  let possibleNames =
    filter (all looksLikeName . words) wordPairs

  print possibleNames
```

6. The resulting output after running the code is as follows:

$ runhaskell Main.hs

["Dr Erickson","Mark Norell","American Museum","Natural History","History Philip","Philip Currie","Peter Makovicky","Field Museum"]

How it works...

The =~ function takes in a string and a regular expression and returns a target that we parse as Bool. In this recipe, the ^[A-Z][a-z]{1,30}$ regular expression matches the words that start with a capital letter and are between 2 and 31 letters long.

In order to determine the usefulness of the algorithm presented in this recipe, we will introduce two metrics of relevance: **precision** and **recall**. Precision is the percent of retrieved data that is relevant. Recall is the percent of relevant data that is retrieved.

Out of a total of 45 words in the input.txt file, four correct names are produced and a total eight candidates are retrieved. It has a precision of 50 percent and a recall of 100 percent. This is not bad at all for a simple regular expression trick.

See also

Instead of running regular expressions on a string, we can pass them through a lexical analyzer. The next recipe entitled *Lexing and parsing an e-mail address* will cover this in detail.

Lexing and parsing an e-mail address

An elegant way to clean data is by defining a lexer to split up a string into tokens. In this recipe, we will parse an e-mail address using the attoparsec library. This will naturally allow us to ignore the surrounding whitespace.

Getting ready

Import the attoparsec parser combinator library:

```
$ cabal install attoparsec
```

How to do it...

Create a new file, which we will call Main.hs, and perform the following steps:

1. Use the GHC OverloadedStrings language extension to more legibly use the Text data type throughout the code. Also, import the other relevant libraries:

    ```
    {-# LANGUAGE OverloadedStrings #-}
    import Data.Attoparsec.Text
    import Data.Char (isSpace, isAlphaNum)
    ```

2. Declare a data type for an e-mail address:

```
data E-mail = E-mail
  { user :: String
  , host :: String
  } deriving Show
```

3. Define how to parse an e-mail address. This function can be as simple or as complicated as required:

```
e-mail :: Parser E-mail
e-mail = do
  skipSpace
  user <- many' $ satisfy isAlphaNum
  at <- char '@'
  hostName <- many' $ satisfy isAlphaNum
  period <- char '.'
  domain <- many' (satisfy isAlphaNum)
  return $ E-mail user (hostName ++ "." ++ domain)
```

4. Parse an e-mail address to test the code:

```
main :: IO ()
main = print $ parseOnly e-mail "nishant@shukla.io"
```

5. Run the code to print out the parsed e-mail address:

```
$ runhaskell Main.hs

Right (E-mail {user = "nishant", host = "shukla.io"})
```

How it works...

We create an e-mail parser by matching the string against multiple tests. An e-mail address must contain some alphanumerical username, followed by the 'at' sign (@), then an alphanumerical hostname, a period, and lastly the top-level domain.

The various functions used from the `attoparsec` library can be found in the `Data.Attoparsec.Text` documentation, which is available at `https://hackage.haskell.org/package/attoparsec/docs/Data-Attoparsec-Text.html`.

Deduplication of nonconflicting data items

Duplication is a common problem when collecting large amounts of data. In this recipe, we will combine similar records in a way that ensures no information is lost.

Getting ready

Create an `input.csv` file with repeated data:

glasses		60
jacket	brown	
shirt		
glasses	black	
jacket		89.99
shirt	red	15

How to do it...

Create a new file, which we will call `Main.hs`, and perform the following steps:

1. We will be using the `CSV`, `Map`, and `Maybe` packages:

   ```
   import Text.CSV (parseCSV, Record)
   import Data.Map (fromListWith)
   import Control.Applicative ((<|>))
   ```

2. Define the `Item` data type corresponding to the CSV input:

   ```
   data Item = Item   { name :: String
                      , color :: Maybe String
                      , cost :: Maybe Float
                      } deriving Show
   ```

3. Get each record from CSV and put them in a map by calling our `doWork` function:

   ```
   main :: IO ()
   main = do
     let fileName = "input.csv"
     input <- readFile fileName
     let csv = parseCSV fileName input
     either handleError doWork csv
   ```

4. If we're unable to parse CSV, print an error message; otherwise, define the `doWork` function that creates a map from an association list with a collision strategy defined by `combine`:

   ```
   handleError = print

   doWork :: [Record] -> IO ()
   doWork csv = print $
                fromListWith combine $
                map parseToTuple csv
   ```

5. Use the `<|>` function from `Control.Applicative` to merge the nonconflicting fields:

```
combine :: Item -> Item -> Item

combine item1 item2 =
    Item { name = name item1
         , color = color item1 <|> color item2
         , cost = cost item1 <|> cost item2 }
```

6. Define the helper functions to create an association list from a CSV record:

```
parseToTuple :: [String] -> (String, Item)
parseToTuple record = (name item, item)
    where item = parseItem record


parseItem :: Record -> Item
parseItem record =
    Item { name = record !! 0
         , color = record !! 1
         , cost = case reads(record !! 2)::[(Float,String)] of
             [(c, "")] -> Just c
             _ -> Nothing   }
```

7. Executing the code shows a map filled with combined results:

```
$ runhaskell Main.hs

fromList
[ ("glasses",
    Item {name = "glasses", color = "black", cost = Just 60.0})
, ("jacket",
    Item {name = "jacket", color = "brown", cost = Just 89.99})
, ("shirt",
    Item {name = "shirt", color = "red", cost = Just 15.0})
]
```

How it works...

The `Map` data type offers a convenient function `fromListWith :: Ord k => (a -> a -> a) -> [(k, a)] -> Map k a` to easily combine data in the map. We use it to find out whether a key already exists. If so, we combine the fields in the old and new items and store them under the key.

The true hero in this recipe is the `<|>` function form `Control.Applicative`. The `<|>` function takes its arguments and returns the first one that is not *empty*. Since both `String` and `Maybe` implement `Applicative typeclass`, we can reuse the `<|>` function for a more manageable code. Here are a couple of examples of it in use:

```
$ ghci

Prelude> import Control.Applicative

Prelude Control.Applicative> (Nothing) <|> (Just 1)
Just 1

Prelude Control.Applicative> (Just 'a') <|> (Just 'b')
Just 'a'

Prelude Control.Applicative> "" <|> "hello"
"hello"

Prelude Control.Applicative> "" <|> ""
""
```

There's more...

If you're dealing with larger numbers, it may be wise to use `Data.Hashmap.Map` instead because the running time for *n* items is $O(min(n, W))$, where *W* is the number of bits in an integer (32 or 64).

For even better performance, `Data.Hashtable.Hashtable` provides $O(1)$ performance for lookups but adds complexity by being in an I/O monad.

See also

If the corpus contains inconsistent information about duplicated data, see the next recipe on *Deduplication of conflicting data items*.

Deduplication of conflicting data items

Unfortunately, information about an item may be inconsistent throughout the corpus. Collision strategies are often domain-dependent, but one common way to manage this conflict is by simply storing all variations of the data. In this recipe, we will read a CSV file that contains information about musical artists and store all of the information about their songs and genres in a set.

Getting ready

Create a CSV input file with the following musical artists. The first column is for the name of the artist or band. The second column is the song name, and the third is the genre. Notice how some musicians have multiple songs or genres.

Daft Punk	Around the World	French house
Madeon	Icarus	French house
Daft Punk	Get Lucky	
Justice	Genesis	Electro
Junior Boys	Bits & Pieces	Synthpop
Justice		Electronic rock

How to do it...

Create a new file, which we will call `Main.hs`, and perform the following steps:

1. We will be using the `CSV`, `Map`, and `Set` packages:

   ```
   import Text.CSV (parseCSV, Record)
   import Data.Map (fromListWith)
   import qualified Data.Set as S
   ```

2. Define the `Artist` data type corresponding to the CSV input. For fields that may contain conflicting data, store the value in its corresponding list. In this case, song- and genre-related data are stored in a set of strings:

   ```
   data Artist = Artist { name :: String
                        , song :: S.Set String
                        , genre :: S.Set String
                        } deriving Show
   ```

3. Extract data from CSV and insert it in a map:

   ```
   main :: IO ()
   main = do
     let fileName = "input.csv"
     input <- readFile fileName
     let csv = parseCSV fileName input
     either handleError doWork csv
   ```

4. Print out any error that might occur:

   ```
   handleError = print
   ```

5. If no error occurs, then combine the data from the CSV and print it out:

   ```
   doWork :: [Record] -> IO ()
   doWork csv = print $
                fromListWith combine $
                map parseToTuple csv
   ```

6. Create a map from an association list with a collision strategy defined by `combine`:

```
combine :: Artist -> Artist -> Artist
combine artist1 artist2 =
    Artist { name = name artist1
           , song = S.union (song artist1) (song artist2)
           , genre = S.union (genre artist1)
             (genre artist2) }
```

7. Make the helper functions create an association list from the CSV records:

```
parseToTuple :: [String] -> (String, Artist)
parseToTuple record = (name item, item)
  where item = parseItem record


parseItem :: Record -> Artist
parseItem record =
  Artist { name = nameStr
         , song = if null songStr
                  then S.empty
                  else S.singleton songStr
         , genre = if null genreStr
                   then S.empty
                   else S.singleton genreStr
         }
  where nameStr  = record !! 0
        songStr  = record !! 1
        genreStr = record !! 2
```

8. The output of the program will be a map with the following information that will be collected:

```
fromList [
("Daft Punk", Artist
  {  name = "Daft Punk",
    song = fromList ["Get Lucky","Around the World"],
    genre = fromList ["French house"] }),
("Junior Boys", Artist
  {  name = "Junior Boys",
    song = fromList ["Bits & Pieces"],
    genre = fromList ["Synthpop"] }),
("Justice", Artist
  {  name = "Justice",
    song = fromList ["Genesis"],
    genre = fromList ["Electronic rock","Electro"] }),
("Madeon", Artist
  {  name = "Madeon",
    song = fromList ["Icarus"],
    genre = fromList ["French house"] })]
```

How it works...

The `Map` data type offers a convenient function `fromListWith :: Ord k => (a -> a -> a) -> [(k, a)] -> Map k a` to easily combine data in `Map`. We use it to find out whether a key already exists. If so, we combine the fields in the old and new items and store them under the key.

We use a set to efficiently combine these data fields.

There's more...

If dealing with larger numbers, it may be wise to use `Data.Hashmap.Map` instead because the running time for *n* items is *O(min(n, W))*, where *W* is the number of bits in an integer (32 or 64).

For even better performance, `Data.Hashtable.Hashtable` provides *O(1)* performance for lookups but adds complexity by being in an I/O monad.

See also

If the corpus contains nonconflicting information about duplicated data, see the previous section on *Deduplication of nonconflicting data items*.

Implementing a frequency table using Data.List

A frequency map of values is often useful to detect outliers. We can use it to identify frequencies that seem out of the ordinary. In this recipe, we will be counting the number of different colors in a list.

How to do it...

Create a new file, which we will call `Main.hs`, and perform the following steps:

1. We will use the `group` and `sort` functions from `Data.List`:

   ```
   import Data.List (group, sort)
   ```

2. Define a simple data type for colors:

   ```
   data Color = Red | Green | Blue deriving (Show, Ord, Eq)
   ```

3. Create a list of these colors:
```
main :: IO ()
main = do
    let items = [Red, Green, Green, Blue, Red, Green, Green]
```

4. Implement the frequency map and print it out:
```
    let freq =
        map (\x -> (head x, length x)) . group . sort $ items
    print freq
```

How it works...

Grouping identical items after sorting the list is the central idea.

See the following step-by-step evaluation in ghci:

Prelude> sort items

[Red,Red,Green,Green,Green,Green,Blue]
Prelude> group it

[[Red,Red],[Green,Green,Green,Green],[Blue]]

Prelude> map (\x -> (head x, length x)) it

[(Red,2),(Green,4),(Blue,1)]

 As we may expect, sorting the list is the most expensive step.

See also

A cleaner version of the code is possible by using `Data.MultiSet` described in the next recipe, *Implementing a frequency table using Data.MultiSet*.

Implementing a frequency table using Data.MultiSet

A frequency map of values is often useful to detect outliers. We will use an existing library that does much of the work for us.

Getting ready

We will be using the `multiset` package from Hackage:

```
$ cabal install multiset
```

How to do it...

Create a new file, which we will call `Main.hs`, and perform the following steps:

1. We will use the `fromList` and `toOccurList` functions from `Data.MultiSet`:

    ```
    import Data.MultiSet (fromList, toOccurList)
    ```

2. Define a simple data type for colors:

    ```
    data Color = Red | Green | Blue deriving (Show, Ord, Eq)
    ```

3. Create a list of these colors:

    ```
    main :: IO ()
    main = do
        let items = [Red, Green, Green, Blue, Red, Green, Green]
    ```

4. Implement the frequency map and print it out:

    ```
    let freq = toOccurList . fromList $ items
    print freq
    ```

5. Run the code to display the frequency list:

    ```
    $ runhaskell Main.hs


    [ (Red, 2), (Green, 4), (Blue, 1) ]
    ```

How it works...

The `toOccurList :: MultiSet a -> [(a, Int)]` function creates a frequency map from a list. We construct `MuliSet` using the provided `fromList` function.

See also

If importing a new library is not desired, see the previous recipe on *Implementing a frequency map using Data.List*.

Computing the Manhattan distance

Defining a distance between two items allows us to easily interpret clusters and patterns. The Manhattan distance is one of the easiest to implement and is used primarily due to its simplicity.

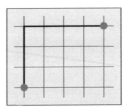

The Manhattan distance (or Taxicab distance) between two items is the sum of the absolute differences of their coordinates. So if we are given two points (1, 1) and (5, 4), then the Manhattan distance will be $|1\text{-}5| + |1\text{-}4| = 4 + 3 = 7$.

We can use this distance metric to detect whether an item is unusually *far away* from everything else. In this recipe, we will detect outliers using the Manhattan distance. The calculations merely involve addition and subtraction, and therefore, it performs exceptionally well for a very large amount of data.

Getting ready

Create a list of comma-separated points. We will compute the smallest distance between these points and a test point:

```
$ cat input.csv


0,0
10,0
0,10
10,10
5,5
```

How to do it...

Create a new file, which we will call `Main.hs`, and perform the following steps:

1. Import the CSV and List packages:

   ```
   import Text.CSV (parseCSV)
   ```

2. Read in the following points:

```
main :: IO ()
main = do
  let fileName = "input.csv"
  input <- readFile fileName
  let csv = parseCSV fileName input
```

3. Represent the data as a list of floating point numbers:

```
let points = either (\e -> []) (map toPoint . myFilter)
  csv
```

4. Define a couple of points to test the function:

```
let test1 = [2,1]
let test2 = [-10,-10]
```

5. Compute the Manhattan distance on each of the points and find the smallest result:

```
if (not.null) points then do
  print $ minimum $ map (manhattanDist test1) points
  print $ minimum $ map (manhattanDist test2) points
else putStrLn "Error: no points to compare"
```

6. Create a helper function to convert a list of strings to a list of floating point numbers:

```
toPoint record = map (read :: String -> Float) record
```

7. Compute the Manhattan distance between two points:

```
manhattanDist p1 p2 =
  sum $ zipWith (\x y -> abs (x - y)) p1 p2
```

8. Filter out records that are of incorrect size:

```
myFilter = filter (\x -> length x == 2)
```

9. The output will be the shortest distance between the test points and the list of points:

```
$ runhaskell Main.hs

3.0
20.0
```

See also

If the distance matches more closely to the traditional geometric space, then read the next recipe on *Computing the Euclidean distance*.

Computing the Euclidean distance

Defining a distance between two items allows us to easily interpret clusters and patterns. The Euclidean distance is one of the most geometrically natural forms of distance to implement. It uses the Pythagorean formula to compute how far away two items are, which is similar to measuring the distance with a physical ruler.

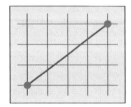

We can use this distance metric to detect whether an item is unusually *far away* from everything else. In this recipe, we will detect outliers using the Euclidean distance. It is slightly more computationally expensive than measuring the Manhattan distance since it involves multiplication and square roots; however, depending on the dataset, it may provide more accurate results.

Getting ready

Create a list of comma-separated points. We will compute the smallest distance between these points and a test point.

```
$ cat input.csv

0,0
10,0
0,10
10,10
5,5
```

How to do it...

Create a new file, which we will call `Main.hs`, and perform the following steps:

1. Import the CSV and List packages:

    ```
    import Text.CSV (parseCSV)
    ```

2. Read in the following points:

```
main :: IO ()
main = do
  let fileName = "input.csv"
  input <- readFile fileName
  let csv = parseCSV fileName input
```

3. Represent the data as a list of floating point numbers:

```
let points = either (\e -> []) (map toPoint .
  myFilter) csv
```

4. Define a couple of points to test out the function:

```
let test1 = [2,1]
let test2 = [-10,-10]
```

5. Compute the Euclidean distance on each of the points and find the smallest result:

```
if (not.null) points then do
  print $ minimum $ map (euclidianDist test1) points
  print $ minimum $ map (euclidianDist test2) points
else putStrLn "Error: no points to compare"
```

6. Create a helper function to convert a list of strings to a list of floating point numbers:

```
toPoint record = map (read String -> Float) record
```

7. Compute the Euclidean distance between two points:

```
euclidianDist p1 p2 = sqrt $ sum $
                      zipWith (\x y -> (x - y)^2) p1 p2
```

8. Filter out records that are of incorrect size:

```
myFilter = filter (\x -> length x == 2)
```

9. The output will be the shortest distance between the test points and the list of points:

```
$ runhaskell Main.hs
```

```
2.236068
```

```
14.142136
```

See also

If a more computationally efficient distance calculation is required, then take a look at the previous recipe, *Computing the Manhattan distance*.

Comparing scaled data using the Pearson correlation coefficient

Another way to measure how closely two items relate to each other is by examining their individual trends. For example, two items that both show an upward trend are more closely related. Likewise, two items that both show a downward trend are also closely related. To simplify the algorithm, we will only consider linear trends. This calculation of correlation is called the Pearson correlation coefficient. The closer the coefficient is to zero, the less correlated the two data sets will be.

The Pearson correlation coefficient for a sample is calculated using the following formula:

$$r_{xy} = \frac{n \sum x_i y_i - \sum x_i \, y_i}{\sqrt{n \sum x_i^2 - (\sum x_i)^2} \sqrt{n \sum y_i^2 - (\sum y_i)^2}}$$

How to do it...

Create a new file, which we will call `Main.hs`, and perform the following steps:

1. Implement `main` to compute the correlation coefficient between two lists of numbers:

```
main :: IO ()
main = do
  let d1 = [3,3,3,4,4,4,5,5,5]
  let d2 = [1,1,2,2,3,4,4,5,5]
  let r = pearson d1 d2
  print r
```

2. Define the function to compute the Pearson coefficient:

```
pearson xs ys = (n * sumXY - sumX * sumY) /
                sqrt ( (n * sumX2 - sumX*sumX) *
                       (n * sumY2 - sumY*sumY) )

where n = fromIntegral (length xs)
      sumX = sum xs
      sumY = sum ys
      sumX2 = sum $ zipWith (*) xs xs
      sumY2 = sum $ zipWith (*) ys ys
      sumXY = sum $ zipWith (*) xs ys
```

3. Run the code to print the coefficient.

```
$ runhaskell Main.hs
```

```
0.9128709291752768
```

How it works...

The Pearson correlation coefficient measures the degree of linear relationship between two variables. The magnitude of this coefficient describes how strongly the variables are related. If positive, the two variables change together. If negative, as one variable increases, the other decreases.

Comparing sparse data using cosine similarity

When a data set has multiple empty fields, comparing the distance using the Manhattan or Euclidean metrics might result in skewed results. Cosine similarity measures how closely two vectors are oriented with each other. For example, the vectors (82, 86) and (86, 82) essentially point in the same direction. In fact, their cosine similarity is equivalent to the cosine similarity between (41, 43) and (43, 41). A cosine similarity of 1 corresponds to vectors that point in the exact same direction, and 0 corresponds to vectors that are completely orthogonal to each other.

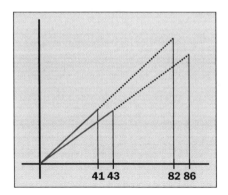

As long as the angles between the two vectors are equal, their cosine similarity is equivalent. Applying a distance metric such as the Manhattan distance or Euclidean distance in this case produces a significant difference between the two sets of data.

The cosine similarity between the two vectors is the dot product of the two vectors divided by the product of their magnitudes.

$$cosineSimilarity(\vec{a}, \vec{b}) = \frac{\vec{a} \cdot \vec{b}}{||\vec{a}||\,||\vec{b}||}$$

$$\vec{a} \cdot \vec{b} = \sum_i a_i b_i$$

$$||\vec{a}|| = \sqrt{\vec{a} \cdot \vec{a}}$$

How to do it...

Create a new file, which we will call `Main.hs`, and perform the following steps:

1. Implement `main` to compute the cosine similarity between two lists of numbers.

   ```
   main :: IO ()
   main = do
     let d1 = [3.5, 2, 0, 4.5, 5, 1.5, 2.5, 2]
     let d2 = [  3, 0, 0,   5, 4, 2.5,   3, 0]
   ```

2. Compute the cosine similarity.

   ```
   let similarity = dot d1 d2 / (eLen d1 * eLen d2)
   print similarity
   ```

3. Define the dot product and Euclidean length helper functions.

   ```
   dot a b = sum $ zipWith (*) a b
   eLen a = sqrt $ dot a a
   ```

4. Run the code to print the cosine similarity.

   ```
   $ runhaskell Main.hs


   0.924679432210068
   ```

See also

If the data set is not sparse, consider using the Manhattan or Euclidean distance metrics instead, as detailed in the recipes *Computing the Manhattan distance* and *Computing the Euclidean distance*.

3
The Science of Words

In this chapter, we will cover the following recipes:

- ▶ Displaying a number in another base
- ▶ Reading a number from another base
- ▶ Searching for a substring using Data.ByteString
- ▶ Searching a string using the Boyer–Moore–Horspool algorithm
- ▶ Searching a string using the Rabin-Karp algorithm
- ▶ Splitting a string on lines, words, or arbitrary tokens
- ▶ Finding the longest common subsequence
- ▶ Computing a phonetic code
- ▶ Calculating the edit distance between two strings
- ▶ Computing the Jaro–Winkler distance between two strings
- ▶ Finding strings within one-edit distance
- ▶ Fixing spelling mistakes using edit distance

Introduction

Many interesting analysis techniques can be used on a large corpus of words. Whether it be examining the structure of a sentence or the content of a book, these recipes will introduce us to some useful tools.

When manipulating strings for data analysis, some of the most common functions are among substring search and edit distance computations. Since numbers are often found in a corpus of text, this chapter will start by showing how to represent numbers in an arbitrary base as a string. We will cover a couple of string-searching algorithms and then focus on extracting text to study not only the words but also how the words are used together.

Many practical applications can be constructed given the simple set of tools provided in this section. For example, in the last recipe, we will demonstrate a way to correct spelling mistakes. How we use these algorithms is entirely up to our creativity, but at least having them at our disposal is an excellent start.

Displaying a number in another base

Strings are a natural way to represent numbers in different bases due to the inclusion of letters as digits. This recipe will tell us how to convert a number to a string that can be printed as output.

How to do it...

1. We will need to import the following two functions:

```
import Data.Char (intToDigit, chr, ord)
import Numeric (showIntAtBase)
```

2. Define a function to represent a number in a particular base as follows:

```
n 'inBase' b = showIntAtBase b numToLetter n ""
```

3. Define the mapping between numbers and letters for digits larger than nine as follows:

```
numToLetter :: Int -> Char
numToLetter n
  | n < 10 = intToDigit n
  | otherwise = chr (ord 'a' n - 10)
```

4. Print out the result using the following code snippet:

```
main :: IO ()
main = do
   putStrLn $ 8 'inBase' 12
   putStrLn $ 10 'inBase' 12
   putStrLn $ 12 'inBase' 12
   putStrLn $ 47 'inBase' 12
```

5. The following is the printed output when running the code:

```
$ runhaskell Main.hs


8

a

10

3b
```

How it works...

The showIntAtBase function takes in a base, the desired number, and its mapping from number to printable digit. We order our digits in the following manner: 0, 1, 2, 3, 4, 5, 6, 7, 8, 9, a, b, c, d, e, f, and so on, up to 36 characters. Putting it all together, we get a convenient way to represent a decimal number in any base.

See also

To read a string representing a number from another base as a decimal integer, refer to the *Reading a number from another base* recipe.

Reading a number from another base

Decimal, binary, and hexadecimal are widely used numeral systems that are often represented using a string. This recipe will show how to convert a string representation of a number in an arbitrary base to its decimal integer. We use the `readInt` function, which is the dual of the `showIntAtBase` function described in the previous recipe.

How to do it...

1. Import `readInt` and the following functions for character manipulation as follows:

```
import Data.Char (ord, digitToInt, isDigit)
import Numeric (readInt)
```

2. Define a function to convert a string representing a number in a particular base to a decimal integer as follows:

```
str 'base' b = readInt b isValidDigit letterToNum str
```

3. Define the mapping between letters and numbers for larger digits, as shown in the following code snippet:

```
letterToNum :: Char -> Int
letterToNum d
  | isDigit d = digitToInt d
  | otherwise = ord d - ord 'a' + 10

isValidDigit :: Char -> Int
isValidDigit d = letterToNum d >= 0
```

4. Print out the result using the following line of codes:

```
main :: IO ()
main = do
  print $ "8" 'base' 12
  print $ "a" 'base' 12
  print $ "10" 'base' 12
  print $ "3b" 'base' 12
```

5. The printed output is as follows:

```
[(8,"")]
[(10,"")]
[(12,"")]
[(47,"")]
```

How it works...

The `readInt` function reads an unsigned integral value and converts it to the specified base. It takes in the base as the first argument, valid characters as the second argument, and its mapping from character to number as the third argument. We order our digits in the following order: 0, 1, 2, 3, 4, 5, 6, 7, 8, 9, a, b, c, d, e, f, and so on up to 36 characters. Putting it all together, we get a convenient way to convert a string representation of a number in an arbitrary base to a decimal number.

> This recipe assumes that a valid string is passed into the `base` function for conversion. Further error checks are necessary to ensure that erroneous input such as `"a"` `'base'` 4 should not result in an answer.

See also

To do the reverse, refer to the *Displaying a number in another base* recipe.

Searching for a substring using Data.ByteString

There are many algorithms to search for a string within another string. This recipe will use an existing `breakSubstring` function in the `Data.ByteString` library to do most of the heavy lifting.

The `ByteString` documentation establishes its merits by declaring the following claim:

> *"[A ByteString is] a time- and space-efficient implementation of byte vectors using packed Word8 arrays, suitable for high performance use, both in terms of large data quantities, or high speed requirements. Byte vectors are encoded as strict Word8 arrays of bytes, held in a ForeignPtr, and can be passed between C and Haskell with little effort."*

More information and documentation can be obtained on the package web page at `http://hackage.haskell.org/package/bytestring/docs/Data-ByteString.html`.

How to do it...

1. Import the `breakSubstring` function as well as the `Data.ByteString.Char8` package as follows:

```
import Data.ByteString (breakSubstring)
import qualified Data.ByteString.Char8 as C
```

2. Pack the strings as a `ByteString` and feed them into `breakSubstring` which has the following type: `ByteString -> ByteString -> (ByteString, ByteString)`. Then determine whether the string is found:

    ```
    substringFound :: String -> String -> Bool

    substringFound query str =
      (not . C.null . snd) $
      breakSubstring (C.pack query) (C.pack str)
    ```

3. Try out some tests in `main` as follows:

    ```
    main = do
      print $ substringFound "scraf" "swedish scraf mafia"
      print $ substringFound "flute" "swedish scraf mafia"
    ```

4. Executing `main` will print out the following results:

    True

    False

How it works...

The `breakSubstring` function recursively checks if the pattern is a prefix of the string. To lazily find the first occurrence of a string, we can call `snd (breakSubstring pat str)`.

There's more...

Another elegant way to quickly find a substring is by using the `isInfixOf` function provided by both `Data.List` and `Data.ByteString`. Moreover, we can also use the `OverloadedStrings` language extension to remove verbiage, as shown in the following code snippet:

```
{-# LANGUAGE OverloadedStrings #-}
import Data.ByteString (isInfixOf)

main = do
  print $ isInfixOf "scraf" "swedish scraf mafia"
  print $ isInfixOf "flute" "swedish scraf mafia"
```

See also

Depending on the length of the pattern we're trying to find and the length of the whole string itself, other algorithms may provide better performance. Refer to the *Searching a string using the Boyer-Moore-Horspool algorithm* and *Searching a string using the Rabin-Karp algorithm* recipes for more details.

Searching a string using the Boyer-Moore-Horspool algorithm

When searching for a pattern in a string, we refer to the pattern as the **needle** and the whole corpus as the **haystack**. The Horspool string search algorithm implemented in this recipe performs well for almost all pattern lengths and alphabet sizes, but is ideal for large alphabet sizes and large needle sizes. Empirical benchmarks can be found by navigating to the following URL:

```
http://orion.lcg.ufrj.br/Dr.Dobbs/books/book5/chap10.htm
```

By preprocessing the query, the algorithm is able to efficiently skip redundant comparisons. In this recipe, we will implement a simplified version called Horspool's algorithm, which achieves the same average best case as the Boyer-Moore algorithm, benefits from having a smaller overhead cost, but may in very rare circumstances suffer the same worst-case running time as the naive search when the algorithm performs too many matches. The Boyer-Moore algorithms should only be used if the extra prepossessing time and space required are acceptable.

How to do it...

1. We will be using a couple `Data.Map` functions as follows:

    ```
    import Data.Map (fromList, (!), findWithDefault)
    ```

2. For convenience, define tuples representing character indices as follows:

    ```
    indexMap xs = fromList $ zip [0..] xs

    revIndexMap xs = fromList $ zip (reverse xs) [0..]
    ```

3. Define the search algorithm to use the recursive `bmh'` function as follows:

    ```
    bmh :: Ord a => [a] -> [a] -> Maybe Int

    bmh pat xs = bmh' (length pat - 1) (reverse pat) xs pat
    ```

4. Recursively find the pattern in the current index until the index moves past the length of the string, as shown in the following code snippet:

    ```
    bmh' :: Ord a => Int -> [a] -> [a] -> [a] -> Maybe Int

    bmh' n [] xs pat = Just (n + 1)
    bmh' n (p:ps) xs pat
      | n >= length xs   = Nothing
      | p == (indexMap xs) ! n = bmh' (n - 1) ps xs pat
      | otherwise              = bmh' (n + findWithDefault
    ```

```
                                    (length pat)  (sMap ! n) pMap)
                                    (reverse pat)  xs pat
        where sMap = indexMap xs
              pMap = revIndexMap pat
```

5. Test out the function as follows:

```
main :: IO ()
main = print $ bmh "Wor" "Hello World"
```

6. The following printed output displays the first index of the matching substring:

```
Just 6
```

How it works...

This algorithm compares the desired pattern to a moving window through the text. The efficiency comes from how quickly the moving window shifts left to right through this text. In the Horspool algorithm, the query is compared to the current window character by character from right to left, and the window shifts by the size of the query in the best case.

Another version of the Horspool algorithm designed by Remco Niemeijer can be found at http://bonsaicode.wordpress.com/2009/08/29/programming-praxis-string-search-boyer-moore.

There's more...

The Boyer-Moore algorithm ensures a faster worst case, but also endures slightly more initial overhead. Refer to the following commands to use the Boyer-Moore algorithm from the Data.ByteString.Search package:

```
$ cabal install stringsearch
```

Import the following libraries:

```
import Data.ByteString.Search
import qualified Data.ByteString.Char8 as C
```

Feed two ByteString types to the indices function to run the search as follows:

```
main = print $ indices (C.pack "abc") (C.pack "bdeabcdabc")
```

This will print out the following indices:

```
[3,7]
```

By benchmarking the performance of this library, we can see that longer search needles really improve runtime. We modify the code to search through a huge corpus of words from a file called `big.txt` to find multiple needles. Here, we use the `deepseq` function to force evaluation, so Haskell's lazy nature won't ignore it, as shown in the following code:

```
shortNeedles = ["abc", "cba"]
longNeedles = ["very big words", "some long string"]

main = do
  corpus <- BS.readFile "big.txt"
  map (\x -> (not.null) (indices x corpus)) shortNeedles
    'deepseq' return ()
```

We can compile this code with special runtime system (RTS) control for easy profiling as follows:

```
$ ghc -O2 Main.hs -rtsopts
```

```
$ ./Main +RTS -sstder
```

We use the text from `norvig.com/big.txt` as our corpus. Searching for 25 long needles takes just about 0.06 seconds; however, searching for 25 short needles takes a sluggish 0.19 seconds.

See also

For another efficient string searching algorithm, refer to the *Searching a string using the Rabin-Karp algorithm* recipe.

Searching a string using the Rabin-Karp algorithm

The Rabin-Karp algorithm finds a pattern in a body of text by matching a unique representation of the pattern against a moving window. The unique representation, or hash, is computed by considering a string as a number written in an arbitrary base of 26 or greater.

The advantage of Rabin-Karp is in searching for many needles in a haystack. It's not very efficient to search for just a single string. After the initial preprocessing of the corpus, the algorithm can quickly find matches.

Getting ready

Install the `Data.ByteString.Search` library from Cabal as follows:

```
$ cabal install stringsearch
```

How to do it...

1. Use the `OverloadedStrings` language extension to facilitate the `ByteString` manipulations in our code as follows. It essentially allows polymorphic behavior for strings so that the GHC compiler may infer it as a `ByteString` type when necessary:

   ```
   {-# LANGUAGE OverloadedStrings #-}
   ```

2. Import the Rabin-Karp algorithms as follows:

   ```
   import Data.ByteString.Search.KarpRabin (indicesOfAny)
   import qualified Data.ByteString as BS
   ```

3. Define a couple of patterns to find and obtain the corpus from a `big.txt` file, as shown in the following code snippet:

   ```
   main = do
     let needles = [ "preparing to go away"
                   , "is some letter of recommendation"]
     haystack <- BS.readFile "big.txt"
   ```

4. Run the Rabin-Karp algorithm on all the search patterns as follows:

   ```
   print $ indicesOfAny needles haystack
   ```

5. The code prints out all indices found for each needle as a list of tuples. The first element of the tuple is the position in the haystack that the needle was found. The second element of the tuple is a list of indices of the needles. In our recipe, we find one instance of "preparing to go away" and two instances of "is some letter of recommendation."

   ```
   $ runhaskell Main.hs
   ```

   ```
   [(3738968,[1]),(5632846,[0]),(5714386,[0])]
   ```

How it works...

In Rabin-Karp, a fixed window moves from left to right, comparing the unique hash values for efficient comparisons. The hash function converts a string to its numerical representation. Here's an example of converting a string into base b equal to 256: *"hello"* = $h' * b^4 + e' * b^3 + l' * b^2 + l' * b^1 + o' * b^0$ (which results in 448378203247), where each letter `h'` = `ord h` (which results in 104), and so on.

See also

To see another efficient string searching algorithm, refer to the *Searching a string using the Boyer-Moore-Horspool algorithm* recipe.

Splitting a string on lines, words, or arbitrary tokens

Useful data is often interspersed between delimiters, such as commas or spaces, making string splitting vital for most data analysis tasks.

Getting ready

Create an `input.txt` file similar to the following one:

```
$ cat input.txt


first line
second line
words are split by space
comma,separated,values
or any delimiter you want
```

Install the `split` package using Cabal as follows:

```
$ cabal install split
```

How to do it...

1. The only function we will need is `splitOn`, which is imported as follows:

   ```
   import Data.List.Split (splitOn)
   ```

2. First we split the string into lines, as shown in the following code snippet:

   ```
   main = do
      input <- readFile "input.txt"
      let ls = lines input
      print $ ls
   ```

3. The lines are printed in a list as follows:

   ```
   [ "first line","second line"
   , "words are split by space"
   , "comma,separated,values"
   , "or any delimiter you want"]
   ```

4. Next, we separate a string on spaces as follows:

   ```
   let ws = words $ ls !! 2
   print ws
   ```

5. The words are printed in a list as follows:

   ```
   ["words","are","split","by","space"]
   ```

6. Next, we show how to split a string on an arbitrary value using the following lines of code:

   ```
   let cs = splitOn "," $ ls !! 3
   print cs
   ```

7. The values are split on the commas as follows:

   ```
   ["comma","separated","values"]
   ```

8. Finally, we show splitting on multiple letters as shown in the following code snippet:

   ```
   let ds = splitOn "an" $ ls !! 4
   print ds
   ```

9. The output is as follows:

   ```
   ["or any d","limit","r you want"]
   ```

Finding the longest common subsequence

One way to compare string similarity is by finding their longest common subsequence. This is useful in finding differences between mutations of data such as source code or genome sequences.

A subsequence of a string is the same string with zero or more of the indices removed. So, some possible subsequences of "BITCOIN" could be "ITCOIN", "TON", "BIN", or even "BITCOIN" itself, as shown in the following figure:

The longest common subsequence is exactly what it sounds like. It is the longest subsequence common to both strings. For example, the longest common subsequence of "find the lights" and "there are four lights" is "the lights."

Getting ready

Install the `data-memocombinators` package from Cabal. This allows us to minimize redundant computations to improve runtime as follows:

```
$ cabal install data-memocombinators
```

How to do it...

1. The only import we will need is this handy package to easily support memoization:

    ```
    import qualified Data.MemoCombinators as Memo
    ```

2. Create a convenience function to enable memoization of functions that take in two string arguments, as shown in the following code snippet:

    ```
    memoize :: (String -> String -> r) -> String -> String -> r
    memoize = Memo.memo2
        (Memo.list Memo.char) (Memo.list Memo.char)
    ```

3. Define the largest common subsequence function as follows:

```
lcs :: String -> String -> String

lcs = memoize lcs'
  where lcs' xs'@(x:xs) ys'@(y:ys)
        | x == y = x : lcs xs ys
        | otherwise = longer (lcs xs' ys) (lcs xs ys')
        lcs' _ _ = []
```

4. Internally, define a function that returns the longer length string.

```
longer as bs
  | length as > length bs = as
  | otherwise = bs
```

5. Run the function on two strings as follows.

```
main :: IO ()
main = do
  let xs = "find the lights"
  let ys = "there are four lights"
  print $ lcs xs ys
```

6. The following is the longest common subsequence between the two strings:

"the lights"

How it works...

The algorithm is implemented naively, with memoization added to the recursive calls. If the first two items of a list are the same, then the longest common subsequence is the lcs function applied to the remaining parts of the list. Otherwise, the longest common subsequence is the longer of the two possibilities.

Naively, this algorithm will stall when given two strings as small as 10 characters each. Since the code breaks down to multiple identical subproblems, we can easily use a simple memoize function that remembers already computed values, improving the runtime dramatically.

Computing a phonetic code

If we're dealing with a corpus of English words, then we can categorize them into phonetic codes to see how similar they sound. Phonetic codes work for any alphabetical strings, not just actual words. We will use the Text.PhoneticCode package to compute the Soundex and Phoneix phonetic codes. The package documentation can be found on Hackage at http://hackage.haskell.org/package/phonetic-code.

Getting ready

Install the phonetic code library from Cabal as follows:

```
$ cabal install phonetic-code
```

How to do it...

1. Import the phonetic code functions as follows:

    ```
    import Text.PhoneticCode.Soundex (soundexNARA,
      soundexSimple)
    import Text.PhoneticCode.Phonix (phonix)
    ```

2. Define a list of similar-sounding words as follows:

    ```
    ws = ["haskell", "hackle", "haggle", "hassle"]
    ```

3. Test out the phonetic codes on these words, as shown in the following code snippet:

    ```
    main :: IO ()
    main = do
      print $ map soundexNARA ws
      print $ map soundexSimple ws
      print $ map phonix ws
    ```

4. The output will be printed as follows:

    ```
    $ runhaskell Main.hs


    ["H240","H240","H240","H240"]


    ["H240","H240","H240","H240"]


    ["H82","H2","H2","H8"]
    ```

Notice how `phonix` produces a finer categorization than `soundex`.

How it works...

The algorithms perform simple string manipulations based on heuristic English-language-dependent patterns.

There's more...

Metaphone is an improvement over the Soundex algorithm and can be found at `http://aspell.net/metaphone`.

Computing the edit distance

The edit distance or Levenshtein distance is the minimum number of simple string operations required to convert one string into another. In this recipe, we will compute the edit distance based on only insertions, deletions, and substitutions of characters.

Getting ready

Review the equation shown in the following figure obtained from the Wikipedia article about the Levenshtein distance (`http://en.wikipedia.org/wiki/Levenshtein_distance`):

$$\mathrm{lev}_{a,b}(i,j) = \begin{cases} \max(i,j) & \text{if } \min(i,j) = 0, \\ \min \begin{cases} \mathrm{lev}_{a,b}(i-1,j)+1 \\ \mathrm{lev}_{a,b}(i,j-1)+1 & \text{otherwise.} \\ \mathrm{lev}_{a,b}(i-1,j-1)+1_{(a_i \neq b_j)} \end{cases} \end{cases}$$

Here, *a* and *b* are the two strings, and i and j are numbers representing their lengths.

The Haskell code will be a direct translation of this mathematical formula.

Also, install the `data-memocombinators` package from Cabal. This allows us to minimize redundant computations to improve runtime.

```
$ cabal install data-memocombinators
```

How to do it...

1. The only import we will need is the ability to easily memoize functions using the following line of code:

    ```
    import qualified Data.MemoCombinators as Memo
    ```

2. Define the Levenshtein distance function exactly as described in the formula using the following code snippet:

    ```
    lev :: Eq a => [a] -> [a] -> Int
    lev a b = levM (length a) (length b)
      where levM = memoize lev'
        lev' i j
          | min i j == 0 = max i j
          | otherwise    = minimum
    ```

```
          [ ( 1 + levM (i-1) j )
          , ( 1 + levM i (j-1) )
          , ( ind i j + levM (i-1) (j-1) ) ]
```

3. Define the indicator function that returns 1 if the characters don't match.

    ```
    ind i j
      | a !! (i-1) == b !! (j-1) = 0
      | otherwise = 1
    ```

4. Create a convenience function to enable memoization of functions that take in two string arguments:

    ```
    memoize = Memo.memo2 (Memo.integral) (Memo.integral)
    ```

5. Print out the edit distance between two strings:

    ```
    main = print $ lev "mercury" "sylvester"
    ```

6. The result is as follows:

    $ runhaskell Main.hs

    8

How it works...

This algorithm recursively tries all deletions, insertions, and substitutions and finds the minimum distance from one string to another.

See also

Another measurement is described in the *Computing the Jaro-Winkler distance between two strings* recipe.

Computing the Jaro-Winkler distance between two strings

The Jaro-Winkler distance measures string similarity represented as a real number between 0 and 1. The value 0 corresponds to no similarity, and 1 corresponds to an identical match.

Getting ready

The algorithm behind the function comes from the following mathematical formula presented in the Wikipedia article about the Jaro-Winkler distance `http://en.wikipedia.org/wiki/Jaro%E2%80%93Winkler_distance`:

$$d_j = \begin{cases} 0 & \text{if } m = 0 \\ \frac{1}{3}\left(\frac{m}{|s1|} + \frac{m}{|s2|} + \frac{m-t}{m}\right) & \text{otherwise} \end{cases}$$

In the preceding formula, the following are the representations of the variables used:

► *s1* is the first string.

► *s2* is the second string.

► *m* is the number of identical characters within a distance of at the most half the length of the longer string. These are called matching characters.

► *t* is half the number of matching characters that are not in the same index. In other words, it is half the number of transpositions.

How to do it...

1. We will need access to the `elemIndices` function, which is imported as follows:

   ```
   import Data.List (elemIndices)
   ```

2. Define the Jaro-Winkler function based on the following formula:

   ```
   jaro :: Eq a => [a] -> [a] -> Double

   jaro s1 s2
       | m == 0     = 0.0
       | otherwise = (1/3) * (m/ls1 + m/ls2 + (m-t)/m)
   ```

3. Define the variables used, as follows:

   ```
   where ls1 = toDouble $ length s1

         ls2 = toDouble $ length s2

         m' = matching s1 s2 d

         d = fromIntegral $
         max (length s1) (length s2) 'div' 2 - 1

         m = toDouble m'

         t = toDouble $ (m' - matching s1 s2 0) 'div' 2
   ```

4. Define a helper function to convert an integer to `Double` type:

```
toDouble :: Integral a => a -> Double

toDouble n = (fromIntegral n) :: Double
```

5. Define a helper function to find the number of matching characters within a specified distance, as shown in the following code snippet:

```
matching :: Eq a => [a] -> [a] -> Int -> Int

matching s1 s2 d = length $ filter
    (\(c,i) -> not (null (matches s2 c i d)))
    (zip s1 [0..])
```

6. Define a helper function to find the number of matching characters from a specific character at a specified index as follows.

```
matches :: Eq a => [a] -> a -> Int -> Int -> [Int]

matches str c i d = filter (<= d) $
    map (dist i) (elemIndices c str)
    where dist a b = abs $ a - b
```

7. Test out the algorithm by printing out a couple of examples as follows:

```
main = do
    print $ jaro "marisa" "magical"
    print $ jaro "haskell" "hackage"
```

8. The similarities are printed out as such, implying "marisa" is closer to "magical" than "haskell" is to "hackage".

$ runhaskell Main.hs

```
0.746031746031746
```

```
0.7142857142857142
```

See also

Another way to compute string similarity is defined in the previous recipe entitled *Computing the Edit Distance*.

Finding strings within one-edit distance

This recipe will demonstrate how to find strings that are one-edit distance away from a specified string. This function can be used to correct spelling.

Getting ready

The algorithm in this recipe is based heavily on Peter Norvig's spell corrector algorithm described at `http://norvig.com/spell-correct.html`. Take a look at and study the `edits1` Python function implemented there.

How to do it...

1. Import a couple of character and list functions as follows:

    ```
    import Data.Char (toLower)
    import Data.List (group, sort)
    ```

2. Define a function to return strings that are one-edit distance away, as shown in the following code snippet:

    ```
    edits1 :: String -> [String]

    edits1 word = unique $
                  deletes ++ transposes ++ replaces ++ inserts
      where splits  = [ (take i word', drop i word') |
          i <- [0..length word']]
    ```

3. Create a list of strings with one character deleted, as follows:

    ```
    deletes = [ a ++ (tail b) |
        (a,b) <- splits, (not.null) b]
    ```

4. Create a list of strings with two characters swapped, as follows:

    ```
    transposes = [a ++ [b!!1] ++ [head b] ++ (drop 2 b) |
        (a,b) <- splits, length b > 1 ]
    ```

5. Create a list of strings with one of the characters replaced by another letter in the alphabet, as follows:

    ```
    replaces  = [ a ++ [c] ++ (drop 1 b)
        | (a,b) <- splits
        , c <- alphabet
        , (not.null) b ]
    ```

6. Create a list of strings with one character inserted anywhere, as follows:

```
inserts = [a ++ [c] ++ b
| (a,b) <- splits
, c <- alphabet ]
```

7. Define the alphabet and a helper function to convert a string to lowercase as follows:

```
alphabet = ['a'..'z']
word' = map toLower word
```

8. Define a helper function to obtain unique elements from a list, as follows:

```
unique :: [String] -> [String]
unique = map head.group.sort
```

9. Print out all possible strings that are one-edit distance away from the following string, as follows:

```
main = print $ edits1 "hi"
```

The result is, as follows:

```
["ahi","ai","bhi","bi","chi","ci","dhi","di","ehi","ei","fhi","fi","ghi",
"gi","h","ha","hai","hb","hbi","hc","hci","hd","hdi","he","hei","hf","hfi
","hg","hgi","hh","hhi","hi","hia","hib","hic","hid","hie","hif","hig","h
ih","hii","hij","hik","hil","him","hin","hio","hip","hiq","hir","his","hi
t","hiu","hiv","hiw","hix","hiy","hiz","hj","hji","hk","hki","hl","hli","
hm","hmi","hn","hni","ho","hoi","hp","hpi","hq","hqi","hr","hri","hs","hs
i","ht","hti","hu","hui","hv","hvi","hw","hwi","hx","hxi","hy","hyi","hz"
,"hzi","i","ih","ihi","ii","jhi","ji","khi","ki","lhi","li","mhi","mi","n
hi","ni","ohi","oi","phi","pi","qhi","qi","rhi","ri","shi","si","thi","ti
","uhi","ui","vhi","vi","whi","wi","xhi","xi","yhi","yi","zhi","zi"]
```

More intuitively, we've created a neighborhood of words that are different by only 1 insertion, deletion, or substitution, or transpositions. The following figure tries to show this neighborhood:

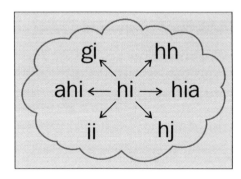

There's more...

We can recursively apply `edit1` to find strings that are an arbitrary edit distance away. However, for values of *n* greater than three, this will take an unacceptably long time. In the following code, `edits1'` is a function that takes in a list of strings and produces all strings that are one-edit distance away from these. Then in `editsN`, we simply apply the `edits1'` function iteratively as follows:

```
edits1' :: [String] -> [String]
edits1' ls = unique $ concat $ map edits1 ls

editsN :: String -> Int -> [String]
editsN word n = iterate edits1' (edits1 word) !! n
```

See also

This function is very useful in implementing a spell corrector described in the *Fixing spelling mistakes* recipe.

Fixing spelling mistakes

When gathering human-provided data, spelling mistakes may sneak in. This recipe will correct a misspelled word using Peter Norvig's simple heuristic spellchecker described at http://norvig.com/spell-correct.html.

This recipe is just one approach to a very difficult problem in machine learning. We can use it as a starting point or as an influence to implement a more powerful solution with better results.

Getting ready

Refer to Norvig's spell-correction Python algorithm located at http://norvig.com/spell-correct.html.

The core algorithm works as follows:

▸ Transform raw text into lowercase alphabetical words

▸ Compute a frequency map of all the words

▸ Define functions to produce all strings within an edit distance of one or two

▸ Find all possible candidates of a misspelling by looking up valid words within this edit distance of one or two

▸ Finally, pick out the candidate with the highest frequency of occurrence in the trained corpus

The Haskell algorithm below mimics this Python code.

How to do it...

1. Import the following functions:

    ```
    import Data.Char (isAlpha, isSpace, toLower)
    import Data.List (group, sort, maximumBy)
    import Data.Ord (comparing)
    import Data.Map (fromListWith, Map, member, (!))
    ```

2. Define a function to automatically correct the spelling of each word in a sentence:

    ```
    autofix :: Map String Int -> String -> String

    autofix m sentence = unwords $
                    map (correct m) (words sentence)
    ```

3. Get the words from a body of text.

    ```
    getWords :: String -> [String]

    getWords str = words $
                filter (\x -> isAlpha x || isSpace x) lower

        where lower = map toLower str
    ```

4. Compute a frequency map of the words provided, as follows:

    ```
    train :: [String] -> Map String Int

    train = fromListWith (+) . ('zip' repeat 1)
    ```

5. Find strings one-edit distance away as follows:

    ```
    edits 1 :: String -> [String]

    edits1 word = unique $
                deletes ++ transposes ++ replaces ++ inserts

        where splits = [ (take i word', drop i word')
                    | i <- [0..length word']]

        deletes = [ a ++ (tail b)
                    | (a,b) <- splits
                    , (not.null) b ]

        transposes = [ a ++ [b !! 1] ++ [head b] ++ (drop 2 b)
    ```

```
                          | (a,b) <- splits, length b > 1 ]

    replaces = [ a ++ [c] ++ (drop 1 b)
                      | (a,b) <- splits, c <- alphabet
                      , (not.null) b ]

    inserts = [a ++ [c] ++ b |
                      (a,b) <- splits, c <- alphabet ]

    alphabet = ['a'..'z']

    word' = map toLower word
```

6. Find words that are apart by an edit distance of two:

```
knownEdits2 :: String -> Map String a -> [String]

knownEdits2 word m = unique $ [ e2
                              | e1 <- edits1 word
                              , e2 <- edits1 e1
                              , e2 'member' m]
```

7. Define a helper function to obtain unique elements from a list, as follows:

```
unique :: [String] -> [String]

unique = map head.group.sort
```

8. Find known words from a list of strings as follows:

```
known :: [String] -> Map String a -> [String]

known ws m = filter ('member' m) ws
```

9. Correct a spelling mistake by returning the most common candidate as follows:

```
correct :: Map String Int -> String -> String

correct m word = maximumBy (comparing (m!)) candidates
  where candidates = head $ filter (not.null)
                    [ known [word] m
                    , known (edits1 word) m
                    , knownEdits2 word m
                    , [word] ]
```

10. Gather a list of known words used in common literature from `big.txt`. The file is available at `http://norvig.com/big.txt`, or we can make our own. Test out the spell corrector as follows:

```
main :: IO ()

main = do
  rawText <- readFile "big.txt"
  let m = train $ getWords rawText
  let sentence = "such codez many hsakell very spel so korrect"
  print $ autofix m sentence
```

11. The correct spellings are printed out as follows:

```
$ runhaskell Main.hs


"such code many haskell very spell so correct"
```

How it works...

The algorithm assumes that spelling mistakes occur one- or two-edit distances away. It establishes a list of known words within one- or two-edit distances and returns the most commonly used word based on the frequency map generated by reading in a corpus of real-world text.

There's more...

This algorithm runs quickly, but it is very simplistic. This recipe provides a starting point to implement a spell corrector, but is certainly not state of the art. Some improvements that can be added to the code could involve parallelizing, caching, or designing better heuristics.

See also

For more in-depth analysis about the `edit1` function, refer to the *Finding strings within one-edit distance* recipe.

4
Data Hashing

In this chapter, we will cover the following recipes:

- ▶ Hashing a primitive data type
- ▶ Hashing a custom data type
- ▶ Running popular cryptographic hash functions
- ▶ Running a cryptographic checksum on a file
- ▶ Performing fast comparisons between data types
- ▶ Using a high-performance hash table
- ▶ Using Google's CityHash hash functions for strings
- ▶ Computing Geohash for location coordinates
- ▶ Using a bloom filter to remove unique items
- ▶ Running MurmurHash, a simple but speedy hashing algorithm
- ▶ Measuring image similarity with perceptual hashes

Introduction

A **hash** is a lossy way of representing an object into a small and typically fixed-length value. Hashing data embellishes us with speedy lookups and lightweight handling of massive datasets.

The output of a hashing function is referred to as a **digest**. One of the principal properties of a good hashing function is that it must be deterministic, which means a given input must always produce the same corresponding output. Sometimes, two different inputs may end up producing the same output, and we call that a **collision**. Given a hash alone, we cannot invert the process to rediscover the object within an adequate time. To minimize the chances of a collision, another property of a hash function called **uniformity** is used. In other words, the probability of each output occurring should be nearly the same.

We will start by first producing a simple digest from an input. Then in the next recipe, we will run the hashing algorithm on our custom-made data type.

Another important application of hashing is in cryptography. We will cover some of the most popular cryptographic hashing algorithms such as SHA-512. We will also apply these hashes on files for computing checksums to ensure file integrity.

Lastly, we will cover many nontraditional hashing approaches including CityHash, GeoHashing, bloom filters, MurmurHash, and pHash.

Hashing a primitive data type

This recipe demonstrates how to use a simple hash function on various primitive data types.

Getting ready

Install the `Data.Hashable` package from Cabal as follows:

```
$ cabal install hashable
```

How to do it...

1. Import the hashing function with the following line:

    ```
    import Data.Hashable
    ```

2. Test the `hash` function on a string as follows; this function is actually a wrapper around the `hashWithSalt` function with a default salt value:

    ```
    main = do
      print $ hash "foo"
    ```

3. Test out the `hashWithSalt` functions using different initial salt values as follows:

    ```
    print $ hashWithSalt 1 "foo"
    print $ hashWithSalt 2 "foo"
    ```

4. We can also hash tuples and lists as follows:

    ```
    print $ hash [ (1 :: Int, "hello", True)
                 , (0 :: Int, "goodbye", False) ]
    ```

5. Notice in the following output how the first three hashes produce different results even though their input is the same:

    ```
    $ runhaskell Main.hs

    7207853227093559468
    367897294438771247
    6879415431139326482
    6768682186886785615
    ```

How it works...

Hashing with a salt means applying the hash function only after slightly modifying it. It's as if we "salted up" the input before processing it through the hash function. Even the slightest change in salt values produces dramatically different hashed digests.

We need this concept of a salt for better password security. Hash functions always produce the same output for the same input, and this is both good and bad. There are databases of rainbow tables for every commonly used password in existence for all major hashing algorithms. If a website with a login system service (such as Packt Publishing) stores the password using cryptographic hashes, but without being salted, then it's no better than plain text if the password itself is considered weak. If a service such as Packt Publishing uses salt in its cryptographic hashing (and it should), then it's an added layer of security and rainbow tables are rendered useless.

There's more...

The previous code produced a hash of a string, but the algorithm is not limited to just strings. The following data types also implement `hashable`:

- Bool
- Char
- Int
- Int8
- Int16
- Int32
- Int64
- Word
- Word8
- Word16
- Word32
- Word64
- ByteString
- List of hashable items
- Tuple of hashable items
- Maybe of a hashable item

See also

For using a hash function on a custom-made data type, refer to the *Hashing a custom data type* recipe.

Hashing a custom data type

Even a custom-defined data type can be hashed easily. Dealing with hashed digests is often useful when the data itself is too space consuming to manage directly. By referencing a data by its digest, we can easily skip the cost of carrying around whole data types. This is especially useful in data analysis.

Getting ready

Install the `Data.Hashable` package from Cabal as follows:

```
$ cabal install hashable
```

How to do it...

1. Use the GHC language extension `DeriveGeneric` to autodefine the hash functions for our custom data types as follows:

    ```
    {-# LANGUAGE DeriveGeneric #-}
    ```

2. Import the relevant packages using the following lines of code:

    ```
    import GHC.Generics (Generic)
    import Data.Hashable
    ```

3. Create a custom data type and let GHC autodefine its hashable instance as follows:

    ```
    data Point = Point Int Int
               deriving (Eq, Generic)

    instance Hashable Point
    ```

4. In `main`, create three points. Let two of them be the same, and let the third point be different, as shown in the following code snippet:

    ```
    main = do
        let p1 = Point 1 1
        let p2 = Point 1 1
        let p3 = Point 3 5
    ```

5. Print the hash values of identical points as follows:

    ```
    if p1 == p2
      then putStrLn "p1 = p2"
      else putStrLn "p1 /= p2"
      if hash p1 == hash p2
      then putStrLn "hash p1 = hash p2"
      else putStrLn "hash p1 /= hash p2"
    ```

6. Print the hash values of different points as follows:

```
if p1 == p3
  then putStrLn "p1 = p3"
  else putStrLn "p1 /= p3"
if hash p1 == hash p3
  then putStrLn "hash p1 = hash p3"
  else putStrLn "hash p1 /= hash p3"
```

7. The output will be as follows:

```
$ runhaskell Main.hs


p1 = p2

hash p1 = hash p2

p1 /= p3

hash p1 /= hash p3
```

There's more...

We can define a custom hashing function on our own data types by providing an instance for Hashable. The Hashable instance only requires the implementation of `hashWithSalt :: Int -> a -> Int`. To help implement `hashWithSalt`, we also have two useful functions:

► Hashing a pointer with salt is performed as shown in the following code snippet:

```
hashPtrWithSalt :: Ptr a    --  pointer to the data to hash
                -> Int      --  length, in bytes
                -> Int      --  salt
                -> IO Int   --  hash value
```

► Hashing a byte array with salt is performed as shown in the following code snippet:

```
hashByteArrayWithSalt
    :: ByteArray#   --  data to hash
    -> Int          --  offset, in bytes
    -> Int          --  length, in bytes
    -> Int          --  salt
    -> Int          --  hash value
```

See also

To hash a built-in primitive, refer to the *Hashing a primitive data type* recipe.

Running popular cryptographic hash functions

A cryptographic hash function has specific properties that make it different from other hash functions. First of all, producing a possible input message from a given hash digest output should be intractable, meaning that it must take an exponentially long time to solve in practice.

For example, if a hash produces the digest `66fc01ae071363ceaa4178848c2f6224`, then in principle, discovering the content used to generate a digest should be difficult.

In practice, some hash functions are easier to crack than others. For example, MD5 and SHA-1 are considered trivial to crack and should not be used, but are demonstrated later for completeness. More information about how MD5 and SHA-1 are insecure can be found at `http://www.win.tue.nl/hashclash/rogue-ca` and `https://www.schneier.com/blog/archives/2005/02/cryptanalysis_o.html` respectively.

Getting ready

Install the `Crypto.Hash` package from Cabal as follows:

```
$ cabal install cryptohash
```

How to do it...

1. Import the cryptographic hash function library as follows:

    ```
    import Data.ByteString.Char8 (ByteString, pack)
    import Crypto.Hash
    ```

2. Define each hash functions by explicitly associating the data types as follows:

    ```
    skein512_512 :: ByteString -> Digest Skein512_512
    skein512_512 bs = hash bs

    skein512_384 :: ByteString -> Digest Skein512_384
    skein512_384 bs = hash bs

    skein512_256 :: ByteString -> Digest Skein512_256
    skein512_256 bs = hash bs

    skein512_224 :: ByteString -> Digest Skein512_224
    ```

```
skein512_224 bs = hash bs

skein256_256 :: ByteString -> Digest Skein256_256
skein256_256 bs = hash bs

skein256_224 :: ByteString -> Digest Skein256_224
skein256_224 bs = hash bs

sha3_512 :: ByteString -> Digest SHA3_512
sha3_512 bs = hash bs

sha3_384 :: ByteString -> Digest SHA3_384
sha3_384 bs = hash bs

sha3_256 :: ByteString -> Digest SHA3_256
sha3_256 bs = hash bs

sha3_224 :: ByteString -> Digest SHA3_224
sha3_224 bs = hash bs

tiger :: ByteString -> Digest Tiger
tiger bs = hash bs

whirlpool :: ByteString -> Digest Whirlpool
whirlpool bs = hash bs

ripemd160 :: ByteString -> Digest RIPEMD160
ripemd160 bs = hash bs

sha512 :: ByteString -> Digest SHA512
sha512 bs = hash bs

sha384 :: ByteString -> Digest SHA384
sha384 bs = hash bs

sha256 :: ByteString -> Digest SHA256
sha256 bs = hash bs

sha224 :: ByteString -> Digest SHA224
```

```
sha224 bs = hash bs

sha1 :: ByteString -> Digest SHA1
sha1 bs = hash bs

md5 :: ByteString -> Digest MD5
md5 bs = hash bs

md4 :: ByteString -> Digest MD4
md4 bs = hash bs

md2 :: ByteString -> Digest MD2
md2 bs = hash bs
```

3. Test out each cryptographic hash function on the same input, as shown in the following code snippet:

```
main = do
  let input = pack "haskell data analysis"
  putStrLn $ "Skein512_512: " ++ (show.skein512_512) input
  putStrLn $ "Skein512_384: " ++ (show.skein512_384) input
  putStrLn $ "Skein512_256: " ++ (show.skein512_256) input
  putStrLn $ "Skein512_224: " ++ (show.skein512_224) input
  putStrLn $ "Skein256_256: " ++ (show.skein256_256) input
  putStrLn $ "Skein256_224: " ++ (show.skein256_224) input
  putStrLn $ "SHA3_512: " ++ (show.sha3_512) input
  putStrLn $ "SHA3_384: " ++ (show.sha3_384) input
  putStrLn $ "SHA3_256: " ++ (show.sha3_256) input
  putStrLn $ "SHA3_224: " ++ (show.sha3_224) input
  putStrLn $ "Tiger: " ++ (show.tiger) input
  putStrLn $ "Whirlpool: " ++ (show.whirlpool) input
  putStrLn $ "RIPEMD160: " ++ (show.ripemd160) input
  putStrLn $ "SHA512: " ++ (show.sha512) input
  putStrLn $ "SHA384: " ++ (show.sha384) input
  putStrLn $ "SHA256: " ++ (show.sha256) input
  putStrLn $ "SHA224: " ++ (show.sha224) input
  putStrLn $ "SHA1: " ++ (show.sha1) input
  putStrLn $ "MD5: " ++ (show.md5) input
  putStrLn $ "MD4: " ++ (show.md4) input
  putStrLn $ "MD2: " ++ (show.md2) input
```

4. The final output can be seen in the following screenshot:

```
$ runhaskell Main.hs
```

```
$ runhaskell Main.hs
Skein512_512: dcf428af92736789b2c8cd235dd64335a836af1807c6801142945cec4c45e1afff
4e01c09a4af11f64c723a600e07c3e247a863950d7f659ab678d55cbdc4575
Skein512_384: 76f432fad4ce6004f47214966f9cb4ab9d6adf2cb15091d210d8ef4364b33eaeec
78a329180ec577eb8923987ce93fcb
Skein512_256: 45bfe259cd152b2a588b9afe41bf57ce60881eb8f9d4a92239ccc248902aea7a
Skein512_224: 1dd7251b1a057eebd479eeaf04d118a6518b2c360db2a7272d53fb8a
Skein256_256: 89bc6f0c10c5db27ca76c2c42509e3e6885822db0835b5db9e5c7703d44afa7e
Skein256_224: 1ced6f95ac295247ee3fc5ead125af5de2a1eed2e5a79d2bb92e271e
SHA3_512: 2c83ffb8af309c59e58485bf3f76ab1c280c88981e918d9c9f91c5dba365ababa9f652
3fd0d75002d8b7d55c7378cd7749af0e7f7c367813e0aed3cdf944100e4
SHA3_384: 3613ad4834e7dbf0358c9ff747b1cd3f73b6e63c0332af9c54877863c7c151ad2146f9
32a985969d554f0942fc9f5572
SHA3_256: 62439d86ff208b211e44cc9ba1acf123f7cfa975ffebf4e61a92bbba5a04b9f1
SHA3_224: d4a25ed3bfd43d8d26737a90889dea0b8e3a2598571e914955a54e1a
Tiger: e856bc222ec2a3aaa9656e3338e467df585038f8cbed70a8
Whirlpool: 53316c4794bc1d9c4b4bebba111571e44e0e9d44c7c019e664f4038f4400b955c092a
dece5aeaa1079dd975a5be8f272baca91f03d19e9263119ac0e56140837
RIPEMD160: 59dd1c6e6e3ff2f42e099d929fd574c025d38d5b
SHA512: ec1bc5ccb27752d9b48c7fda881c287e6f694c4cae923bb04c33188bf438f83fc7c435d1
45151b7156fe36e664802fb6b3c8090f9e5a8cf561f8efdf8a3b877c
SHA384: b8d9ea6184fa2161dad67dfded1365d1bbddef503dd156cecc3f0d6b9d37f63d1d3cad0c
416acb755043525960111662
SHA256: 3bf92740ac996a83c3159adf1efbd044427bb257842bf1e21d3220ae1e2930f6
SHA224: 4d04165d1916c09dc74fe7d35b114321ccfe1f6feb36063104597a82
SHA1: 96d350822480f0d578ec9cb27905664edc8a2a47
MD5: 66fc01ae071363ceaa4178848c2f6224
MD4: 16ad0b01d310eb31a39090303eb2e37e
MD2: f35fbf11e7f4eced2f69195240af2bf6
```

See also

To run one of these cryptographic hash functions on a file to perform an integrity check, refer to the *Running a cryptographic checksum on a file* recipe.

Running a cryptographic checksum on a file

One of the most effective methods to determine whether a file on a computer is different from another file elsewhere is by comparing their cryptographic hashes. If the two hashes are equal, it's only highly probable that the files are equal, but not strictly necessary due to the possibility of collisions.

After downloading a file online, such as Arch Linux from `https://www.archlinux.org/download`, it is a good idea to ensure the cryptographic hashes match up. For example, have a look at the following screenshot:

Checksums

File integrity checksums for the latest releases can be found below:

- PGP signature
- **MD5:** 4881f5e2d9ae745c5abacec1b068a0c2
- **SHA1:** 007654f3f18da66f761611c1e645fca2fb194c5b

The preceding screenshot shows the corresponding hashes for the Arch Linux download as of late May, 2014.

Notice how both MD5 and SHA1 hashes are provided. This recipe will show how to compute these hashes in Haskell to ensure data integrity.

We will compute the SHA256, SHA512, and MD5 hashes of its own source file.

Getting ready

Install the `Crypto.Hash` package from Cabal as follows:

```
$ cabal install cryptohash
```

How to do it...

Create a file named `Main.hs` and insert the following code:

1. Import the relevant packages as follows:

   ```
   import Crypto.Hash
   import qualified Data.ByteString as BS
   ```

2. Define the MD5 hash function as follows:

   ```
   md5 :: BS.ByteString -> Digest MD5
   md5 bs = hash bs
   ```

3. Define the SHA256 hash function as follows:

   ```
   sha256 :: BS.ByteString -> Digest SHA256
   sha256 bs = hash bs
   ```

4. Define the SHA512 hash function as follows:

   ```
   sha512 :: BS.ByteString -> Digest SHA512
   sha512 bs = hash bs
   ```

5. Open a file of the `ByteString` type using the `readFile` function provided by the `Data.ByteString` package as follows:

```
main = do
  byteStr <- BS.readFile "Main.hs"
```

6. Test out the various hashes on the file as follows:

```
putStrLn $ "MD5: " ++ (show.md5) byteStr
putStrLn $ "SHA256: " ++ (show.sha256) byteStr
putStrLn $ "SHA512: " ++ (show.sha512) byteStr
```

7. The following output is generated:

```
$ runhaskell Main.hs


MD5: 242334e552ae8ede926de9c164356d18


SHA256:

50364c25e0e9a835df726a056bd5370657f37d20aabc82e0b1719a343ab505d8


SHA512: 1ad6a9f8922b744c7e5a2d06bf603c267ca6becbf52b2b22f8e5a8e2d
82fb52d87ef4a13c9a405b06986d5d19b170d0fd05328b8ae29f9d92ec0bca
80f7b60e7
```

See also

To apply the cryptographic hash functions on data types instead, refer to the *Running popular cryptographic hash functions* recipe.

Performing fast comparisons between data types

The `StableName` package allows us to establish constant time comparisons of arbitrary data types. The Hackage documentation elegantly describes this (http://hackage.haskell.org/package/base-4.7.0.0/docs/System-Mem-StableName.html):

> *"Stable names solve the following problem: suppose you want to build a hash table with Haskell objects as keys, but you want to use pointer equality for comparison; maybe because the keys are large and hashing would be slow, or perhaps because the keys are infinite in size. We can't build a hash table using the address of the object as the key, because objects get moved around by the garbage collector, meaning a re-hash would be necessary after every garbage collection."*

How to do it...

1. Import the built-in `StableName` package as follows:

```
import System.Mem.StableName
```

2. Create a custom data type as follows:

```
data Point = Point [Int]
```

3. In `main`, define two points as follows:

```
main = do
   let p1 = Point [1..]
   let p2 = Point [2,4]
```

4. Get the stable name of each point and display it using the following set of commands:

```
sn1 <- makeStableName p1
sn2 <- makeStableName p2
print $ hashStableName sn1
print $ hashStableName sn2
```

5. Notice in the following result how we can easily obtain the stable name of arbitrary data types:

```
$ runhaskell Main.hs


22

23
```

Using a high-performance hash table

Haskell already comes with a `Data.Map` module based on size-balanced binary trees. There exist better-optimized hash table libraries such as `Data.HashMap` from the unordered-containers package.

For example, both `Data.Map` and `Data.HashMap` have insertion and lookup time complexities of O(log n); however, the latter uses a large base, so in practice these operations are constant time. More documentation on `Data.HashMap` can be found at `http://hackage.haskell.org/package/unordered-containers-0.2.4.0/docs/Data-HashMap-Lazy.html`.

In this recipe, we will use the unordered-contains library from Hackage to create a mapping of word size to a set of words of that size.

Getting ready

Download a large corpus of text and name the file `big.txt` as follows:

```
$ wget norvig.com/big.txt
```

Install the `Data.HashMap` package using Cabal as follows:

```
$ cabal install unordered-containers
```

How to do it...

1. Import the `HashMap` package as follows:

```
import Data.HashMap.Lazy
import Data.Set (Set)
import qualified Data.Set as Set
```

2. Create a helper function to define an empty hash map using the following line of code:

```
emptyMap = empty :: HashMap Int (Set String)
```

3. Define a function to insert a word to the hash map using the following code snippet:

```
insertWord m w = insertWith append key val m
  where append new old = Set.union new old
    key = length w
    val = Set.singleton w
```

4. Find all words of a specific length from a map as follows:

```
wordsOfLength len m = Set.size(lookupDefault Set.empty len
  m )
```

5. Construct the hashmap from a corpus of text using the following line of code:

```
constructMap text = foldl (\m w -> insertWord m w) emptyMap
  (words text)
```

6. Read the large corpus of text, construct the hash map, and print the number of words of each length, as shown in the following code snippet:

```
main = do
  text <- readFile "big.txt"
  let m = constructMap text
  print [wordsOfLength s m | s <- [1..30]]
```

7. The output is as follows:

```
$ runhaskell Main.hs
```

```
[59,385,1821,4173,7308,9806,11104,11503,10174,7948,5823,4024,2586,
1597,987,625,416,269,219,139,115,78,51,50,27,14,17,15,11,7]
```

If we plot the data, we can discover an interesting trend as shown in the following figure:

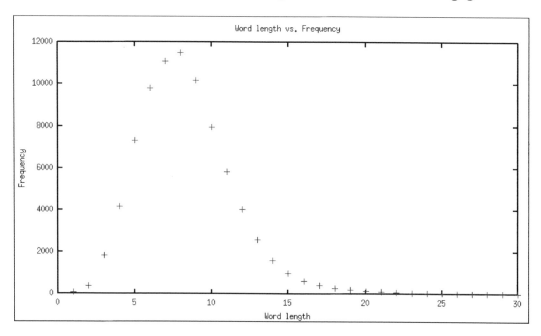

How it works...

Technical specifics about the library are explained in the following blog post by the author:

```
http://blog.johantibell.com/2012/03/announcing-unordered-
containers-02.html
```

Using Google's CityHash hash functions for strings

Google's CityHash hash functions are optimized for hashing strings, but are not meant to be cryptographically secure. CityHash is ideal for implementing a hash table dealing with strings. We will use it in this recipe to produce both 64-bit and 128-bit digests.

Getting ready

Install the `cityhash` package from Cabal as follows:

```
$ cabal install cityhash
```

How to do it...

1. Import the relevant packages as follows:

```
import Data.Digest.CityHash
import Data.ByteString.Char8 (pack)
import Data.Word (Word64)
import Data.LargeWord (Word128)
```

2. Test the various hashing function on an input string using the following code snippet:

```
main = do
  (pack str) (1 :: Word128)   let str = "cityhash"
  print $ cityHash64 (pack str)
  print $ cityHash64WithSeed (pack str) (1 :: Word64)
  print $ cityHash64WithSeed (pack str) (2 :: Word64)
  print $ cityHash128 (pack str)
  print $ cityHash128WithSeed
  print $ cityHash128WithSeed (pack str) (2 :: Word128)
```

3. Display the output as follows:

```
$ runhaskell Main.hs
```

```
11900721293443925155
10843914211836357278
12209340445019361150
116468032688941434670559074973810442908
218656848647432546431274347445469875003
450749526477220732143925569572 68553766
```

How it works...

Google describes its package on its blog announcement at `http://google-opensource.blogspot.com/2011/04/introducing-cityhash.html` as follows:

> *"The key advantage of our approach is that most steps contain at least two independent mathematical operations. Modern CPUs tend to perform best with this type of code."*

See also

To see a more generic hashing function, refer to the *Hashing a primitive data type* and *Hashing a custom data type* recipes.

Computing a Geohash for location coordinates

A Geohash is a practical encoding of latitude-longitude coordinates. It does not behave like a typical hash function since minor changes in location only produce minor changes in the output digest. Geohash allows efficient proximity search and arbitrary precision determined by the specified length of the digest.

Getting ready

Install the Geohashing library as follows:

```
$ cabal install geohash
```

How to do it...

1. Import the `Geohash` library as follows:

   ```
   import Data.Geohash
   ```

2. Create a geohash of a latitude-longitude coordinate pair as follows:

   ```
   main = do
     let geohash1 = encode 10 (37.775, -122.419)
     putStrLn $ "geohash1 is " ++ (show geohash1)
   ```

3. Display the geohash using the following code snippet:

   ```
   case geohash1 of
     Just g -> putStrLn $ "decoding geohash1: " ++
       (show.decode) g
     Nothing -> putStrLn "error encoding"
   ```

4. Create a geohash of another similar latitude-longitude coordinate pair as follows:

```
let geohash2 = encode 10 (37.175, -125.419)
putStrLn $ "geohash2 is " ++ (show geohash2)
```

5. Display the geohash using the following code snippet:

```
case geohash2 of
Just g -> putStrLn $ "decoding geohash2: " ++ (show.decode)
  g
Nothing -> putStrLn "error encoding"
```

6. The output is as follows. Notice how the geohash appears to share the same prefix due to their closeness.

```
$ runhaskell Main.hs


geohash1 is Just "9q8yyk9pqd"


decoding geohash1: Just (37.775000631809235,-122.4189966917038)


geohash2 is Just "9nwg6p88j6"


decoding geohash2: Just (37.175001204013824,-
   125.4190045595169)
```

Using a bloom filter to remove unique items

A bloom filter is an abstract data type that tests whether an item exists in a set. Unlike a typical hash map data structure, a bloom filter only takes up a constant amount of space. The advantage comes in handy when dealing with billions of data, such as representations of DNA strands as strings: "GATA", "CTGCTA", and so on.

In this recipe, we will use a bloom filter to try to remove unique DNA strands from a list. This is often desired because a typical DNA sample may contain thousands of strands that only appear once. The major disadvantage of a bloom filter is that false positive results for membership are possible. The bloom filter may accidentally claim that an element exists. Though false negatives are not possible: a bloom filter will never claim that an element does not exist when it actually does.

Getting ready

Import the bloom filter package from Cabal as follows:

```
$ cabal install bloomfilter
```

How to do it...

1. Import the bloom filter package as follows:

```
import Data.BloomFilter (fromListB, elemB, emptyB, insertB)
import Data.BloomFilter.Hash (cheapHashes)
import Data.Map (Map, empty, insertWith)
import qualified Data.Map as Map
```

2. Create a function to remove the unique elements from a list. First check to see if each item exists in the bloom filter; if so, add it to a hash map. If not, add it to the bloom filter, as presented in the following code snippet:

```
removeUniques strands = foldl bloomMapCheck
                              (emptyBloom, emptyMap) strands

    where emptyBloom = emptyB (cheapHashes 3) 1024
          emptyMap = empty :: Map String Int
          bloomMapCheck (b, m) x
          | elemB x b = (b, insertWith (+) x 1 m)
          | otherwise = (insertB x b, m)
```

3. Run the algorithm on a couple of DNA strand examples as follows:

```
main = do
let strands = ["GAT", "GATC", "CGT", "GAT"
                    , "GAT", "CGT", "GAT", "CGT"]
print $ snd $ removeUniques strands
```

4. We see the following strands that likely occur at least twice:

```
$ runhaskell Main.hs


fromList [("CGT",2),("GAT",3)]
```

How it works...

A bloom filter is composed of a couple of hashing functions and a list of numbers initialized at zero. When inserting an element to this data structure, hashes are computed from each of the hashing functions and the corresponding item in the list is updated. Membership tests on a bloom filter are conducted by computing each of the hash functions in the input and testing whether all corresponding list elements are above some threshold value.

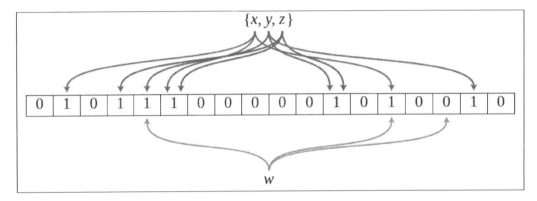

For example, in the preceding figure, three hash functions are applied to every input. When a hash is calculated for **x**, **y**, and **z**, the corresponding element in the list representing the bloom filter is incremented. We can determine whether **w** exists in this bloom filter by computing the three hashes and checking if corresponding indices are all at a desired value. In this case, **w** does not exist in the bloom filter.

Running MurmurHash, a simple but speedy hashing algorithm

Sometimes, the priority of a hashing function should be in maximizing its computation speed. The MurmurHash algorithm exists for this reason. When dealing with massive **data sets**, speed is essential.

There are negative qualities of a fast hashing algorithm. If hashing algorithm A is 10 times faster than hashing algorithm B, then it's also 10 times faster to stumble upon the content used to create a digest with A than with B using a random content search. A hashing algorithm should be fast, but not so fast as to impact the security of the algorithm.

Getting ready

Install the Murmur hashing algorithm from Cabal as follows:

```
$ cabal install murmur-hash
```

How to do it...

1. Import the Murmur hashing algorithm as follows:

    ```
    import Data.Digest.Murmur32
    ```

2. Define a custom data type and implement an instance to use Murmur as follows:

    ```
    data Point = Point Int Int
      instance (Hashable32 Point) where
      hash32Add (Point x y) h = x `hash32Add` (y `hash32Add` h)
    ```

3. Run the hashing algorithm on various inputs, using the following code snippet:

    ```
    main = do
      let p1 = Point 0 0
      let p2 = Point 2 3
      putStrLn $ "hash of string: "
                            ++ (show.hash32) "SO FAST WOW."
      putStrLn $ "hash of a data-type: " ++ (show.hash32) p1
      putStrLn $ "hash of another data-type: " ++ (show.hash32)
        p2
    ```

4. The following hashes are produced:

    ```
    $ runhaskell Main.hs


    hash of string: Hash32 0xa18fa3d2


    hash of a data-type: Hash32 0x30408e22


    hash of another data-type: Hash32 0xfda11257
    ```

Measuring image similarity with perceptual hashes

A perceptual hash produces a small digest from an image file where slight changes in the images only produce a slight change in the hash. This can be useful to quickly compare thousands of images.

Getting ready

Install the pHash library from www.phash.org. On a Debian-based system, we can install it by using apt-get as follows:

```
$ sudo apt-get install libphash0-dev
```

Install the phash library from Cabal as follows:

```
$ cabal install phash
```

Find three nearly identical images. We will use the following image:

This is the second image that we will be using

And the following image is the third:

How to do it...

1. Import the `phash` library as follows:

```
import Data.PHash
import Data.Maybe (fromJust, isJust)
```

2. Hash an image as follows:

```
main = do
  phash1 <- imageHash "image1.jpg"
  putStrLn $ "image1: " ++ show phash1
```

3. Hash a similar image as follows:

```
  phash2 <- imageHash "image2.jpg"
    putStrLn $ "image2: " ++ show phash2
```

4. Hash a slightly different image as follows:

```
  phash3 <- imageHash "image3.jpg"
  putStrLn $ "image3: " ++ show phash3
```

5. Compute the similarity of the first two images using the following code snippet:

```
if isJust phash1 && isJust phash2
  then do putStr "hamming distance between image1 and
    image2: "
  print $ hammingDistance (fromJust phash1) (fromJust
    phash2)
else print "Error, could not read images"
```

6. Compute the similarity of the first to the third image as follows:

```
if isJust phash1 && isJust phash3
  then do putStr "hamming distance between image1 and
    image3: "
  print $ hammingDistance
  (fromJust phash1) (fromJust phash3)
else print "Error, could not read images"
```

7. The output hashes are as follows:

```
$ runhaskell Main.hs

image1: Just (PHash 14057618708811251228)

image2: Just (PHash 14488838648009883164)

image3: Just (PHash 9589915937059962524)

hamming distance between image1 and image2: 4

hamming distance between image1 and image3: 10
```

How it works...

It's much easier to visualize how similar these hashes are in hexadecimal (or binary), since Hamming distance operates in bits.

The hexadecimal representation of the three images are as follows:

- **Image 1**: c316b1bc36947e1c
- **Image 2**: c912b1fc36947e1c
- **Image 3**: 851639bc3650fe9c

By comparing these values, we can see that images 1 and 2 differ by only four, whereas images 1 and 3 differ by a whopping 10 characters.

5
The Dance with Trees

Everything from creating simple binary trees to practical applications such as Huffman encoding is covered in this section:

- ▶ Defining a binary tree data type
- ▶ Defining a rose tree (multiway tree) data type
- ▶ Traversing a tree depth-first
- ▶ Traversing a tree breadth-first
- ▶ Implementing a Foldable instance for a tree
- ▶ Calculating the height of a tree
- ▶ Implementing a binary search tree data structure
- ▶ Verifying the order property of a binary search tree
- ▶ Using a self-balancing tree
- ▶ Implementing a min-heap data structure
- ▶ Encoding a string using a Huffman tree
- ▶ Decoding a Huffman code

Introduction

Trees are a common data structure used in a variety of data analysis techniques. A **tree** is a hierarchical connection of nodes under one all-encompassing mighty root node. Every node can have zero or more children, but each child node associates with only one parent. Also, the root is the only special case that has no parent node. All nodes without children are also referred to as **leaf** nodes.

In Haskell, we can very gracefully represent a tree since the recursive nature of the data structure makes use of the recursive nature of functional programming. This section will cover creating our own trees as well as using existing implementations from libraries.

We will implement heaps and Huffman trees, which are some of the most notable examples of trees in data analysis. In other chapters throughout the book, we also run into HTML/XML traversal, hierarchical clustering, and decision trees, which all depend heavily on the tree data structure.

Defining a binary tree data type

In a binary tree, each node has at most two children. We will define a data structure to encompass the left and right subtrees of each node.

Getting ready

The code in the recipe will represent the following tree. The root node is labeled **n3** with a value of **3**. It has a left node **n1** of value **1**, and a right node **n2** of value **2**.

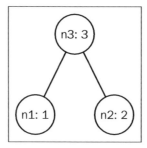

How to do it...

1. This code requires no imports. We can jump in and define the data structure recursively. A tree can either be a node with values or null/empty:

```
data Tree a = Node { value :: a
                   , left  :: (Tree a)
                   , right:: (Tree a) }
            | Leaf
            deriving Show
```

2. In `main`, create the tree shown in the preceding diagram and print it out:

```
main = do
  let n1 = Node { value = 1, left = Leaf, right = Leaf }
  let n2 = Node { value = 2, left = Leaf, right = Leaf }
  let n3 = Node { value = 3, left = n1,   right = n2 }
  print n3
```

3. The full tree is printed out as follows:

```
$ runhaskell Main.hs


Node { value = 3
     , left = Node  { value = 1
                    , left = Leaf
                    , right = Leaf }
     , right = Node { value = 2
                    , left = Leaf
                    , right = Leaf }

     }
```

See also

If the nodes in a tree need more than two children, then see the next section, *Defining a rose tree (multiway tree) data type.*

Defining a rose tree (multiway tree) data type

A rose tree relaxes the limitation of at most two children per node. It can have an arbitrary number of elements. Rose trees are common when parsing HTML to represent the **Document Object Model** (**DOM**).

Getting ready

We will be representing the following tree in this recipe. The root node has three children:

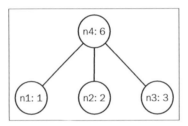

How to do it...

We will not need any imports for this recipe:

1. The rose tree data type is similar to that of the binary tree, except that instead of left and right children, it will store an arbitrary list of children:

```
data Tree a = Node { value    :: a
                   , children :: [Tree a] }
                   deriving Show
```

2. Construct the tree from the preceding diagram and print it out:

```
main = do
  let n1 = Node { value = 1, children = [] }
  let n2 = Node { value = 2, children = [] }
  let n3 = Node { value = 3, children = [] }
  let n4 = Node { value = 6, children = [n1, n2, n3] }
  print n4
```

3. The printed output will be as follows:

```
$ runhaskell Main.hs


Node { value = 6
    , children = [ Node { value = 1
                        , children = [] }
                 , Node { value = 2
                        , children = [] }
                 , Node { value = 3
                        , children = [] } ]
    }
```

How it works...

Instead of using dedicated left and right fields to represent child nodes, a rose tree uses a list data structure to represent an arbitrary number of children. A rose tree can be used to emulate a binary tree if each node is restricted to have at most two children.

See also

To represent a binary tree, it may be simpler to use the previous recipe, *Defining a binary tree data type*.

Traversing a tree depth-first

This recipe will demonstrate one way to traverse through a tree. The algorithm starts at the root node and continues exploring nodes along the entire length of a branch before going back to explore more shallow nodes.

Since we will examine each node before recursively examining its child nodes, we call this a **pre-order traversal**. Instead, if we examine each node afterwards, then we call this approach **post-order traversal**. Anything in-between is an **in-order traversal**, but naturally, there is no unique in-order traversal for rose trees.

The biggest advantage in using the depth-first approach is the minimal space complexity. Video game AIs often use depth-first approaches in determining the ideal move to take against an opponent. However, in enormous or infinite trees, a depth-first search may never terminate if we keep visiting subsequent child nodes.

Getting ready

We will traverse the following tree in a depth-first fashion. Starting at node **r**, we first explore node **n1**, followed by **n2**, then go back up to find **n3**, and backtrack all the way to finally end at **n4**.

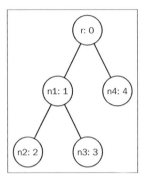

How to do it...

1. We will use an existing rose tree implementation from `Data.Tree`:

   ```
   import Data.Tree (rootLabel, subForest, Tree(..))
   import Data.List (tails)
   ```

2. This function will traverse a tree depth-first:

   ```
   depthFirst :: Tree a -> [a]

   depthFirst (Node r forest) =
     r : concat [depthFirst t | t <- forest]
   ```

3. Here's a depth-first implementation of adding all the values in a tree:

   ```
   add :: Tree Int -> Int

   add (Node r forest) = r + sum [add t | t <- forest]
   ```

4. Define a tree to represent the preceding diagram:

   ```
   someTree :: Tree Int

   someTree = r
     where r  = Node { rootLabel = 0, subForest = [n1, n4] }
           n1 = Node { rootLabel = 1, subForest = [n2, n3] }
           n2 = Node { rootLabel = 2, subForest = [] }
           n3 = Node { rootLabel = 3, subForest = [] }
           n4 = Node { rootLabel = 4, subForest = [] }
   ```

5. Test out the depth-first functions:

```
main = do
  print $ depthFirst someTree
  print $ add someTree
```

6. This will print the following two lines of output:

$ runhaskell Main.hs

```
[0,1,2,3,4]
10
```

How it works...

In this recipe, we use the built-in rose tree data structure from `Data.Tree`. Similar to our implementation in the previous recipe, it has the `Tree` data type having the following constructor:

```
data Tree a = Node { rootLabel :: a
                   , subForest :: Forest a }
```

We recursively run the `depthFirst` algorithm on every child node and append it to the node's value, thereby creating a list that represents the tree traversal.

See also

If traversing a tree by the tree level is preferred, then take a look at the next section, *Traversing a tree breadth-first*.

Traversing a tree breadth-first

In a breadth-first search approach to traversing a tree, nodes are visited in the order of the depth of the tree. The root is visited, then its children, then each of their children, and so on and so forth. This process requires a greater space complexity than the depth-first traversal but comes in handy for optimizing search algorithms.

For example, imagine trying to find all relevant topics from a Wikipedia article. Traversing all the links within the article in a breadth-first fashion will help ensure the topics start out with relevance.

Getting ready

Examine the tree in the following diagram. A breadth-first traversal will start at the root node **r**, then continue to the next level, encountering **n1** and **n4**, finally followed by **n2** and **n3**.

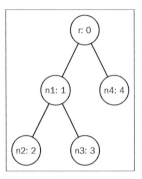

How to do it...

1. We will be using an existing implementation of a rose tree from `Data.Tree`:

    ```
    import Data.Tree (rootLabel, subForest, Tree(..))
    import Data.List (tails)
    ```

2. Implement the breadth-first traversal of a tree:

    ```
    breadthFirst :: Tree a -> [a]

    breadthFirst t = bf [t]
       where bf forest | null forest = []
                       | otherwise   = map rootLabel forest ++
                                bf (concat (map subForest forest))
    ```

3. For demonstration, implement a function to add the values of each node in a tree.

    ```
    add :: Tree Int -> Int

    add t = sum $ breadthFirst t
    ```

4. Create a tree based on the preceding diagram:

    ```
    someTree :: Tree Int

    someTree = root
       where root = Node { rootLabel = 0, subForest = [n1, n4] }
             n1   = Node { rootLabel = 1, subForest = [n2, n3] }
             n2   = Node { rootLabel = 2, subForest = [] }
             n3   = Node { rootLabel = 3, subForest = [] }
             n4   = Node { rootLabel = 4, subForest = [] }
    ```

5. Test out the breadth-first algorithms in `main`:

    ```
    main = do
      print $ breadthFirst someTree
      print $ add someTree
    ```

6. The printed output is as follows:

    $ runhaskell Main.hs


    ```
    [0,1,4,2,3]
    10
    ```

How it works...

In this recipe, we use the built-in rose tree data structure from `Data.Tree`. Similar to our implementation in one of the previous recipes, it has the `Tree` data type with the following constructors:

```
data Tree a = Node { rootLabel :: a
                   , subForest :: Forest a }
```

We perform the breadth-first search by creating a list that begins with the values of the node's direct children. Then, the values of the children's children are appended, and so on until the tree is fully traversed.

See also

If space complexity becomes an issue, then the previous recipe, *Traversing a tree depth-first*, might offer a better approach.

Implementing a Foldable instance for a tree

The idea of traversing a tree can be generalized by implementing a `Foldable` instance. Usually, folds are used on lists; for example, `foldr1 (+)` `[1..10]` traverses a list of numbers to produce a grand sum. Similarly, we can apply `foldr1 (+)` tree to find the sum of all nodes in a tree.

Getting ready

We will be folding through the following tree to obtain a sum of all node values.

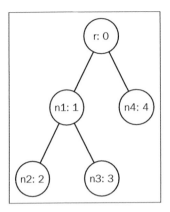

How to do it...

1. Import the following built-in packages:

   ```
   import Data.Monoid (mempty, mappend)
   import qualified Data.Foldable as F
   import Data.Foldable (Foldable, foldMap)
   ```

2. The tree from `Data.Tree` already implements `Foldable`, so we will define our own tree data type for demonstration purposes:

   ```
   data Tree a = Node { value :: a
                      , children :: [Tree a] }
                      deriving Show
   ```

3. Implement the `foldMap` function for the `Foldable` instance. This implementation will give us a post-order traversal of the tree:

   ```
   instance Foldable Tree where
     foldMap f Null = mempty
     foldMap f (Node val xs) = foldr mappend (f val)
                               [foldMap f x | x <- xs]
   ```

4. Define a function to fold through a tree to find the sum of all nodes:

   ```
   add :: Tree Integer -> Integer

   add = F.foldr1 (+)
   ```

5. Construct a tree that represents the one in the preceding diagram:

    ```
    someTree :: Tree Integer

    someTree = root
      where root = Node { value = 0, children = [n1, n4] }
            n1   = Node { value = 1, children = [n2, n3] }
            n2   = Node { value = 2, children = [] }
            n3   = Node { value = 3, children = [] }
            n4   = Node { value = 4, children = [] }
    ```

6. Test out the folding by running the `add` function on a tree:

    ```
    main :: IO ()
    main = print $ add someTree
    ```

7. The result gets printed out as follows:

    ```
    $ runhaskell Main.hs


    10
    ```

How it works...

The function that is necessary to define a `Foldable` instance is either `foldMap` or `foldr`. In this recipe, we define the `foldMap :: (Foldable t, Data.Monoid.Monoid m) => (a -> m) -> t a -> m` function that essentially maps a function `f` over every node in a tree, and glues it together using `mappend` from `Data.Monoid`.

See also

Other ways to traverse through elements of a tree are discussed in the previous two sections, *Traversing a tree depth-first* and *Traversing a tree breadth-first*.

Calculating the height of a tree

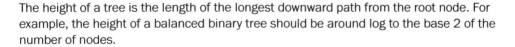

The height of a tree is the length of the longest downward path from the root node. For example, the height of a balanced binary tree should be around log to the base 2 of the number of nodes.

Getting ready

As long as we're consistent, the height of a tree can be defined as either the number of nodes or the number of edges in the longest path. In this recipe, we will count by using the number of nodes. The longest path of this tree contains three nodes and two edges. Therefore, this tree has a height of three units.

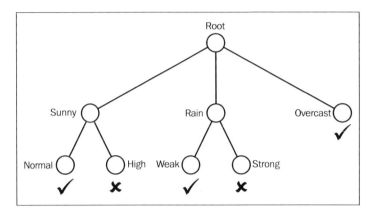

How to do it...

1. Import the `maximum` function from `Data.List` and the built-in tree data structure from `Data.Tree`:

   ```
   import Data.List (maximum)
   import Data.Tree
   ```

2. Define a function to calculate the height of a tree:

   ```
   height :: Tree a -> Int

   height (Node val []) = 1
   height (Node val xs) = 1 + maximum (map height xs)
   ```

3. Construct a tree on which we will run our algorithm:

   ```
   someTree :: Tree Integer

   someTree = root
     where root = 0 [n1, n4]
           n1   = 1 [n2, n3]
           n2   = 2 []
           n3   = 3 []
           n4   = 4 []
   ```

4. Test out the function in `main`:

```
main = print $ height someTree
```

5. The height of the tree will be printed as follows:

```
$ runhaskell Main.hs
```

3

How it works...

The `height` function recursively finds the maximum height among its child trees and returns one plus that value.

Implementing a binary search tree data structure

A binary search tree restricts an order property on a binary tree. This order property requires that among every node, the nodes in the left subtree must not be greater, and that the nodes in the right subtree must not be less than the current node.

How to do it...

1. Create a binary `BSTree` module to expose our binary search tree data structure. Insert the following code in a file called `BSTree.hs`:

```
module BSTree (insert, find, single) where
```

2. Define the data structure for a binary tree:

```
data Tree a = Node  {value :: a
                    , left    :: (Tree a)
                    , right   :: (Tree a)}
            | Null
            deriving (Eq, Show)
```

3. Define a convenience function to create a one-node tree:

```
single :: a -> Tree a

single n = Node n Null Null
```

4. Implement a function to insert new values in the binary search tree:

```
insert :: Ord a => Tree a -> a -> Tree a

insert (Node v l r) v'
```

```
        | v' < v        = Node v (insert l v') r
        | v' > v        = Node v l (insert r v')
        | otherwise     = Node v l r

insert _ v' = Node v' Null Null
```

5. Implement a function to find a node with a specific value in a binary search tree:

```
find :: Ord a => Tree a -> a -> Bool

find (Node v l r) v'
    | v' < v        = find l v'
    | v' > v        = find r v'
    | otherwise     = True

find Null v' = False
```

6. Now, test out the BSTree module by creating a new file that can be called Main.hs with the following code:

```
import BSTree
```

7. In main, construct a binary search tree by calling the insert function on various values:

```
main = do
  let tree = single 5
  let nodes = [6,4,8,2,9]
  let bst = foldl insert tree nodes
```

8. Print out the tree and test out the find function:

```
print bst
print $ find bst 1
print $ find bst 2
```

9. The output should be as follows:

$ runhaskell Main.hs

```
Node { value = 5
     , left = Node { value = 4
                   , left = Node { value = 2
                                 , left = Null
                                 , right = Null }
                   , right = Null }
     , right = Node { value = 6
```

```
                              , left = Null

                              , right = Node { value = 8

                                               , left = Null

                                               , right = Node { value = 9

                                                                , left = Null

                                                                , right = Null }

                                             }

                            }

                 }
```

```
False
```

```
True
```

How it works...

The core functions of a binary search tree data structure are `insert` and `find`, and are used for inserting and finding elements in a binary search tree respectively. Finding a node is accomplished by traversing the tree and taking advantage of its order property. If the value is lower than expected, it will check the left node; otherwise, if the value is greater, it will check the right node. Eventually, this recursive algorithm either finds the desired node or ends up at a leaf node and consequently does not find the node.

A binary search tree does not guarantee the tree to be balanced, and therefore, a speedy O(log n) lookup is not to be expected. There is always a possibility for a binary search tree to end up looking like a list data structure (consider, for example, when we insert nodes in the following order [1,2,3,4,5] and examine the resulting structure).

See also

Given a binary tree, the order property can be verified using the following recipe titled *Verifying the order property of a binary search tree*. To use a balanced binary tree, refer to the recipe, *Using a self-balancing tree*.

Verifying the order property of a binary search tree

Given a binary tree, this recipe will cover how to verify if it actually satisfies the order property such that all elements in the left subtree are of lesser value, and that all values of the right subtree are of greater value.

Getting ready

We will be verifying whether or not the following tree is a binary search tree:

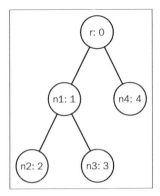

How to do it...

No imports are necessary for this recipe. Perform the following steps to find if the tree is a binary search tree:

1. Define a data structure for a binary tree:

   ```
   data Tree a = Node { value  :: a
                      , left   :: (Tree a)
                      , right  :: (Tree a)}
               | Null
        deriving (Eq, Show)
   ```

2. Construct a tree based on the preceding diagram:

   ```
   someTree :: Tree Int

   someTree = root
     where root = Node 0 n1 n4
           n1   = Node 1 n2 n3
           n2   = Node 2 Null Null
           n3   = Node 3 Null Null
           n4   = Node 4 Null Null
   ```

3. Define the function to verify whether or not a tree obeys the binary order property:

   ```
   valid :: Ord t => Tree t -> Bool

   valid (Node v l r) = leftValid && rightValid
     where leftValid  = if notNull l
   ```

```
                              then valid l && value l <= v
                              else True
              rightValid = if notNull r
                              then valid r && v <= value r
                              else True
          notNull t  =  t /= Null
```

4. Test out the function in `main`:

   ```
   main = print $ valid someTree
   ```

5. Clearly, the tree does not obey the order property, and therefore, the output is as follows:

   ```
   $ runhaskell Main.hs


   False
   ```

How it works...

The `valid` function recursively checks if the left subtree contains elements less than the current node and if the right subtree contains elements greater than the current node.

Using a self-balancing tree

An AVL tree is a balanced binary search tree. The heights of each subtree differ by at most one. On each insertion or deletion, the tree shifts around its nodes through a series of rotations to become balanced. A balanced tree ensures the height is minimized, which guarantees lookups and insertions to be within *O(log n)* time. In this recipe, we will use an AVL tree package directly, but self-balancing trees also exist within the `Data.Set` and `Data.Map` implementations.

Getting ready

We will be using the `AvlTree` package to use `Data.Tree.AVL`:

```
$ cabal install AvlTree
```

How to do it...

1. Import the relevant AVL tree packages:

   ```
   import Data.Tree.AVL
   import Data.COrdering
   ```

2. Set up an AVL tree from a list of values and read the minimum and maximum values from it:

```
main = do
  let avl  = asTree fstCC [4,2,1,5,3,6]
  let min  = tryReadL avl
  let max  = tryReadR avl
  print min
  print max
```

3. The minimum and maximum values are printed out as follows:

```
$ runhaskell Main.hs


Just 1

Just 6
```

How it works...

The asTree :: (e -> e -> COrdering e) -> [e] -> AVL e-function takes in an ordering property and a list of elements to produce an AVL tree out of the corresponding elements. The function fstCC :: Ord a => a -> a -> COrdering a comes from Data.Cordering and is defined as:

> A combining comparison for an instance of 'Ord' which keeps the first argument if they are deemed equal. The second argument is discarded in this case.

There's more...

The implementation of Haskell's Data.Set and Data.Map functions efficiently uses balanced binary trees. We can rewrite the recipe by simply using Data.Set:

```
import qualified Data.Set as S

main = do
  let s = S.fromList [4,2,1,5,3,6]
  let min = S.findMin s
  let max = S.findMax s
  print min
  print max
```

Implementing a min-heap data structure

A heap is a binary tree with both a shape property and a heap property. The shape property enforces the tree to behave in a balanced way by defining each node to have two children unless the node is in the very last level. The heap property ensures that each node is less than or equal to either of its child nodes if it is a min-heap, and vice versa in case of a max-heap.

Heaps are used for constant time lookups for maximum or minimum elements. We will use a heap in the next recipe to implement our own Huffman tree.

Getting started

Install the lens library for easy data manipulation:

```
$ cabal install lens
```

How to do it...

1. Define the `MinHeap` module in a file `MinHeap.hs`:

   ```
   module MinHeap (empty, insert, deleteMin, weights) where

   import Control.Lens (element, set)
   import Data.Maybe (isJust, fromJust)
   ```

2. We will use a list to represent a binary tree data structure for demonstration purposes only. It is best to implement the heap as an actual binary tree (as we have done in the previous sections), or we should use an actual array that will give us constant time access to its elements. For simplicity, we will define the root node to start at index 1. Given a node at index `i`, the left child will always be located at $2*i$, and the right child at $2*i + 1$:

   ```
   data Heap v = Heap { items :: [Node v] }
                  deriving Show

   data Node v = Node { value :: v, weight :: Int }
                  deriving Show
   ```

3. We define a convenience function to initiate an empty heap:

   ```
   empty = Heap []
   ```

4. Insertion of a node in a heap is done by appending the node to the end of the array and percolating it up:

   ```
   insert v w (Heap xs) = percolateUp position items'
     where items'    = xs ++ [Node v w]
           position = length items' - 1
   ```

5. Deleting a node from a heap is done by swapping the root node with the last element, and then percolating down from the root node:

```
deleteMin (Heap xs) = percolateDown 1 items'
   where items' = set (element 1) (last xs) (init xs)
```

6. Create a function to view the minimum:

```
viewMin heap@(Heap (_:y:_)) =
   Just (value y, weight y, deleteMin heap)
viewMin _                    = Nothing
```

7. Percolating down from a node means ensuring the heap property holds for the current node; otherwise, swap the node with the greater or lesser (depending on the max or min heap) child. This process is recursively applied all the way down to the leaf nodes:

```
percolateDown i items
    | isJust left && isJust right = percolateDown i'
                                        (swap i i' items)
    | isJust left = percolateDown l (swap i l items)
    | otherwise = Heap items
```

8. Define the `left`, `right`, `i'`, `l`, and `r` variables:

```
where left   = if l >= length items
                   then Nothing
                   else Just $ items !! l
      right  = if r >= length items
                   then Nothing
                   else Just $ items !! r
      i'     = if (weight (fromJust left)) <
                     (weight (fromJust right))
                 then l else r
      l      = 2*i
      r      = 2*i + 1
```

9. Percolating a node up means to recursively swap a node with its parent until the heap property of the tree holds:

```
percolateUp i items
   | i == 1 = Heap items
   | w < w' = percolateUp c (swap i c items)
   | otherwise = Heap items
  where  w  = weight $ items !! i
         w' = weight $ items !! c
         c  = i `div` 2
```

10. We define a convenience function to swap items at two indices in a list:

```
swap i j xs = set (element j) vi (set (element i) vj xs)
  where vi = xs !! i
        vj = xs !! j
```

11. To view the weights of each node in the array representation of a heap, we can define the following function:

```
weights heap = map weight ((tail.items) heap)
```

12. Finally, in a different file that we can name `Main.hs`, we can test out the min-heap:

```
import MinHeap

main = do
  let heap = foldr (\x -> insert x x)
                   empty [11, 5, 3, 4, 8]
  print $ weights heap
  print $ weights $ iterate deleteMin heap !! 1
  print $ weights $ iterate deleteMin heap !! 2
  print $ weights $ iterate deleteMin heap !! 3
  print $ weights $ iterate deleteMin heap !! 4
```

13. The output of the weights in the array representation of the heap is as follows:

```
$ runhaskell Main.hs

[3,5,4,8,11]
[4,5,11,8]
[5,8,11]
[8,11]
[11]
```

There's more...

The code in this recipe is for understanding the heap data structure, but it is by no means efficient. Better implementations of heaps exist on Hackage, including the `Data.Heap` library that we will explore:

1. Import the heap library:

```
import Data.Heap (MinHeap, MaxHeap, empty, insert, view)
```

2. Define a helper function to construct a min-heap from a list:

```
minheapFromList :: [Int] -> MinHeap Int
minheapFromList ls = foldr insert empty ls
```

3. Define a helper function to construct a max-heap from a list:

```
maxheapFromList :: [Int] -> MaxHeap Int
maxheapFromList ls = foldr insert empty ls
```

4. Test out the heaps:

```
main = do
  let myList = [11, 5, 3, 4, 8]
  let minHeap = minheapFromList myList
  let maxHeap = maxheapFromList myList
  print $ view minHeap
  print $ view maxHeap
```

5. The view functions return a tuple in a `Maybe` data structure. The first element of the tuple is the value from performing a lookup, and the second element is the new heap with that value removed:

```
$ runhaskell Main.hs

Just (3, fromList [(4,()),(11,()),(5,()),(8,())])

Just (11, fromList [(8,()),(3,()),(5,()),(4,())])
```

Encoding a string using a Huffman tree

A **Huffman tree** allows efficient encoding of data by calculating a probability distribution of characters to optimize the space taken per character. Imagine compressing this book into one piece of paper and back without any information loss. Huffman trees allow this type of optimal lossless data compression based on statistics.

In this recipe, we will implement a Huffman tree from a source of text and produce a string representation of its Huffman codes.

For example, the string "hello world" contains 11 characters, which, depending on the encoding and architecture, may take up as few as 11 bytes of space to represent. The code in this recipe will transform the string into just 51 bits, or 6.375 bytes.

Getting ready

Make sure to be connected to the Internet since this recipe will download text from `http://norgiv.com/big.txt` to analyze probability distribution of many characters. We will be using the min-heap that was implemented in the previous recipe by importing `MinHeap`.

How to do it...

1. Import the following packages. We will be using our previous `MinHeap` module, so be sure to include the code from the previous recipe:

```
import Data.List (group, sort)
import MinHeap
import Network.HTTP ( getRequest, getResponseBody
                    , simpleHTTP )
import Data.Char (isAscii)
import Data.Maybe (fromJust)
import Data.Map (fromList, (!))
```

2. Define a function to return an association list of characters to its frequency:

```
freq xs = map (\x -> (head x, length x)) .
             group . sort $ xs
```

3. The data structure of a Huffman tree is simply a binary tree:

```
data HTree   =  HTree { value :: Char
                      , left  :: HTree
                      , right :: HTree }
             | Null
             deriving (Eq, Show)
```

4. Construct a Huffman tree with one value:

```
single v = HTree v Null Null
```

5. Define a function to construct a Huffman tree from a min-heap:

```
htree heap = if length (items heap) == 2
             then case fromJust (viewMin heap) of
                  (a,b,c) -> a
             else htree $ insert newNode (w1 + w2) heap3

   where (min1, w1, heap2) = fromJust $ viewMin heap
         (min2, w2, heap3) = fromJust $ viewMin heap2
         newNode           = HTree { value = ' '
                                   , left  = min1
                                   , right = min2 }
```

6. Get a map of Huffman codes from the Huffman tree:

```
codes htree = codes' htree ""

  where codes' (HTree v l r) str
           | l==Null && r==Null = [(v, str)]
           | r==Null            = leftCodes
           | l==Null            = rightCodes
           | otherwise          = leftCodes ++ rightCodes
          where  leftCodes  = codes' l ('0':str)
                 rightCodes = codes' r ('1':str)
```

7. Define a function to encode a string to text using the Huffman codes:

```
encode str m = concat $ map (m !) str
```

8. Test out the entire process by executing the following in `main`. Downloading and calculating the frequency might take a couple of minutes:

```
main = do
  rsp <- simpleHTTP (getRequest
            "http://norvig.com/big.txt")
  html <- fmap (takeWhile isAscii) (getResponseBody rsp)
  let freqs = freq html
  let heap = foldr (\(v,w) -> insert (single v) w)
              empty freqs
  let m = fromList $ codes $ htree heap
  print $ encode "hello world" m
```

9. The string representation of the Huffman tree is then printed as follows:

```
$ runhaskell Main.hs


"0100011100111101111100010111010001000110110111110010"
```

How it works...

First, we obtain a source of data to analyze by downloading the text from `http://norvig.com/big.txt`. Next, we obtain the frequency map of each character and throw it in a heap. The Huffman tree is constructed from this min-heap by combining the two lowest frequency nodes until only one node is left in the min-heap. Finally, the Huffman codes are used on a sample "hello world" string to see the encoding.

See also

To read an encoded Huffman value, see the next section, *Decoding a Huffman code*.

Decoding a Huffman code

This code relies heavily on the previous recipe, *Encoding a string using a Huffman tree*. The same Huffman tree data structure is used next to decode a string representation of a Huffman coding.

Getting ready

Read the previous recipe, *Encoding a string using a Huffman tree*. The same `HTree` data structure is used in this recipe.

How to do it...

We traverse down the tree until we hit a leaf node. Then, we prepend the character found and restart from the root node. This process continues until no input is available:

```
decode :: String -> HTree -> String
decode str htree = decode' str htree
  where   decode' "" _ = ""
      decode' ('0':str) (HTree _ l _)
        | leaf l    = value l : decode' str htree
        | otherwise = decode' str l
      decode' ('1':str) (HTree v _ r)
        | leaf r    = value r : decode' str htree
        | otherwise = decode' str r
      leaf tree = left tree == Null && right tree == Null
```

See also

To encode data using a Huffman tree, see the previous recipe, *Encoding a string using a Huffman tree*.

6
Graph Fundamentals

In this chapter, we will cover the following recipes:

- ▸ Representing a graph from a list of edges
- ▸ Representing a graph from an adjacency list
- ▸ Conducting a topological sort on a graph
- ▸ Traversing a graph depth-first
- ▸ Traversing a graph breadth-first
- ▸ Visualizing a graph using Graphviz
- ▸ Using Directed Acyclic Word Graphs
- ▸ Working with hexagonal and square grid networks
- ▸ Finding maximal cliques in a graph
- ▸ Determining whether any two graphs are isomorphic

Introduction

This section on graphs is a natural extension to the previous one about trees. Graphs are an essential data structure for representing networks, and this chapter will cover some important algorithms.

A graph relieves some of the restrictions from a tree, which allows one to represent network data such as biological gene relationship, social networks, and road topologies. Haskell supports multiple graph data structure libraries with various helpful tools and algorithms. This section will cover basic topics such as graph representation, topological sort, traversal, and graph-specific packages.

Representing a graph from a list of edges

A graph can be defined by a list of edges, where an edge is a tuple of vertices. In the `Data.Graph` package, a vertex is simply `Int`. In this recipe, we use the `buildG` function to construct a graph data structure out of a list of edges.

Getting ready

We will be constructing the graph represented in the following diagram:

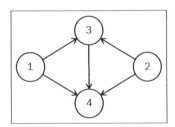

How to do it...

Create a new file, which we will name `Main.hs`, and insert the following code:

1. Import the `Data.Graph` package:

```
import Data.Graph
```

2. Construct a graph using the `buildG` function from the imported library:

```
myGraph :: Graph

myGraph= buildG bounds edges
   where   bounds = (1,4)
        edges = [ (1,3), (1,4)
                , (2,3), (2,4)
                , (3,4) ]
```

3. Print out the graph, its edges, and its vertices:

```
main = do
   print $ "The edges are " ++ (show.edges) myGraph
   print $ "The vertices are " ++ (show.vertices) myGraph
```

How it works...

A list of edges is fed to the `buildG :: Bounds -> [Edge] -> Graph` function to form a graph data structure. The first argument specifies the lower and upper bounds for the vertices, and the second argument specifies the list of edges that make up the graph.

This graph data type is actually a Haskell array of vertices to a list of vertices. It uses the built-in `Data.Array` package, meaning we can use all the functions provided in `Data.Array` in our graphs.

See also

For another way to construct a graph, see the next recipe, *Representing a graph from an adjacency list*.

Representing a graph from an adjacency list

It may be more convenient to construct a graph given an adjacency list. In this recipe, we will use the built-in package `Data.Graph` to read a mapping of a vertex to a list of connected vertices.

Getting ready

We will be constructing the graph represented in the following diagram:

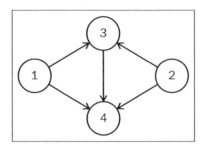

How to do it...

Create a new file, which we will name `Main.hs`, and insert the following code:

1. Import the `Data.Graph` package:

    ```
    import Data.Graph
    ```

2. Use the `graphFromEdges'` function to obtain a tuple that contains the graph. A graph data structure, `Graph`, is in the first element of the tuple returned. The second element of the tuple contains mappings from a vertex number to its corresponding value, `Vertex -> (node, key, [key])`:

    ```
    myGraph :: Graph

    myGraph = fst $ graphFromEdges'   [ ("Node 1", 1, [3, 4] )
                                      , ("Node 2", 2, [3, 4])
                                      , ("Node 3", 3, [4])
                                      , ("Node 4", 4, []) ]
    ```

3. Print out some graph computations:

    ```
    main = do
      putStrLn $ "The edges are "++ (show.edges) myGraph
      putStrLn $ "The vertices are "++ (show.vertices) myGraph
    ```

4. Running the code displays the edges and vertices of the graph:

    ```
    $ runhaskell Main.hs
    ```

    ```
    The edges are [(0,2), (0,3), (1,2), (1,3), (2,3)]
    The vertices are [0, 1, 2, 3]
    ```

How it works...

We may notice that the keys of each vertex have been automatically assigned by the algorithm. The `graphFromEdges'` function actually returns a tuple of the type `(Graph, Vertex -> (node, key, [key]))`, where the first element is the graph data structure, and the second element is a mapping of the vertex number to its actual key.

Just like the previous recipe, this graph data structure is actually an array from the `Data.Array` package, meaning we can use all the functions provided in `Data.Array` in our graphs.

See also

If we instead wish to create a graph from a list of edges, the previous recipe, *Representing a graph from an adjacency list* does the job.

Conducting a topological sort on a graph

If a graph is directed, the topological sort is one of the natural orderings of the graph. In a network of dependencies, the topological sort will reveal a possible enumeration through all the vertices that satisfy such dependencies.

Haskell's built-in graph package comes with a very useful function, `topSort`, to conduct a topological sort over a graph. In this recipe, we will be creating a graph of dependencies and enumerating a topological sort through it.

Getting ready

We will be reading the data from the user input. Each pair of lines will represent a dependency.

Create a file `input.txt` with the following pairs of lines:

```
$ cat input.txt

understand Haskell
do Haskell data analysis
understand data analysis
do Haskell data analysis
do Haskell data analysis
find patterns in big data
```

This file describes a list of dependencies, which are as follows:

- One must understand Haskell in order to do Haskell data analysis
- One must understand data analysis to do Haskell data analysis
- One must do Haskell data analysis to find patterns in big data

 We will use the `topsort` algorithm provided by `Data.Graph`. Beware, this function does not detect cyclic dependencies.

How to do it...

In a new file, which we will call `Main.hs`, insert the following code:

1. Import the following from the graph, map, and list packages:

```
import Data.Graph
import Data.Map (Map, (!), fromList)
import Data.List (nub)
```

2. Read from the input and construct a graph from the dependencies. Run our topological sort on the graph and print out a valid order:

```
main = do
  ls <- fmap lines getContents
  let g = graph ls
  putStrLn $ showTopoSort ls g
```

3. Construct a graph from a list of strings, where each pair of lines represents a dependency:

```
graph :: Ord k => [k] -> Graph

graph ls = buildG bounds edges
  where bounds = (1, (length.nub) ls)
    edges = tuples $ map (mappingStrToNum !) ls
    mappingStrToNum = fromList $ zip (nub ls) [1..]
    tuples (a:b:cs) = (a, b) : tuples cs
    tuples _ = []
```

4. Sort the graph topologically and print out a valid ordering of the items:

```
showTopoSort :: [String] -> Graph -> String

showTopoSort ls g =
  unlines $ map (mappingNumToStr !) (topSort g)
  where mappingNumToStr = fromList $ zip [1..] (nub ls)
```

5. Compile the code and feed it with the text file of dependencies:

```
$ runhaskell Main.hs < input.txt
```

```
understand data analysis
understand Haskell
do Haskell data analysis
find patterns in big data
```

Traversing a graph depth-first

Using depth-first search, one can traverse a graph to view the nodes in the desired order. Implementing a topological sort, solving mazes, and finding connected components are all examples of useful algorithms that rely on a depth-first traversal of a graph.

How to do it...

Start editing a new source file, which we will name `Main.hs`:

1. Import the required packages:

```
import Data.Graph
import Data.Array ((!))
```

2. Construct the graph from the adjacency list:

```
graph :: (Graph, Vertex -> (Int, Int, [Int]))

graph = graphFromEdges'  [ (1, 1, [3, 4] )
                         , (2, 2, [3, 4])
                         , (3, 3, [4])
                         , (4, 4, []) ]
```

3. Scan the graph depth-first:

```
depth g i = depth' g [] i
depth' g2 (gShape, gMapping) seen i =
   key : concat (map goDeeper adjacent)
   where goDeeper v = if v `elem` seen
                      then []
                      else depth' g (i:seen) v
         adjacent = gShape ! i
         (_, key, _) = gMapping i
```

4. Print out the list of vertices visited:

```
main = print $ depth graph 0
```

5. Run the algorithm to see the order of traversal.

```
$ runhaskell Main.hs

[1, 3, 4, 4]
```

We start at node 1 (which is at index 0). We traverse the first edge to 3. From number 3, we traverse to the first edge to 4. Since 4 has no outbound edges, we traverse back to 3. Since 3 has no remaining outbound edges, we traverse back to 1. From 1, we traverse the second edge to 4.

Traversing a graph breadth-first

Using breadth-first search, one can traverse a graph to view the nodes in the desired order. In an infinite graph, a depth-first traversal may never return back to the starting node. One of the most notable examples of a breadth-first traversal algorithm is finding the shortest path between two nodes.

In this recipe, we will print out the breadth-first traversal of the nodes in a graph.

How to do it...

Insert the following code in a new file, which can be called `Main.hs`:

1. Import the required packages:

```
import Data.Graph
import Data.Array ((!))
```

2. Construct the graph from a list of edges:

```
graph :: Graph
graph = buildG bounds edges
  where   bounds = (1,7)
          edges = [ (1,2), (1,5)
                  , (2,3), (2,4)
                  , (5,6), (5,7)
                  , (3,1) ]
```

3. Scan the graph breadth-first:

```
breadth g i = bf [] [i]
  where bf :: [Int] -> [Int] -> [Int]
        bf seen forest | null forest = []
                       | otherwise   = forest ++
                                       bf (forest ++ seen)
```

```
                              (concat (map goDeeper forest))
              where goDeeper v = if elem v seen
                                 then [] else (g ! v)
```

4. Print out the list of vertices visited depth-first:

```
main = do
  print $ breadth graph 1
```

5. Running the code shows the traversal:

```
$ runhaskell Main.hs
```

```
[1, 5, 2, 7, 6, 4, 3, 1]
```

Visualizing a graph using Graphviz

One can easily draw an image that represents a graph using the graphviz library. In the world of data analysis, visually interpreting an image can reveal peculiarities about the data that the human eye can easily pick up. This recipe will let us construct a diagram out of the data we are dealing with. More visualization techniques are explained in *Chapter 11, Visualizing Data*.

Getting ready

Install the graphviz library from http://www.graphviz.org/Download.php as the Haskell package requires it.

Next, install the package from cabal by running the following command:

```
$ cabal install graphviz
```

How to do it...

In a new file, insert the following code. We will name our file Main.hs:

1. Import the package:

```
import Data.GraphViz
```

2. Create the graph from nodes and edges:

```
graph :: DotGraph Int

graph = graphElemsToDot graphParams nodes edges
```

3. Use the default parameters for creating the graph. This function can be modified to modify the graph's visual parameters:

    ```
    graphParams :: GraphvizParams Int String Bool () String
    ```

    ```
    graphParams = defaultParams
    ```

4. Create the code from the corresponding edges:

    ```
    nodes :: [(Int, String)]
    ```

    ```
    nodes = map (\x -> (x, "")) [1..4]
    ```

    ```
    edges:: [(Int, Int, Bool)]
    ```

    ```
    edges= [ (1, 3, True)
           , (1, 4, True)
         , (2, 3, True)
         , (2, 4, True)
         , (3, 4, True)]
    ```

5. Execute `main` to output the graph:

    ```
    main = addExtension (runGraphviz graph) Png "graph"
    ```

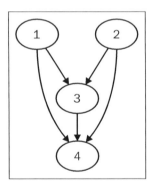

Using Directed Acyclic Word Graphs

We use **Directed Acyclic Word Graphs** (**DAWG**) to retrieve very quickly from a large corpus of strings at an extremely small cost in space complexity. Imagine compressing all words in a dictionary using a DAWG to perform efficient lookups for words. It is a powerful data structure that can come in handy when dealing with a large corpus of words. A very nice introduction to DAWGs can be found in Steve Hanov's blog post here: `http://stevehanov.ca/blog/index.php?id=115`.

We can use this recipe to incorporate a DAWG in our code.

Getting ready

Install the DAWG package using cabal:

```
$ cabal install dawg
```

How to do it...

We name a new file `Main.hs` and insert the following code:

1. Import the following packages:

   ```
   import qualified Data.DAWG.Static as D
   import Network.HTTP ( simpleHTTP, getRequest,
                          getResponseBody)
   import Data.Char (toLower, isAlphaNum, isSpace)
   import Data.Maybe (isJust)
   ```

2. In `main`, download a large corpus of text to store:

   ```
   main = do
     let url = "http://norvig.com/big.txt"
     body <- simpleHTTP (getRequest url) >>= getResponseBody
   ```

3. Look up some strings from the DAWG constructed by the corpus:

   ```
   let corp = corpus body
   print $ isJust $ D.lookup "hello" corp
   print $ isJust $ D.lookup "goodbye" corp
   ```

4. Construct a getter function:

   ```
   getWords :: String -> [String]

   getWords str = words $ map toLower wordlike
     where wordlike =
             filter (\x -> isAlphaNum x || isSpace x) str
   ```

5. Create a DAWG from the corpus dictionary:

   ```
   corpus :: String -> D.DAWG Char () ()

   corpus str = D.fromLang $ getWords str
   ```

6. Running the code reveals that the two words indeed exist in the massive corpus. Notice that there will be a time-consuming prepossessing step to build the DAWG:

   ```
   $ runhaskell Main.hs


   True

   True
   ```

A naive approach may be to use the `isInfixOf` function from `Data.List` to perform a substring search. On a typical ThinkPad T530 with 8 GB RAM on an Intel i5 processor, performing the `isInfixOf` operation takes around 0.16 seconds on average. However, if we preprocess a DAWG data structure, lookups take less than 0.01 seconds!

Working with hexagonal and square grid networks

Sometimes, the graph we're dealing with has a strict structure, such as a hexagonal or square grid. Many video games use a hexagonal grid layout to facilitate diagonal movement because moving diagonally in a square grid complicates the values of the traveled distance. On the other hand, square grid structures are often used within graphs to traverse pixels for image manipulation algorithms such as flood fill.

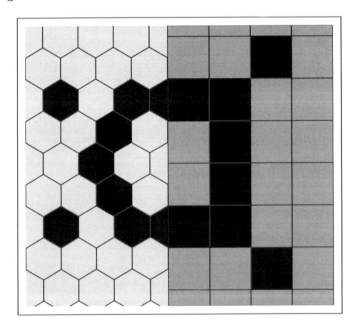

There is a very useful library in the Haskell package listing to deal with such topologies. We can obtain the indices of a grid to traverse the world, which is essentially a path embedded in a graph. For each grid index, we can query the library to find the neighboring indices, effectively using grids as a graph.

Getting started

Review the package documentation located at `https://github.com/mhwombat/grid/wiki`.

Install the grid package using cabal:

```
$ cabal install grid
```

How to do it...

In a new file, which we will name `Main.hs`, insert the following code:

1. Import the following libraries:

   ```
   import Math.Geometry.Grid (indices, neighbours)
   import Math.Geometry.Grid.Hexagonal (hexHexGrid)
   import Math.Geometry.Grid.Square (rectSquareGrid)
   import Math.Geometry.GridMap ((!))
   import Math.Geometry.GridMap.Lazy (lazyGridMap)
   ```

2. In `main`, print out some examples of hexagonal and grid functions:

   ```
   main = do
     let putStrLn' str = putStrLn ('\n':str)
     putStrLn' "Indices of hex grid:"
     print $ indices hex
     putStrLn' "Neighbors around (1,1) of hex grid:"
     print $ neighbours hex (1,1)
     putStrLn' "Indices of rect grid:"
     print $ indices rect
     putStrLn' "Neighbors around (1,1) of rect grid:"
     print $ neighbours rect (1,1)
     putStrLn' "value of hex at index (1,1)"
     print $ hexM ! (1,1)
   ```

3. Use a helper function to construct a hexagonal grid:

   ```
   hex = hexHexGrid 4
   ```

4. Use a helper function to construct a square grid:

   ```
   rect = rectSquareGrid 3 5
   ```

5. Create a hexagonal grid with the associated numerical values:

   ```
   hexM = lazyGridMap hex [1..]
   ```

Finding maximal cliques in a graph

Haskell comes with a luxury of vital graph libraries, conveniently one of which is the clique detection library from `Data.Algorithm.MaximualCliques`. A **clique** in a graph is a subgraph where all the nodes have connections between themselves, and is depicted as follows:

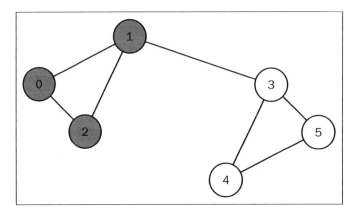

For example, the preceding graph contains two cliques shaded in different colors. Perhaps, the graph represents web pages that link to each other. We can visually infer that there might be two clusters of Internet communities due to the structure of the graph. As the network of connections increases, finding the greatest clique becomes an exponentially difficult problem.

In this recipe, we will use an efficient implementation of the maximal clique problem.

Getting started

Install the clique library using cabal:

```
$ cabal install maximal-cliques
```

How to do it...

Write the following code in a new file, which we will name `Main.hs`:

1. Import the required library:

   ```
   import Data.Algorithm.MaximalCliques
   ```

2. In `main`, print out the max cliques:

   ```
   main = print $ getMaximalCliques edges nodes
   ```

3. Create the following graph:

```
edges 1 5 = True
edges 1 2 = True
edges 2 3 = True
edges 2 5 = True
edges 4 5 = True
edges 3 4 = True
edges 4 6 = True
edges _ _ = False
```

4. Determine the node range:

```
nodes = [1..6]
```

How it works...

The library applies the recursive Bron-Kerbosch pivoting algorithm for identifying a maximal clique in an undirected graph. The core idea in the algorithm is to intelligently backtrack until a maximum clique is found.

Determining whether any two graphs are isomorphic

Graphs can have arbitrary labels, but their topology may be isomorphic. In the world of data analysis, we can examine different graphical networks and identify clusters of nodes that have identical connection patterns. This helps us discover when two seemingly different graphical networks end up with the same network mapping. Maybe then we can declare a one-to-one isomorphism between the nodes and learn something profound about the nature of the graphs.

We will use the `isIsomorphic` function from `Data.Graph.Automorphism` to detect whether two graphs are identical in their connection.

In this recipe, we will let the library calculate whether the two graphs in the following diagram are isomorphic in their connections:

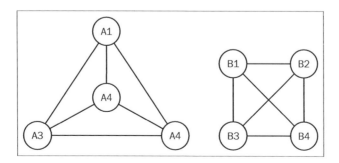

Getting started

Install the Automorphism library:

```
$ cabal install hgal
```

How to do it...

Write the following code in a new file, which we will name `Main.hs`:

1. Import the following packages:

    ```
    import Data.Graph
    import Data.Graph.Automorphism
    ```

2. Construct a graph:

    ```
    graph = buildG (0,4) [ (1, 3), (1, 4)
                         , (1, 2), (2, 3)
                         , (2, 4), (3, 4) ]
    ```

3. Construct another graph:

    ```
    graph' = buildG (0,4) [ (3, 1), (3, 2)
                          , (3, 4), (4, 1)
                          , (4, 2), (1, 2) ]
    ```

4. Check whether the graphs have the same topology:

    ```
    main = print $ isIsomorphic graph graph'
    ```

7
Statistics and Analysis

One core motivation to analyze big data is to find intrinsic patterns. This chapter contains recipes that answer questions about data deviation from the norm, existence of linear and quadratic trends, and probabilistic values of a network. Some of the most fascinating results can be uncovered by the following recipes:

- ▶ Calculating a moving average
- ▶ Calculating a moving median
- ▶ Approximating a linear regression
- ▶ Approximating a quadratic regression
- ▶ Obtaining the covariance matrix from samples
- ▶ Finding all unique pairings in a list
- ▶ Using the Pearson correlation coefficient
- ▶ Evaluating a Bayesian network
- ▶ Creating a data structure for playing cards
- ▶ Using a Markov chain to generate text
- ▶ Creating *n*-grams from a list
- ▶ Constructing a neural network perception

Introduction

The first two recipes deal with summarizing a series of data. For example, assume someone asks, "How old is everyone?". A valid response could be to enumerate through the age of each person, but depending on the number of people, this could take minutes if not hours. Instead, we can answer in terms of the average or in terms of the median to summarize all the age values in one simple number.

The next two recipes are about approximating an equation that most closely fits a collection of points. Given two series of coordinates, we can use a linear or quadratic approximation to predict other points.

We can detect relationships between numerical data through covariance matrices and Pearson correlation calculations as demonstrated in the corresponding recipes.

The `Numeric.Probability.Distribution` library has many useful functions for deeper statistical understanding as demonstrated in the Bayesian network and playing cards recipes.

We will also use Markov chains and *n*-grams for further interesting results.

Finally, we will create a neural network from scratch to learn a labelled set of data.

Calculating a moving average

Summarizing a list of numbers into one representative number can be done by calculating the average. The equation for the arithmetic mean is to add up all the values and divide by the number of values. However, if the values being summed over are extremely large, the total sum may overflow.

In Haskell, the range for `Int` is at least from -2^29 to 2^29-1. Implementations are allowed to have an `Int` type with a larger range. If we try to naively average the numbers 2^29-2 and 2^29-3 by first calculating their sum, the sum may overflow, producing an incorrect calculation for the average.

A moving average (or running average) tries to escape this drawback. We will use an exponential smoothing strategy, which means numbers that were seen previously contribute exponentially less to the value of the running mean. An exponential moving average reacts faster to recent data. It can be used in situations for detecting price oscillations or spiking a neuron in a neural network.

The equation of a running mean is as follows, where α is a smoothening constant, $\mathbf{s_t}$ is the moving average value at time t, and x is the value of the raw data:

$$
\begin{aligned}
s_0 &= x_0 \\
s_t &= \alpha x_{t-1} + (1 - \alpha)s_{t-1}, \ t > 0
\end{aligned}
$$

Getting ready

Create an `input.txt` file with a list of numbers separated by lines. We will be computing the moving average over these numbers:

```
$ cat input.txt
```

```
4
3
2
5
3
4
1
3
12
3
```

How to do it...

1. Create a helper function to convert the raw text input into a list of `Double` as follows:

   ```
   clean raw = map (\s -> read s :: Double) (lines raw)
   ```

2. Calculate the moving average of a list of numbers using an exponential smoothing technique. We **hardcode** the smoothening constant `a` to be `0.95` as shown here:

   ```
   avg :: [Double] -> Double
   avg (x:xs)  = a*x +  (1-a)*(avg xs)
   where a = 0.95
   avg []  = 0
   ```

3. Compute the true arithmetic mean to compare differences in the following manner:

    ```
    mean xs = (sum xs) / (fromIntegral (length xs))
    ```

4. Print out the results of computing the moving average and arithmetic mean to notice how the values are not equal, but reasonably close:

    ```
    main = do
    rawInput <- readFile "input.txt"
    let input = clean rawInput
    print input
    putStrLn $  "mean is " ++ (show.mean) input
    putStrLn $  "moving average is " ++ (show.avg) input
    ```

5. We will see the following output:

    ```
    $ runhaskell Main.hs

    [4.0,3.0,2.0,5.0,3.0,4.0,1.0,3.0,12.0,3.0]
    mean is 4.0
    moving average is 3.9478627675211913
    ```

There's more...

The smoothening constant should be changed according to the fluctuation of the data. A small smoothening constant remembers previous values better and produces an average influenced by the grander structure of the data. On the other hand, a larger value of the smoothening constant puts superior emphasis on recent data, and easily forgets stale data. We should use a larger smoothening constant if we want our average to be more sensitive to new data.

See also

Another way to summarize a list of numbers is explained in the *Calculating a moving median* recipe.

Calculating a moving median

The median of a list of numbers has an equal number of values less than and greater than it. The naive approach of calculating the median is to simply sort the list and pick the middle number. However, on a very large dataset, such a computation would be inefficient.

Another approach of finding a moving median is to use a combination of a **minheap** and a **maxheap** to sort the values while running through the data. We can insert numbers in either heap as they are seen, and whenever needed, the median can be calculated by adjusting the heaps to be of equal or near equal size. When the heaps are of equal size, it is simple to find the middle number, which is the median.

Getting ready

Create a file, `input.txt`, with some numbers:

```
$ cat input.txt
```

3

4

2

5

6

4

2

6

4

1

Also, install a library for dealing with heaps using Cabal as follows:

```
$ cabal install heap
```

How to do it...

1. Import the heap data structure:

    ```
    import Data.Heap
    import Data.Maybe (fromJust)
    ```

2. Convert the raw input as a list of numbers as follows:

    ```
    clean raw = map (\s -> read s :: Int) (lines raw)
    ```

3. Segregate the numbers in the list into the appropriate heaps. Put small numbers in the maxheap, and big numbers in the minheap, as shown in the following code snippet:

    ```
    median (x:xs) maxheap minheap = case viewHead maxheap of
       Just theMax  -> if x < theMax
                 then median xs (insert x maxheap) minheap
                 else median xs maxheap (insert x minheap)
         Nothing -> median xs (insert x maxheap) minheap
    ```

4. When there are no more numbers to read, start manipulating the heaps until both are of equal size. The median will be the number between the values in both heaps, as presented in the following code snippet:

```
median [] maxheap minheap
  | size maxheap + 1 < size minheap =
                median [] (insert minelem maxheap) $
        (snd.fromJust.view) minheap
  | size minheap + 1 < size maxheap =
                median [] ((snd.fromJust.view) maxheap) $
                insert maxelem minheap
  | size maxheap == size minheap =
    (fromIntegral maxelem + fromIntegral minelem)/2.0
  | size maxheap > size minheap = fromIntegral maxelem
  | otherwise = fromIntegral minelem
  where maxelem = fromJust (viewHead maxheap)
        minelem = fromJust (viewHead minheap)
```

5. Test out the code in `main` as follows:

```
main = do
  rawInput <- readFile "input.txt"
  let input = clean rawInput
  print $ input
  print $ median input
          (empty :: MaxHeap Int) (empty :: MinHeap Int)
```

6. The output is as follows:

```
$ runhaskell Main.hs


[3,4,2,5,6,4,2,6,4,1]
4.0
```

How it works...

First, we traverse the list of numbers to build up a minheap and maxheap in an attempt to efficiently separate the stream of incoming numbers. Then we move values between the minheap and maxheap until their sizes differ by at most one item. The median is the extra item, or otherwise the average of the minheap and maxheap values.

See also

For summarizing a list of numbers differently, refer to the *Calculating a moving average* recipe.

Approximating a linear regression

Given a list of points, we can estimate the best fit line using a handy library, `Statistics.LinearRegression`.

It computes the least square difference between points to estimate the best fit line. An example of a linear regression of points can be seen in the following figure:

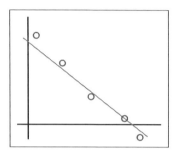

A best-fit line is drawn through five points using linear regression

Getting ready

Install the appropriate library using cabal as follows:

```
$ cabal install statistics-linreg
```

How to do it...

1. Import the following packages:

   ```
   import Statistics.LinearRegression
   import qualified Data.Vector.Unboxed as U
   ```

2. Create a series of points from their coordinates, and feed it to the `linearRegression` function, as shown in the following code snippet:

   ```
   main = do
     let xs =
         U.fromList [1.0, 2.0, 3.0, 4.0, 5.0] :: U.Vector Double
     let ys =
         U.fromList [1.0, 2.0, 1.3, 3.75, 2.25]::U.Vector Double

     let (b, m) = linearRegression xs ys

     print $ concat ["y = ", show m, " x + ", show b]
   ```

3. The resulting linear equation will be as follows:

```
$ runhaskell Main.hs
```

```
"y = 0.425 x + 0.785"
```

How it works...

We can look up the source code for the `linearRegression` function from the `Statistics.LinearRegression` library, `http://hackage.haskell.org/package/statistics-linreg-0.2.4/docs/Statistics-LinearRegression.html`.

The Wikipedia article on least square approximations (`http://en.wikipedia.org/wiki/Linear_least_squares_(mathematics)`) puts it best in writing:

> *"The least squares approach to solving this problem is to try to make as small as possible the sum of squares of "errors" between the right- and left-hand sides of these equations, that is, to find the minimum of the function"*

The core calculations involve finding the mean and variance of the two random variables, as well as the covariance between them. Thorough mathematics behind the algorithm is detailed in `http://www.dspcsp.com/pubs/euclreg.pdf`.

If we take a look at the library's source code, we can discover the underling equations:

$\alpha = \mu Y - \beta * \mu X$

$\beta = covar(X,Y)/\sigma 2X$

$f(x) = \beta x + \alpha$

See also

If the data does not follow a linear trend, try the *Approximating a quadratic regression* recipe.

Approximating a quadratic regression

Given a collection of points, this recipe will try to find a best fit quadratic equation. In the following figure, the curve is a best fit quadratic regression of the points:

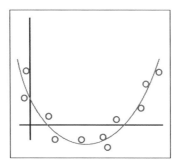

Getting ready

Install the dsp package to use Matrix.LU as follows:

```
$ cabal install dsp
```

In order to perform a quadratic regression, we will use the least square polynomial fitting algorithm described in Wolfram MathWorld available at http://mathworld.wolfram.com/LeastSquaresFittingPolynomial.html.

How to do it...

1. Import the following packages:

```
import Data.Array (listArray, elems)
import Matrix.LU (solve)
```

2. Implement the quadratic regression algorithm, as shown in the following code snippet:

```
fit d vals = elems $ solve mat vec
where mat = listArray ((1,1), (d,d)) $ matrixArray
    vec = listArray (1,d) $ take d vals
    matrixArray = concat [ polys x d
                                | x <- [0..fromIntegral (d-1)]]
        polys x d = map (x**) [0..fromIntegral (d-1)]
```

3. Test out the function as follows, using some **hardcoded** data:

```
main = print $ fit 3 [1,6,17,34,57,86,121,162,209,262,321]
```

4. The following values of the quadratic equation $3x^2 + 2x + 1$ is printed:

```
$ runhaskell Main.hs
```

```
[1.0,2.0,3.0]
```

How it works...

In this recipe, a design matrix, `mat`, multiplied with a parameter vector that we desire to find produces the response vector, `vec`. We can visualize each of these arrays and matrices in the following equation:

$$
\begin{bmatrix} y_1 \\ y_2 \\ y_3 \\ \vdots \\ y_n \end{bmatrix} = \begin{bmatrix} 1 & x_1 & x_1^2 & \cdots & x_1^m \\ 1 & x_2 & x_2^2 & \cdots & x_2^m \\ 1 & x_3 & x_3^2 & \cdots & x_3^m \\ \vdots & \vdots & \vdots & & \vdots \\ 1 & x_n & x_n^2 & \cdots & x_n^m \end{bmatrix} \begin{bmatrix} a_0 \\ a_1 \\ a_2 \\ \vdots \\ a_m \end{bmatrix}
$$

After constructing the design matrix and the response vector, we use the `dsp` library to solve this matrix equation and obtain a list of coefficients for our polynomial.

See also

If the data follows a linear trend, refer to the *Approximating a linear regression* recipe.

Obtaining the covariance matrix from samples

A covariance matrix is a symmetric square matrix whose elements in row *i* and column *j* correspond to how related they are. More specifically, each element is the covariance of the variables represented by its row and column. Variables that move together in the same direction have a positive covariance, and variables with the opposite behavior have a negative covariance.

Let's assume we are given four sets of data of three variables as shown in the following table:

Observation	Feature 1	Feature 2	Feature 3
1	1	0	1
2	1	1	1
3	0	0	0
4	0	1	1

Notice how **Feature 1** and **Feature 3** appear to be similar in their patterns, yet **Feature 1** and **Feature 2** appear to be uncorrelated. Similarly, **Feature 2** and **Feature 3** are significantly correlated.

The covariance matrix will be a 3 x 3 symmetric matrix with the following elements:

$$\begin{bmatrix} var_1 & cov_{1,2} & cov_{1,3} \\ cov_{1,2} & var_2 & cov_{2,3} \\ cov_{1,3} & cov_{2,3} & var_3 \end{bmatrix}$$

Getting ready

Install the `hstats` library using cabal as follows:

```
$ cabal install hstats
```

Alternatively, install the package by performing the following steps:

1. Download the source code of the package from `http://hackage.haskell.org/package/hstats-0.3/hstats-0.3.tar.gz`.

2. Remove the `haskell98` dependency from the cabal file, `hstats.cabal`.

3. In the same directory, run the following command line:

```
$ cabal install
```

How to do it...

1. Import the `hstats` package as follows:

    ```
    import Math.Statistics
    ```

2. Create a matrix out of a list of lists, and run the `covMatrix` function on it using the following code snippet:

    ```
    main = do print $ covMatrix matrixArray
      where matrixArray = [ [1,1,0,0]
                          , [0,1,0,1]
                          , [1,1,0,1] ]
    ```

3. Check the output:

    ```
    $ runhaskell Main.hs


    [ [ 0.333,  0.000,  0.167]
    , [ 0.000,  0.333,  0.167]
    , [ 0.167,  0.167,  0.250] ]
    ```

Notice how the uncorrelated features have a zero value, as we expected.

Finding all unique pairings in a list

Comparing all pairs of items is a common idiom in data analysis. This recipe will cover how to create a list of element pairs out of a list of elements. For example, if there is a list [1, 2, 3], we will create a list of every possible pair-ups [(1, 2), (1, 3), (2, 3)].

Notice that the order of pairing does not matter. We will create a list of unique tuple pairs so that we can compare each item to every other item in the list.

How it works...

Create a new file, which we call `Main.hs`, and insert the code explained in the following steps:

1. Import the following packages:

    ```
    import Data.List (tails, nub, sort)
    ```

2. Construct all unique pairs from a list of items as follows:

    ```
    pairs xs = [(x, y) | (x:ys) <- tails (nub xs), y <- ys]
    ```

3. Print out all unique pairings of the following list:

   ```
   main = print $ pairs [1,2,3,3,4]
   ```

4. The output will be as follows:

   ```
   [(1,2),(1,3),(1,4),(2,3),(2,4),(3,4)]
   ```

See also

We can apply the `pairs` algorithm to the *Using the Pearson correlation coefficient* recipe.

Using the Pearson correlation coefficient

The Pearson correlation coefficient is a number that ranges between -1.0 and 1.0, signifying the linear relationship of two numerical series. A value of 1.0 means strong linear correlation, a -1.0 is a strong negative correlation, and a 0.0 means the series is uncorrelated.

A brilliantly informative diagram was created by Kiatdd on `http://en.wikipedia.org/wiki/File:Correlation_coefficient.gif`, which is shown in the following figure:

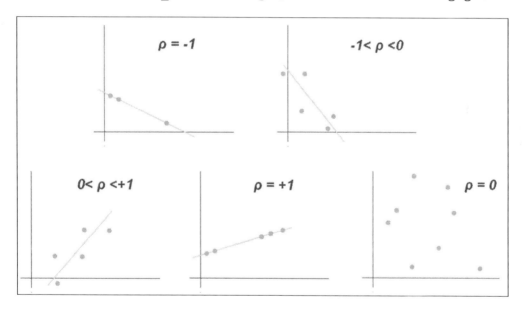

For example, Nick is quite a generous movie critic who consistently awards movies with high ratings. His friend John might be a more dramatic critic who offers a wider range of ratings, yet the two friends tend to always agree on which movies they prefer.

We can use the Pearson correlation coefficient to detect that there is a strong linear correspondence between how these two rate movies.

Getting ready

Install the `hstats` library using cabal as follows:

```
$ cabal install hstats
```

Create a file with five star rating values on each line, corresponding to the rating given by different people.

In our example, three people have given five ratings each, using the following command:

```
$ cat ratings.csv
4,5,4,4,3
2,5,4,3,1
5,5,5,5,5
```

Notice how the first two people rate in similar trends, but the third person has a very different rating trend. The algorithm in this recipe will compute the Pearson correlation coefficient pairwise and sort the results to find the two people who rate most similarly.

How to do it...

1. Import the following packages:

    ```
    import Math.Statistics (pearson)
    import Text.CSV
    import Data.List (tails, nub, sort)
    ```

2. Create a function as follows to calculate the similarities from a list of lists:

    ```
    calcSimilarities (Left err) = error "error parsing"
    calcSimilarities (Right csv) = head $ reverse $ sort $ zip
      [ pearson (convertList a) (convertList b)
      | (a,b) <- pairs csv]
      $ (pairs csv)
    ```

3. Convert a list of `String` to a list of `Double` as follows:

    ```
    convertList :: [String] -> [Double]

    convertList = map read
    ```

4. Create all possible pairs from a list of items as follows:

    ```
    pairs xs = [(x, y) | (x:ys) <- tails (nub xs), y <- ys]
    ```

5. Test the code by finding the two people who rate items most similarly to each other, as shown in the following code snippet:

```
main = do
  let fileName = "ratings.csv"
  input <- readFile filename

  let csv = parseCSV fileName input

  print $ calcSimilarities csv
```

6. The output will be as follows:

```
$ runhaskell Main.hs


(0.89442719909999159,(["4","5","4","4","3"],["2","5","4","3","
  1"]))
```

Evaluating a Bayesian network

A Bayesian network is a graph of probabilistic dependencies. Nodes in the graph are events, and edges represent conditional dependence. We can build a network from prior knowledge to find out new probabilistic properties of the events.

We will use Haskell's probabilistic functional programming library to evaluate such a network and find interesting probabilities.

Getting ready

Install the probability library using cabal as follows:

```
$ cabal install probability
```

We will be representing the following network. Internalize the following figure to get an intuitive grasp of the variable names:

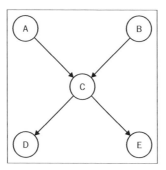

Event **C** depends on events **A** and **B**. Meanwhile, events **D** and **E** depend on event **C**. Through the power of the Probabilistic Functional Programming library, in this recipe, we will find the probability of event **E** given only information about event **D**.

How to do it...

1. Import the following packages:

```
import qualified Numeric.Probability.Distribution as Dist
import Numeric.Probability.Distribution ((??), (?=<<), )
```

2. Create a helper function to define conditional probabilities as follows:

```
prob p = Dist.choose p True False
```

3. Define the probability of variable A, P(A) as follows:

```
a :: Dist.T Rational Bool
a = prob 0.2
```

4. Define the probability of variable B, P(B) as follows:

```
b :: Dist.T Rational Bool
b = prob 0.05
```

5. Define the probability of variable C given A and B, P(C | AB) as follows:

```
c :: Bool -> Bool -> Dist.T Rational Bool
c False False = prob 0.9
c False True = prob 0.5
c True False = prob 0.3
c True True = prob 0.1
```

6. Define the probability of D given C, P(D | C) as follows:

```
d :: Bool -> Dist.T Rational Bool
d False = prob 0.1
d True = prob 0.4
```

7. Define the probability of E given C, P(E | C) as follows:

```
e :: Bool -> Dist.T Rational Bool
e False = prob 0.5
e True = prob 0.2
```

8. Define a data structure for the network as follows:

```
data Network = N {aVal :: Bool
, bVal :: Bool
, cVal :: Bool
, dVal :: Bool
, eVal :: Bool }
deriving (Eq, Ord, Show)
```

9. Construct the network according to the preceding figure:

```
bNetwork :: Dist.T Rational Network
bNetwork = do a' <- a
              b' <- b
              c' <- c a' b'
              d' <- d c'
              e' <- e c'
              return (N a' b' c' d' e')
```

10. Calculate the probability of E given D, P(E | D) as follows:

```
main = print $ eVal ?? dVal ?=<< bNetwork
```

11. The output represented as a fraction is as follows:

```
$ runhaskell Main.hs

3643 % 16430
```

Creating a data structure for playing cards

Many probability and statistic problems are posed using playing cards. In this recipe, we will create a data structure and useful functions for the cards.

There are a total of 52 playing cards in a standard deck. Each card has one of the following four suits:

▶ Spades

▶ Hearts

▶ Diamonds

▶ Clubs

Also, each card has one out of 13 ranks as follows:

▶ Integers between 2 and 10 inclusive

▶ Jack

▶ Queen

▶ King

▶ Ace

Getting ready

Install the `probability` library using cabal as follows:

```
$ cabal install probability
```

Review the sample code on the `probability` package about collections at `http://hackage.haskell.org/package/probability-0.2.4/docs/src/Numeric-Probability-Example-Collection.html`.

The recipe is based heavily on the probability example given in the link.

How to do it...

1. Import the following packages:

   ```
   import qualified Numeric.Probability.Distribution as Dist
   import Numeric.Probability.Distribution ((??))
   import Control.Monad.Trans.State (StateT(StateT, runStateT),
   evalStateT)
   import Control.Monad (replicateM)
   import Data.List (delete)
   ```

2. Create a data structure of the suits on a card as follows:

   ```
   data Suit = Club | Spade | Heart | Diamond
      deriving (Eq,Ord,Show,Enum)
   ```

3. Create a data structure for the ranks of a card as follows:

   ```
   data Rank = Plain Int | Jack | Queen | King | Ace
      deriving (Eq,Ord,Show)
   ```

4. Define a shortcut type for a card to be a tuple of a rank and a suit as follows:

   ```
   type Card = (Rank,Suit)
   ```

5. Describe the plain cards as follows:

   ```
   plains :: [Rank]
   plains = map Plain [2..10]
   ```

6. Describe the face cards as follows:

   ```
   faces :: [Rank]
   faces = [Jack,Queen,King,Ace]
   ```

7. Create a helper function as follows to detect whether it is a face card:

   ```
   isFace :: Card -> Bool
   isFace (r,_) = r `elem` faces
   ```

8. Create a helper function as follows to detect whether it is a plain card:

```
isPlain :: Card -> Bool
isPlain (r,_) = r `elem` plains
```

9. Define all the rank cards as follows:

```
ranks :: [Rank]
ranks = plains ++ faces
```

10. Define the suit cards as follows:

```
suits :: [Suit]
suits = [Club, Spade, Heart, Diamond]
```

11. Create a deck of cards out of ranks and suits as follows:

```
deck :: [Card]
deck = [ (r,s) | r <- ranks, s <- suits ]
```

12. Create a helper function as follows to select an item from a list for probability measurements:

```
selectOne :: (Fractional prob, Eq a) =>
    StateT ([a]) (Dist.T prob) a
selectOne =
    StateT $ Dist.uniform . removeEach
```

13. Create a function as follows to select some cards from the deck:

```
select :: (Fractional prob, Eq a) => Int -> [a] -> Dist.T
    prob [a]
select n = evalStateT (replicateM n selectOne)
```

14. Create a helper function as follows to remove each of the items from a list:

```
removeEach xs = zip xs (map (flip delete xs) xs)
```

15. Test out the deck of cards as follows with the probability functions created:

```
main = print $
Dist.just [(Plain 3, Heart), (Plain 3, Diamond)] ?? select
    2 deck
```

16. The probability of selecting those two cards from the deck is as follows:

```
3.770739064856712e-4
```

Using a Markov chain to generate text

A Markov chain is a system that predicts future outcomes of a system given current conditions. We can train a Markov chain on a corpus of data to generate new text by following the states.

A graphical representation of a chain is shown in the following figure:

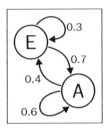

Node E has a 70% probability to end up on node A, and a 30% probability to remain in place

Getting ready

Install the markov-chain library using cabal as follows:

```
$ cabal install markov-chain
```

Download a big corpus of text, and name it big.txt. In this recipe, we will be using the text downloaded from http://norvig.com/big.txt.

How to do it...

1. Import the following packages:

```
import Data.MarkovChain
import System.Random (mkStdGen)
```

2. Train a Markov chain on a big input of text and then run it as follows:

```
main = do
rawText <- readFile "big.txt"
let g = mkStdGen 100
putStrLn $ "Character by character: \n"
putStrLn $ take 100 $ run 3 rawText 0 g
putStrLn $ "\nWord by word: \n"
putStrLn $ unwords $ take 100 $ run 2 (words rawText)0 g
```

3. We can run the Markov chain and see the output as follows:

    ```
    $ runhaskell Main.hs
    ```

    ```
    Generated character by character:
    ```

    ```
    The evaturn bring everice Ana Paciously skuling from to was
    fing, of rant of and sway.
    ```

    ```
    5. Whendent
    ```

    ```
    Generated word by word:
    ```

    ```
    The Project gratefully accepts contributions of money, though
    there was a brief word, showing that he would do so. He could
    hear all that she had to reply; the room scanned Princess Mary's
    heartbeat so violently at this age, so dangerous to life, by the
    friends of the Russians, was trying to free his serfs--and that
    till the eggs mature, when by their Creator with certain small
    vessels but no me...." And the cavalry, Colonel, but I don't wish
    to know which it has a fit, and there was a very large measure,
    attributed to eating this root. But
    ```

How it works...

The code prints our text trained by the corpus, which is fed into the Markov chain.

In the first character-by-character Markov chain, it tries to generate the next letter based on the previous three letters. Notice how most phrases don't make sense and some tokens aren't even English words.

The second Markov chain is generated word by word and only infers based on the previous two words. As we see, it emulates English phrases a bit more naturally.

These texts are purely generated by evaluating probabilities.

Creating n-grams from a list

An *n*-gram is a sequence of *n* items that occur adjacently. For example, in the following sequence of number [1, 2, 5, 3, 2], a possible 3-gram is [5, 3, 2].

n-grams are useful in computing probability tables to predict the next item. In this recipe, we will be creating all possible *n*-grams from a list of items. A Markov chain can easily be trained by using *n*-gram computation from this recipe.

How to do it...

1. Define the *n*-gram function as follows to produce all possible *n*-grams from a list:

```
ngram :: Int -> [a] -> [[a]]
ngram n xs
    | n <= length xs = take n xs : ngram n (drop 1 xs)
    | otherwise = []
```

2. Test it out on a sample list as follows:

```
main = print $ ngram 3 "hello world"
```

3. The printed 3-gram is as follows:

```
["hel","ell","llo","lo ","o w"," wo","wor","orl","rld"]
```

Creating a neural network perceptron

A perceptron is a linear classifier that uses labelled data to converge to its answer. Given a set of inputs and their corresponding expected output, a perceptron tries to linearly separate the input values. If the input is not linearly separable, then the algorithm may not converge.

In this recipe, we will deal with the following list of data:

[(0,0), (0,1), (1,0), (1,1)].

Each item is labelled with an expected output as follows:

▸ (0,0) is expected to output a 0

▸ (0,1) is expected to output a 0

▸ (1,0) is expected to output a 0

▸ (1,1) is expected to output a 1

Graphically, we are trying to find a line that separates these points:

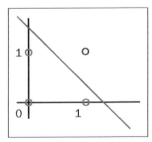

Getting ready

Review the concept of a perceptron by:

- Reading the Wikipedia article on the perceptron available at
  `http://en.wikipedia.org/wiki/Perceptron`

- Skimming the Haskell implementation by Moresmau available at `http://`
  `jpmoresmau.blogspot.com/2007/05/perceptron-in-haskell.html`

How to do it...

1. Import `replicateM`, `randomR`, and `getStdRandom` for handling random number generation in our neural network as follows:

   ```
   import Control.Monad (replicateM)
   import System.Random (randomR, getStdRandom)
   ```

2. Define types to help describe the variables fed into each helper method as follows:

   ```
   type Inputs = [Float]
   type Weights = [Float]
   type Threshold = Float
   type Output = Float
   type Expected = Float
   type Actual = Float
   type Delta = Float
   type Interval = Int
   type Step = (Weights, Interval)
   ```

3. Create a function to generate an output value of a neuron that takes in a series of inputs, corresponding weights, and a threshold value. The neuron fires a `1` if the dot product of the weight vector with the input vector is above the threshold, and `0` otherwise, as presented in the following code snippet:

   ```
   output :: Inputs -> Weights -> Threshold -> Output
   output xs ws t
     | (dot xs ws) > t = 1
     | otherwise = 0
     where dot as bs = sum $ zipWith (*) as bs
   ```

4. Create a function to adjust weights of a neuron given expected and actual results. The weights are updated using a learning rule, as presented in the following code snippet:

```
adjustWeights :: Inputs -> Weights -> Expected -> Actual ->
Weights
adjustWeights xs ws ex ac = add ws delta
  where delta = map (err * learningRate *) xs
        add = zipWith (+)
        err = ex - ac
        learningRate = 0.1
```

5. Step through one iteration of the perceptron cycle to update weights as follows. For this recipe, assume each neuron has a threshold of 0.2:

```
step :: Inputs -> Weights -> Expected -> Weights
step xs ws ex = adjustWeights xs ws ex (output xs ws t)
  where t = 0.2
```

6. Create a helper function as follows to compute weight changes per step:

```
epoch :: [(Inputs, Expected)] -> Weights -> (Weights, Delta)
epoch inputs ws = (newWeights, delta)
  where newWeights = foldl
        (\acc (xs, ex) -> step xs acc ex) ws inputs
        delta = (sum (absSub newWeights ws)) / length' ws
        absSub as bs = map abs $ zipWith (-) as bs
        length' = fromIntegral . length
```

7. Run through the steps using `epoch` until the weights converge. Weight convergence is detected simply by noticing the first instance when weights no longer significantly change values. This is presented in the following code snippet:

```
run :: [(Inputs, Expected)] -> Weights -> Interval -> Step
run inputs ws n
  | delta == 0.0 = (newWeights, n)
  | otherwise = run inputs newWeights (n+1)
  where (newWeights, delta) = epoch inputs ws
```

8. Initialize a weight vector as follows:

```
initialWeights :: Int -> IO [Float]
initialWeights nb = do
  let interval = randomR (-0.5,0.5)
  (replicateM nb (getStdRandom interval))
```

9. Test the perceptron network to separate an AND Boolean structure as follows:

```
main :: IO ()
main = do
  w <- initialWeights 2
```

```
let (ws,i) = run [ ([0,0],0)
                 , ([0,1],0)
                 , ([1,0],0)
                 , ([1,1],1) ] w 1
print (ws,i)
```

10. A valid output may be:

`([0.17867908,3.5879448e-1],8)`

We can verify that this output is correct since the weights sum to a value greater than the threshold value of 0.2, while each weight value individually is less than the threshold of 0.2. Therefore, the output will trigger only when the input is (1, 1) as desired.

8
Clustering and Classification

This chapter demonstrates algorithms that intelligently cluster and categorize data:

- ▶ Implementing the k-means clustering algorithm
- ▶ Implementing hierarchical clustering
- ▶ Using a hierarchical clustering library
- ▶ Finding the number of clusters
- ▶ Clustering words by their lexemes
- ▶ Classifying the parts of speech of words
- ▶ Identifying key words in a corpus of text
- ▶ Training a parts-of-speech tagger
- ▶ Implementing a decision tree classifier
- ▶ Implementing a k-Nearest Neighbors classifier
- ▶ Visualizing points using Graphics.EasyPlot

Introduction

Computer algorithms are becoming better and better at analyzing large datasets. As their performance enhances, their ability to detect interesting patterns in data also improves.

The first few algorithms in this chapter demonstrate how to look at thousands of points and identify clusters. A **cluster** is simply a congregation of points defined by how closely they lie together. This measure of "closeness" is entirely up to us. One of the most popular closeness metrics is the Euclidian distance.

We can understand clusters by looking up at the night sky and pointing at stars that appear together. Our ancestors found it convenient to name "clusters" of stars, of which we refer to as constellations. We will be finding our own constellations in the "sky" of data points.

This chapter also focuses on classifying words. We will label words by their parts of speech as well as topic.

We will implement our own decision tree to classify practical data. Lastly, we will visualize clusters and points using plotting libraries.

Implementing the k-means clustering algorithm

The k-means clustering algorithm partitions data into k different groups. These k groupings are called clusters, and the location of these clusters are adjusted iteratively. We compute the arithmetic mean of all the points in a group to obtain a centroid point that we use, replacing the previous cluster location.

Hopefully, after this succint explanation, the name *k-means clustering* no longer sounds completely foreign. One of the best places to learn more about this algorithm is on Coursera: `https://class.coursera.org/ml-003/lecture/78`.

How to do it...

Create a new file, which we call `Main.hs`, and perform the following steps:

1. Import the following built-in libraries:

```
import Data.Map (Map)
import qualified Data.Map as Map
import Data.List (minimumBy, sort, transpose)
import Data.Ord (comparing)
```

2. Define a type synonym for points shown as follows:

```
type Point = [Double]
```

3. Define the Euclidian distance function between two points:

```
dist :: Point -> Point -> Double

dist a b = sqrt $ sum $ map (^2) $ zipWith (-) a b
```

4. Define the assignment step in the k-means algorithm. Each point will be assigned to its closest centroid:

```
assign :: [Point] -> [Point] -> Map Point [Point]

assign centroids points =
  Map.fromListWith (++) [(assignPoint p, [p]) | p<- points]

  where assignPoint p =
    minimumBy (comparing (dist p)) centroids
```

5. Define the relocation step in the k-means algorithm. Each centroid is relocated to the arithmetic mean of its corresponding points:

```
relocate :: Map Point [Point] -> Map Point [Point]

relocate centroidsMap =
  Map.foldWithKey insertCenter Map.empty centroidsMap
  where insertCenter _ ps m = Map.insert (center ps) ps m
        center [] = [0,0]
        center ps = map average (transpose ps)
        average xs = sum xs / fromIntegral (length xs)
```

6. Run the k-means algorithm repeatedly until the centroids no longer move around:

```
kmeans :: [Point] -> [Point] -> [Point]

kmeans centroids points =
if converged
then centroids
else kmeans (Map.keys newCentroidsMap) points

where converged =
        all (< 0.00001) $ zipWith dist
            (sort centroids) (Map.keys newCentroidsMap)

    newCentroidsMap =
      relocate (assign centroids points)

    equal a b = dist a b < 0.00001
```

7. Test out the clustering with a couple of hardcoded points. The usual way to implement k-means chooses the starting centroids randomly. However, in this recipe, we will simply take the first k points:

```
main = do
let points = [ [0,0], [1,0], [0,1], [1,1]
             , [7,5], [9,6], [8,7] ]
let centroids = kmeans (take 2 points) points
print centroids
```

8. After the algorithm converges, the resulting centroids will be as follows:

    $ runhaskell Main.hs

    ```
    [[0.5,0.5],[8.0,6.0]]
    ```

How it works...

The algorithm repeatedly follows two procedures until the clusters are found. The first procedure is to partition the points by assigning each point to its closest centroid. The following diagram shows the data assignment step. Initially, there are three centroids represented by a star, square, and circle around three different points. The first part of the algorithm assigns each point a corresponding centroid.

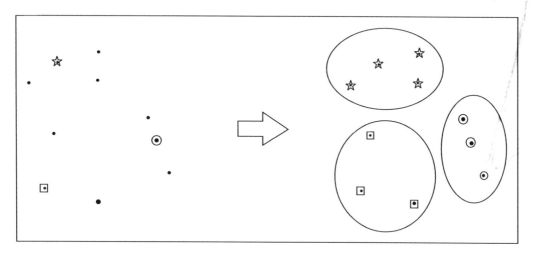

The next step is to relocate the centroids to the center, or arithmetic mean, of their corresponding points. In the following diagram, the arithmetic mean of each cluster is computed, and the centroid is shifted to the new center:

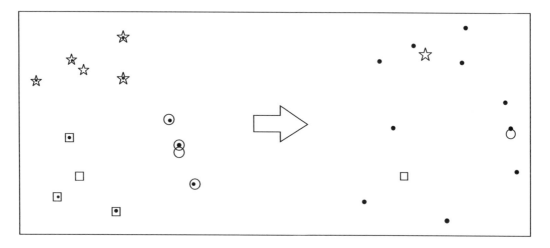

This algorithm continues until the centroids no longer move around. The final categorization of each point is the cluster to which each point belongs.

There's more...

Although easy to implement and understand, this algorithm has a couple of limitations. The output of the k-means clustering algorithm is sensitive to the initial centroids chosen. Also, using the Euclidian distance metric forces the clusters to be described only by circular regions. Another limitation of k-means clustering is that the initial number of clusters k must be specified by the user. The user should visualize the data and use their judgment to determine the number of clusters before beginning the algorithm. Moreover, the convergence condition for the algorithm is an issue for special edge-cases.

See also

For another type of clustering algorithm, see the next recipe on *Implementing hierarchical clustering*.

Implementing hierarchical clustering

Another way to cluster data is by first assuming each data item as its own cluster. We can then take a step back and merge together two of the nearest clusters. This process forms a hierarchy of clusters.

Take, for example, an analogy relating to islands and water level. An island is nothing more than a mountain tip surrounded by water. Imagine we have islands scattered across a sea. If we were to slowly drop the water level of the sea, two nearby small islands would merge into a larger island because they are connected to the same mountain formation. We can stop the water level from dropping any time we have the desired number of larger islands.

How to do it...

In a new file, which we name `Main.hs`, insert this code:

1. Import the built-in functions:

   ```
   import Data.Map (Map, (!), delete)
   import qualified Data.Map as Map
   import Data.Ord (comparing)
   import Data.List (sort, tails, transpose, minimumBy)
   ```

2. Define a type synonym for points:

   ```
   type Point = [Double]
   ```

3. Define a convenience function to compute the arithmetic mean of list of points:

```
center :: [Point] -> Point

center points = map average (transpose points)
  where average xs = sum xs / fromIntegral (length xs)
```

4. Combine the two clusters that are nearest to each other:

```
merge :: Map Point [Point] -> Map Point [Point]

merge m =
        Map.insert (center [a,b]) ((m ! a) ++ (m ! b)) newM

where (a,b) = nearest (Map.keys m)

            newM = Map.delete b (Map.delete a m)

            equal a b = dist a b < 0.00001

            dist a b = sqrt $ sum $ map (^2) $ zipWith (-)
              a b

            nearest points =
                minimumBy (comparing (uncurry dist))
                [(a, b) | (a : rest) <- tails points, b
                  <- rest]
```

5. Run the hierarchical algorithm until there are k clusters:

```
run :: Int -> Map Point [Point] -> Map Point [Point]

run k m = if length (Map.keys m) == k
            then m
            else run k (merge m)
```

6. Initialize so that every point is its own cluster:

```
initialize :: [Point] -> Map Point [Point]

initialize points =
  foldl (\m p -> Map.insert p [p] m) Map.empty points
```

7. Test the clustering algorithm on some input:

```
main = do
        let points = [ [0,0], [1,0], [0,1], [1,1]
                     , [7,5], [9,6], [8,7]]
        let centroids = Map.keys $ run 2 (initialize points)
        print centroids
```

8. The algorithm will output the following centroids:

```
$ runhaskell Main.hs
```

```
[[0.5,0.5],[7.75,5.75]]
```

How it works...

There are two main ways to implement hierarchical clustering. The algorithm described in this recipe implements the *agglomerative* bottom-up approach. Each point is pre-emptively considered to be a cluster, and at each step the two closest clusters merge together. However, another approach to implement is top-down in a *divisive* approach where every point starts in one massive cluster that iteratively splits the clusters.

In this recipe, we begin by first assuming that every point is its own cluster. Then we take a step back and merge two of the nearest clusters. This step repeats until a desired convergence state is reached. In our example, we stop once we have exactly two clusters. The following diagram shows the three iterations of a hierarchical clustering algorithm:

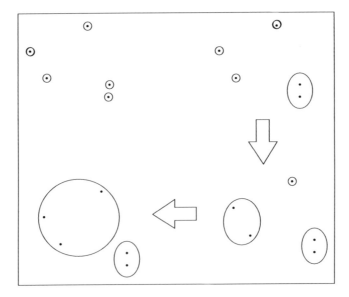

There's more...

Like most clustering algorithms, the choice of distance metric greatly affects the results. In this recipe, we assumed the Euclidean metric, but depending on the data, perhaps the distance metric should be the Manhattan distance or cosine similarity.

See also

For a non-hierarchical clustering algorithm, see the previous recipe on *Implementing the k-means clustering algorithm*.

Using a hierarchical clustering library

We will group together a list of points using a hierarchical clustering approach. We will start by assuming that each point is its own cluster. The two closest clusters merge together and the algorithm repeats until the stopping criteria is met. In this algorithm, we will use a library to run hierarchical clustering until there are a specific number of clusters remaining.

Getting ready

Install the hierarchical clustering package using cabal as follows (documentation is available at http://hackage.haskell.org/package/hierarchical-clustering):

```
$ cabal install hierarchical-clustering
```

How to do it...

Insert the following code in a new file, which we call Main.hs:

1. Import the required library:

   ```
   import Data.Clustering.Hierarchical
   ```

2. Define a Point data type:

   ```
   data Point = Point [Double] deriving Show
   ```

3. Define the Euclidian distance metric:

   ```
   dist :: Point -> Point -> Distance
   dist (Point a) (Point b) = sqrt $ sum $ map (^2) $
                                  zipWith (-) a b
   ```

4. Print out the clusters:

```
printCluster :: Dendrogram Point -> Double -> IO ()

printCluster clusters cut = do
        let es = map elements $ clusters `cutAt` cut
        mapM_ print es
```

5. Test the clustering algorithm on some points:

```
main = do
        let points =
map Point [ [0,0], [1,0], [0,1], [1,1]
            , [7,5], [9,6], [8,7] ]
        let clusters = dendrogram SingleLinkage points dist
        printCluster clusters 2.0
```

6. Each of the three clusters are printed out as lists of points:

```
[Point [0.0,1.0], Point [1.0,0.0], Point [0.0,0.0], Point
[1.0,1.0]]
[Point [7.0,5.0]]
[Point [9.0,6.0], Point [8.0,7.0]]
```

How it works...

The dendogram function has the type `Linkage -> [a] -> (a -> a -> Distance)` `-> Dendrogram a`. The linkage describes how distance is calculated. In this recipe, we use `SingleLinkage` as the first argument, which means that the distance between two clusters is the minimum distance between all their elements.

The second argument is the list of points, followed by a distance metric. The result of this function is a **dendogram**, otherwise referred to as a hierarchical tree diagram. We use the defined `printCluster` function to display the clusters.

There's more...

The other types of linkage in this library include the following mentioned along with their description present on Hackage:

▶ `SingleLinkage`: This is the minimum distance between two clusters.

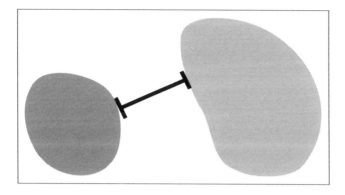

"O(n^2) time and O(n) space, using the SLINK algorithm. This algorithm is optimal in both space and time and gives the same answer as the naive algorithm using a distance matrix."

▸ `CompleteLinkage`: This is the maximum distance between two clusters.

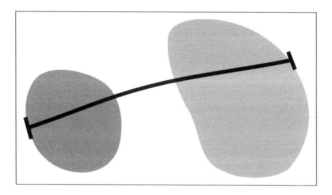

"O(n^3) time and O(n^2) space, using the naive algorithm with a distance matrix. Use CLINK if you need more performance."

▸ Complete linkage with **CLINK** is the same as the previous linkage type, except that it uses a faster but not always optimal algorithm.

"O(n^2) time and O(n) space, using the CLINK algorithm. Note that this algorithm doesn't always give the same answer as the naive algorithm using a distance matrix, but it's much faster."

> ▸ UPGMA is the average distance between the two clusters.

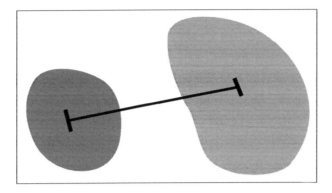

> *"O(n^3) time and O(n^2) space, using the naive algorithm with a distance matrix."*

> ▸ And lastly, FakeAverageLinkage is similar to the previous UPGMA linkage but weighs both clusters equally in its calculations.

> *"O(n^3) time and O(n^2) space, using the naive algorithm with a distance matrix."*

See also

To use our own hierarchical clustering algorithm, see the previous recipe on *Implementing hierarchical clustering*.

Finding the number of clusters

Sometimes, we do not know the number of clusters in a dataset, yet most clustering algorithms require this information a priori. One way to find the number of clusters is to run the clustering algorithm on all possible number of clusters and compute the average variance of the clusters. We can then graph the average variance for the number of clusters, and identify the number of clusters by finding the first fluctuation of the curve.

Getting ready

Review the k-means recipe titled *Implementing the k-means clustering algorithm*. We will be using the kmeans and assign functions defined in that recipe.

Install the Statistics package from cabal:

```
$ cabal install statistics
```

How to do it...

Create a new file and insert the following code. We name this file `Main.hs`.

1. Import the `variance` function and the helper `fromList` function:

    ```
    import Statistics.Sample (variance)
    import Data.Vector.Unboxed (fromList)
    ```

2. Compute the average of the variance of each cluster:

    ```
    avgVar points centroids = avg [variance . fromList $
       map (dist c) ps | (c, ps) <- Map.assocs m]
       where m = assign centroids points
                avg xs = (sum xs) / (fromIntegral (length xs))
    ```

3. In `main`, define a list of points. Notice how there appears to be three clusters:

    ```
    main = do
       let points = [ [0,0], [1,0], [0,1]
                    , [20,0], [21,0], [20,1]
                    , [40,5], [40,6], [40,8] ]
    ```

4. Get the average of the variance of each set of clusters:

    ```
       let centroids = [ kmeans (take k points) points |
                         k <- [1..length points] ]
       let avgVars = map (avgVar points) centroids
       print avgVars
    ```

5. The output will be a list of numbers. Once plotted, we can see that the number of clusters is three, which occurs at the knee, or just before local maxima, of the curve as shown in the following image:

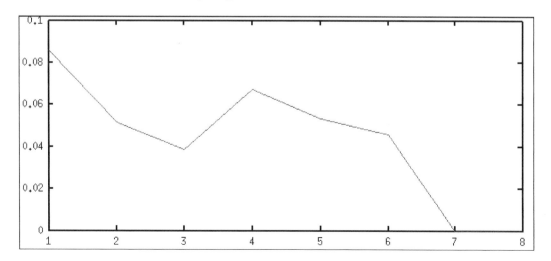

Clustering words by their lexemes

Words that look alike can easily be clustered together. The clustering algorithm in the lexeme-clustering package is based on Janicki's research paper titled, "*A Lexeme-Clustering Algorithm for Unsupervised Learning of Morphology*". A direct link to this paper can be found through the following URL: `http://skil.informatik.uni-leipzig.de/blog/wp-content/uploads/proceedings/2012/Janicki2012.37.pdf`.

Getting ready

An Internet connection is necessary for this recipe to download the package from GitHub.

How to do it...

Follow these steps to install and use the library:

1. Obtain the lexeme-clustering library from GitHub. If Git is installed, enter the following command, otherwise download it from `https://github.com/BinRoot/lexeme-clustering/archive/master.zip`:

   ```
   $ git clone https://github.com/BinRoot/lexeme-clustering
   ```

2. Change into the library's directory:

   ```
   $ cd lexeme-clustering/
   ```

3. Install the package:

   ```
   $ cabal install
   ```

4. Create an input file with a different word on each line:

   ```
   $ cat input.txt
   mama
   papa
   sissy
   bro
   mother
   father
   grandfather
   grandmother
   uncle
   mommy
   daddy
   ```

```
ma

pa

mom

dad

sister

brother
```

5. Run the lexeme-clustering algorithm on the input file:

    ```
    $ dist/build/lexeme-clustering/lexeme-clustering input.txt
    ```

6. The resulting output clusters are then displayed:

    ```
    # Clustering
    bro, brother
    dad, daddy
    grandfather, grandmother
    father, ma, mama, mom, mommy, mother, pa, papa
    sissy, sister
    uncle
    ```

How it works...

The related words are clustered together by carefully looking at each word's **morpheme**, or smallest meaningful component.

Here's a short excerpt from the abstract of the research paper of which this algorithm is based:

> *"Initially, a trie of words is built and each node in the trie is considered a candidate for stem. The suffixes, with which it occurs, are clustered according to mutual information in order to identify inflectional paradigms."*

See also

For clustering points of data, see the previous algorithms on *Implementing the k-means clustering algorithm*, *Implementing hierarchical clustering*, and *Using a hierarchical clustering library*.

Classifying the parts of speech of words

This recipe will demonstrate how to identify the parts of speech of each word in a sentence. We will be using a handy library called **chatter**, which contains very useful **Natural Language Processing (NLP)** tools. It can be obtained from Hackage at `http://hackage.haskell.org/package/chatter`.

NLP is the study of human language embedded in a machine. Our naturally spoken or written language may seem obvious to us in our day-to-day lives, but producing meaning out of words is still a difficult task for computers.

Getting ready

Install the NLP library using cabal:

```
cabal install chatter
```

How to do it...

In a new file, which we name `Main.hs`, enter the following source code:

1. Import the parts of speech library and the pack function:

   ```
   import NLP.POS
   import Data.Text (pack)
   ```

2. Obtain the default tagger provided by the library:

   ```
   main = do
   tagger <- defaultTagger
   ```

3. Feed the `tag` function a tagger and a text to see the corresponding parts of speech per each word:

   ```
   let text = pack "The best jokes have no punchline."
   print $ tag tagger text
   ```

4. The output will be an association list of the word to its part of speech:

   ```
   [[ ("The", Tag "at"),
       ("best", Tag "jjt"),
       ("jokes", Tag "nns"),
       ("have", Tag "hv"),
       ("no", Tag "at"),
       ("punchline",Tag "nn"),
       (".",Tag ".") ]]
   ```

How it works...

A parts of speech tagger is trained from a corpus of text. In this example, we use the default tagger provided by the library, which trains on the corpus in the following directory of the package, `data/models/brown-train.model.gz`. This corpus is called the Brown University Standard Corpus of Present-Day American English, created in the 1960s.

Definitions of each of the abbreviations such as at, `jjt`, or `nns` can be found on `http://en.wikipedia.org/wiki/Brown_Corpus#Part-of-speech_tags_used`.

There's more...

We can also train our own parts of speech taggers by loading a tagger from a file path, `loadTagger :: FilePath -> IO POSTagger`.

See also

To categorize words as something other than parts of speech, see the next recipe on *Identifying key words in a corpus of text*.

Identifying key words in a corpus of text

One way to predict the topic of a paragraph or sentence is by identifying what the words mean. While the parts of speech give some insight about each word, they still don't reveal the connotation of that word. In this recipe, we will use a Haskell library to tag words by topics such as PERSON, CITY, DATE, and so on.

Getting ready

An Internet connection is necessary for this recipe to download the `sequor` package.

Install it from cabal:

```
$ cabal install sequor --prefix=`pwd`
```

Otherwise, follow these directions to install it manually:

1. Obtain the latest version of the sequor library by opening up a browser and visiting the following URL: `http://hackage.haskell.org/package/sequor`.
2. Under the **Downloads** section, download the cabal source package.

3. Extract the contents:

  ❑ On Windows, it is easiest to using 7-Zip, an easy-to-use file archiver. Install it on your machine by going to `http://www.7-zip.org`. Then using 7-Zip, extract the contents of the tarball.

  ❑ On other operating systems, run the following command to extract the tarball. Replace the numbers in the following command to the correct version numbers of your download because a new version (that is, 0.7.3) may be out:

```
$ tar -zxvf sequor-0.7.2.tar.gz
```

4. Go into the directory:

```
$ cd sequor-0.7.2
```

5. Make sure to read the README file:

```
$ cat README.*
```

6. Install the library using the following Cabal command:

```
$ cabal install --prefix=`pwd`
```

How to do it...

We will set up an input file to feed into the program.

1. Create an `input.txt` file using the CoNLL format, which requires one token per line, and sentences separated by a blank line:

```
$ cat input.txt
On
Tuesday
Richard
Stallman
will
visit
Charlottesville
,
Virginia
in
the
United
States
```

2. Now run the word tagging on the input:

   ```
   $ bin/seminer en < input.txt > output.txt
   ```

3. The result is saved in the output.txt file. Open up the file and review the corresponding tags found:

   ```
   $ cat output.txt
   O
   B-DATE
   B-PERSON
   I-PERSON
   O
   O
   B-GPE:CITY
   O
   B-GPE:STATE_PROVINCE
   O
   O
   B-GPE:COUNTRY
   I-GPE:COUNTRY
   ```

How it works...

The library uses Collins' sequence perceptron, based off a paper published in 2002 titled *"Discriminative Training Methods for Hidden Markov Models: Theory and Experiments with Perceptron Algorithms"*. His website (http://www.cs.columbia.edu/~mcollins/) contains comprehensive notes on designing the algorithm used in this recipe.

See also

To use an existing parts of speech tagger, see the previous recipe on *Classifying the parts of speech of words*. To train our own parts-of-speech tagger, see the next recipe on *Training a parts-of-speech tagger*.

Training a parts-of-speech tagger

We will use a Haskell library, sequor, to train our own parts of speech tagger. Then we can use this newly trained model on our own input.

Getting ready

Please refer to the *Getting ready* section of the previous recipe.

How to do it...

In a new file, which we name `Main.hs`, enter the following source code:

1. Use the `sequor` executable to train the parts of speech tagger:

   ❑ The first argument to `sequor` will be `train`, to indicate that we are about to train a tagger

   ❑ The next argument is the template-file, `data/all.features`

   ❑ Then we provide the train-file, `data/train.conll`

   ❑ The last file path we need to provide is the location of where to save the trained model

   ❑ We can specify a learning rate using the `-rate` flag

   ❑ The beam size can be modified using the `-beam` flag

   ❑ Change the number of iterations using the `-iter` flag

   ❑ Use hashing instead of a feature dictionary using the `-hash` flag

   ❑ Provide a path to the held out data using the `-heldout` flag

   ❑ An example of the sequor command in use is as follows:

   ```
   $ ./bin/sequor train data/all.features data/train.conll \
   model --rate 0.1 --beam 10 --iter 5 --hash \
   --heldout data/devel.conll
   ```

2. Test out the trained model on a sample input:

   ```
   $ ./bin/sequor predict model < data/test.conll > \
   data/test.labels
   ```

3. The first few lines of the output `test.labels` file will be:

```
B-NP
I-NP
B-PP
B-NP
I-NP
O
B-VP
B-NP
B-VP
B-NP
```

How it works...

The library uses Collins' sequence perceptron, based off a paper published in 2002 titled *"Discriminative Training Methods for Hidden Markov Models: Theory and Experiments with Perceptron Algorithms"*. The Hackage documentation can be found on `http://hackage.haskell.org/package/sequor`.

See also

To use an existing parts of speech tagger, see the previous recipe on *Classifying the parts of speech of words*.

Implementing a decision tree classifier

A decision tree is a model for classifying data effectively. Each child of a node in the tree represents a feature about the item we are classifying. Traversing down the tree to leaf nodes represent an item's classification. It's often desirable to create the smallest possible tree to represent a large sample of data.

In this recipe, we implement the ID3 decision tree algorithm in Haskell. It is one of the easiest to implement and produces useful results. However, ID3 does not guarantee an optimal solution, may be computationally inefficient compared to other algorithms, and only supports discrete data. While these issues can be addressed by a more complicated algorithm such as C4.5, the code in this recipe is enough to get up and running with a working decision tree.

Getting ready

Create a CSV file representing samples of data. The last column should be the classification. Name this file `input.csv`.

Sunny	Hot	High	Weak	*No*
Sunny	Hot	High	Strong	*No*
Overcast	Hot	High	Weak	*Yes*
Rain	Mild	High	Weak	*Yes*
Rain	Cool	Normal	Weak	*Yes*
Rain	Cool	Normal	Strong	*No*
Overcast	Cool	Normal	Strong	*Yes*
Sunny	Mild	High	Weak	*No*
Sunny	Cool	Normal	Weak	*Yes*
Rain	Mild	Normal	Weak	*Yes*
Sunny	Mild	Normal	Strong	*Yes*
Overcast	Mild	High	Strong	*Yes*
Overcast	Hot	Normal	Weak	*Yes*
Rain	Mild	High	Strong	*No*

The weather data is represented with four attributes, namely outlook, temperature, humidity, and wind. The last column represents whether it is a good idea to play outside.

Import the CSV helper library:

```
$ cabal install csv
```

How to do it...

Insert this code into a new file, which we call `Main.hs`:

1. Import the built-in libraries:

   ```
   import Data.List (nub, elemIndices)
   import qualified Data.Map as M
   import Data.Map (Map, (!))
   import Data.List (transpose)
   import Text.CSV
   ```

2. Define some type synonyms to better understand what data is being passed around:

   ```
   type Class = String
   type Feature = String
   type Entropy = Double
   type DataSet = [([String], Class)]
   ```

3. Define the main function to read in the CSV file and handle any errors:

```
main = do
  rawCSV <- parseCSVFromFile "input.csv"
  either handleError doWork rawCSV

handleError = error "invalid file"
```

4. If the file was read successfully, remove any invalid CSV records and construct a decision tree out of it:

```
doWork csv = do
  let removeInvalids = filter (\x -> length x > 1)
  let myData = map (\x -> (init x, last x)) $
    removeInvalids csv
  print $ dtree "root" myData
```

5. Define helper functions to break up the `DataSet` tuple into a list of samples or a list of classes:

```
samples :: DataSet -> [[String]]
samples d = map fst d



classes :: DataSet -> [Class]
classes d = map snd d
```

6. Calculate the entropy of a list of values:

```
entropy :: (Eq a) => [a] -> Entropy


entropy xs = sum $ map (\x -> prob x * info x) $ nub xs
  where prob x = (length' (elemIndices x xs)) /
      (length' xs)
        info x = negate $ logBase 2 (prob x)
        length' xs = fromIntegral $ length xs
```

7. Split an attribute by its features:

```
splitAttr :: [(Feature, Class)] -> Map Feature [Class]

splitAttr fc = foldl (\m (f,c) ->
  M.insertWith (++) f [c] m)
              M.empty fc
```

8. Obtain each of the entropies from splitting up an attribute by its features:

```
splitEntropy :: Map Feature [Class] ->
  M.Map Feature Entropy

splitEntropy m = M.map entropy m
```

9. Compute the information gain from splitting up an attribute by its features:

```
informationGain :: [Class] -> [(Feature, Class)] -> Double

informationGain s a = entropy s - newInformation
  where eMap = splitEntropy $ splitAttr a
        m = splitAttr a
        toDouble x = read x :: Double
        ratio x y = (fromIntegral x) / (fromIntegral y)
        sumE = M.map (\x -> (fromIntegral.length) x /
          (fromIntegral.length) s) m
        newInformation = M.foldWithKey (\k a b -> b + a*(eMap!k))
          0 sumE
```

10. Determine which attribute contributes the highest information gain:

```
highestInformationGain :: DataSet -> Int
highestInformationGain d = snd $ maximum $
  zip (map ((informationGain . classes) d) attrs) [0..]
  where attrs = map (attr d) [0..s-1]
        attr d n = map (\(xs,x) -> (xs!!n,x)) d
        s = (length . fst . head) d
```

11. Define the data structure for a decision tree that we will soon construct:

```
data DTree = DTree { feature :: String
                   , children :: [DTree] }
           | Node String String
           deriving Show
```

12. Split up the dataset by the attribute that contributes the highest information gain:

```
datatrees :: DataSet -> Map String DataSet
datatrees d =
  foldl (\m (x,n) -> M.insertWith (++) (x!!i)
    [((x `dropAt` i), fst (cs!!n))] m)
    M.empty (zip (samples d) [0..])
  where i = highestInformationGain d
    dropAt xs i = let (a,b) = splitAt i xs in a ++ drop 1 b
        cs = zip (classes d) [0..]
```

13. Define a helper function to determine if all elements of a list are equal. We use this to check if further splitting of the dataset is necessary by checking if its classes are identical:

```
allEqual :: Eq a => [a] -> Bool
allEqual [] = True
allEqual [x] = True
allEqual (x:xs) = x == (head xs) && allEqual xs
```

14. Construct the decision tree from a labeling and a dataset of samples:

```
dtree :: String -> DataSet -> DTree

dtree f d
    | allEqual (classes d) = Node f $ head (classes d)
    | otherwise = DTree f $
            M.foldWithKey (\k a b -> b ++ [dtree k a] ) []
            (datatrees d)
```

15. Run the following code to see the tree printed out:

```
DTree { feature = "root"
      , children = [ DTree { feature = "Sunny"
                           , children = [ Node "Normal" "Yes"
                                        , Node "High" "No"
                                        ]
                    , DTree { feature = "Rain"
                           , children = [ Node "Weak" "Yes"
                                        , Node "Strong" "No"
                                        ]

                           }
                    , Node "Overcast" "Yes"
                    ]

      }
```

It can be visualized using the following diagram:

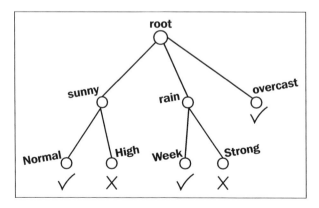

How it works...

The ID3 algorithm uses the concept of Shannon's entropy to divide up a set of samples by the attribute that maximize the information gain. This process is recursively repeated until we're dealing with samples of the same classification or when we run out of attributes.

In the field of Information Theory, **Entropy** is the measure of unpredictability. A fair coin has higher entropy than a biased coin. Entropy can be calculated by taking the expected value of the information content, where information content of a random variable X has the form $- ln(P(X))$. When the logarithm in the equation is to the base of 2, the units of entropy are called *bits*.

Information Gain is the change in entropy from the prior state to the new state. It has the equation $IG = H_1 - H_2$, where H_1 is the original entropy of the sample. And H_2 is the new entropy given an attribute to split.

Implementing a k-Nearest Neighbors classifier

One simple way to classify an item is to look at only its neighboring data. The k-Nearest Neighbors algorithm looks at k items located closest to the item in question. The item is then classified as the most common classification of its k neighbors. This heuristic has been very promising for a wide variety of classification tasks.

In this recipe, we will implement the k-Nearest Neighbors algorithm using a **k-d tree** data structure, which is a binary tree with special properties that allow efficient representation of points in a k-dimensional space.

Imagine we have a web server for our hip new website. Every time someone requests a web page, our web server will fetch the file and present the page. However, bots can easily hammer a web server with thousands of requests, potentially causing a denial of service attack. In this recipe, we will classify whether a web request is being made by a human or a bot.

Getting ready

Install the `KdTree`, `CSV`, and `iproute` packages using cabal:

```
$ cabal install KdTree
$ cabal install CSV
$ cabal install iproute
```

Create a CSV file containing the IP addresses and number of seconds since last access. The last field of each CSV record should be the classification *Human* or *Bot*. We call our file input.csv.

71.190.189.171	8000	Human
71.191.90.170	9000	Human
71.191.91.1	8000	Human
216.239.32.0	5	Bot
216.239.32.10	10	Bot
216.239.32.5	5	Bot

How to do it...

After creating a new file called Main.hs, we perform the following steps:

1. Import the following packages:

```
import Data.Trees.KdTree
import Data.IP (IPv4, fromIPv4)
import Text.CSV
import qualified Data.Map as M
import Data.Maybe (fromJust)
```

2. Convert an IPv4 address string into its 32-bit representation:

```
ipToNum :: String -> Double

ipToNum str = fromIntegral $ sum $
   zipWith (\a b -> a * 256^b) ns [0..]
   where ns = reverse $ fromIPv4 (read str :: IPv4)
```

3. Parse data from a CSV file to obtain a list of points and their associated classifications:

```
parse :: [Record] -> [(Point3d, String)]

parse [] = []
parse xs = map pair (cleanList xs)
   where pair [ip, t, c] =
            (Point3d (ipToNum ip) (read t) 0.0, c)
         cleanList = filter (\x -> length x == 3)
```

4. Find the item in a list that occurs most often:

```
maxFreq :: [String] -> String

maxFreq xs = fst $ foldl myCompare ("", 0) freqs
   where freqs = M.toList $ M.fromListWith (+)
```

```
                                                [(c, 1) | c <- xs]
           myCompare (oldS, oldV) (s,v) = if v > oldV
                                              then (s, v)
                                              else (oldS, oldV)
```

5. Classify a test point given the KdTree, the number of nearest neighbors to use, and the training set of points:

```
test :: KdTree Point3d -> Int -> [(Point3d, String)]
                       -> Point3d -> String


test kdtree k pairList p = maxFreq $ map classify neighbors
  where neighbors = kNearestNeighbors kdtree k p
        classify x = fromJust (lookup x pairList)
```

6. Define `main` to read a CSV file and process the data:

```
main = do
  rawCSV <- parseCSVFromFile "input.csv"
  either handleError doWork rawCSV
```

7. Handle an error if the CSV cannot be read properly:

```
handleError = error "Invalid CSV file"
```

8. Otherwise create a KdTree from the CSV data and test out a couple of examples:

```
doWork rawCSV = do
  let ps = parse rawCSV
  let kdtree = fromList (map fst ps)
  let examples = [ ["71.190.100.100", "2000", "?"]
                 , ["216.239.33.1", "1", "?"] ]
  let examplePts = map fst $ parse examples
  print $ map (test kdtree 2 ps) examplePts
```

9. Run the code to see the resulting classifications of the example points:

```
$ runhaskell Main.hs


["Human", "Bot"]
```

How it works...

The k-Nearest Neighbor algorithm looks at the k closest points from the training set and returns the most frequent classification between these k points. Since we are dealing with points, each of the coordinates should be orderable. Fortunately, an IP address has a faint sense of hierarchy that we can leverage. We convert an IP to its 32-bit number to obtain a useful ordering that we can treat as a coordinate of a point in space.

Visualizing points using Graphics.EasyPlot

Sometimes, it's convenient to simply visualize data points before clustering or classifying to inspect the data. This recipe will feed a list of points to a plotting library to easily see a diagram of the data.

Getting ready

Install easyplot from cabal:

```
$ cabal install easyplot
```

Create a CSV file containing two-dimensional points:

```
$ cat input.csv
```

```
1,2
2,3
3,1
4,5
5,3
6,1
```

How to do it...

In a new file, `Main.hs`, follow these steps:

1. Import the required library to read in CSV data as well the library to plot points:

   ```
   import Text.CSV
   import Graphics.EasyPlot
   ```

2. Create a helper function to convert a list of string records into a list of doubles. For example, we want to convert ["1.0,2.0", "3.5,4.5"] into [(1.0, 2.0), (3.5, 4.5)]:

   ```
   tupes :: [[String]] -> [(Double, Double)]

   tupes records = [ (read x, read y) | [x, y] <- records ]
   ```

3. In `main`, parse the CSV file to be used later on:

   ```
   main = do
     result <- parseCSVFromFile "input.csv"
   ```

4. If the CSV file is valid, plot the points using the `plot :: TerminalType -> a -> IO Bool` function:

```
case result of
  Left err -> putStrLn "Error reading CSV file"
  Right csv -> do
    plot X11 $ Data2D [Title "Plot"] [] (tupes csv)
      return ()
```

How it works...

The first argument to `plot` tells gnuplot where its output should be displayed. For example, we use X11 to output to the X Window System on Linux. Depending on the computer, we can choose between different terminal types. The constructors for `TerminalType` are the following:

- `Aqua`: Output on Mac OS X (Aqua Terminal)
- `Windows`: Output for MS Windows
- `X11`: Output to the X Window System
- `PS FilePath`: Output into a PostScript file
- `EPS FilePath`: Output into an EPS file path
- `PNG FilePath`: Output as Portable Network Graphic into a file
- `PDF FilePath`: Output as Portable Document Format into a file
- `SVG FilePath`: Output as Scalable Vector Graphic into a file
- `GIF FilePath`: Output as Graphics Interchange Format into a file
- `JPEG FilePath`: Output into a JPEG file
- `Latex FilePath`: Output as LaTeX

The second argument to plot is the graph, which may be a `Graph2D`, or `Graph3D`, or a list of these.

9
Parallel and Concurrent Design

In this chapter, we will cover the following recipes:

- ▶ Using the Haskell Runtime System (RTS) options
- ▶ Evaluating a procedure in parallel
- ▶ Controlling parallel algorithms in sequence
- ▶ Forking I/O actions for concurrency
- ▶ Communicating with a forked I/O action
- ▶ Killing forked threads
- ▶ Parallelizing pure functions using the Par monad
- ▶ Mapping over a list in parallel
- ▶ Accessing tuple elements in parallel
- ▶ Implementing MapReduce to count word frequencies
- ▶ Manipulating images in parallel using Repa
- ▶ Benchmarking runtime performance in Haskell
- ▶ Using the criterion package to measure performance
- ▶ Benchmarking runtime performance in the terminal

Introduction

One of the greatest accomplishments in the study of data analysis is the intelligent approach to parallel and concurrent design. As we collect more and more data, we are able to discover more and more patterns. However, this comes at a price of time and space. More data may take more time to compute or more space in terms of memory. It is a very real problem that this chapter will try to solve.

The first few recipes will cover how to evoke pure procedures in parallel and in sequence. The following recipes on forking will deal with concurrency using I/O actions. We will then delve deeper by learning how to access a list and tuple elements in parallel. Then, we will implement MapReduce in Haskell to solve a time-consuming problem efficiently.

We will end the review of parallel and concurrent design by learning how to benchmark runtime performance. Sometimes, the easiest way to discover if code is successfully running in parallel is by timing it against a nonparallel version of the code. If the computation time between the two appears to be the same, then it is very likely that something is wrong. Either the code is not running in parallel or the cost of evoking parallelism outweighs the benefits.

Using the Haskell Runtime System options

The **Runtime System** (**RTS**) in Haskell configures special options such as scheduling, profiling, and managing storage for a compiled Haskell program. In order to write multithreaded code, we must specify our own RTS options as outlined in this recipe.

For further reading, the GHC Commentary on the official Haskell Wiki web page has a very detailed explanation of the runtime system available at `https://ghc.haskell.org/trac/ghc/wiki/Commentary/Rts`.

How to do it...

Open a terminal, compile a code, and run it using the RTS option. Imagine that our file is named `Main.hs`, and issue the following commands:

```
$ ghc -O2 --make Main.hs -threaded -rtsopts

$ ./Main  +RTS -N2
```

How it works...

In order to make use of multiple threads, we must compile our code with the `threaded` and `rtsopts` flags enabled.

Now that it is compiled with `rtsopts`, we can run our program with special instructions placed between the `+RTS` and `-RTS` flags. If there is a `+RTS` flag without a `-RTS` flag, then we assume that the RTS options continue until the end of the line.

We set the number of threads to use by placing `-Nx` within the RTS argument, which stands for "use x threads". So, to use two threads, we should type *-N2*. To use all possible threads, we simply type *-N*.

There's more...

Another way to specify the RTS options is during compile time, using the `--with-rtsopts` flag. More advanced methods include modifying environment variables or overriding runtime system hooks. More information on these can be found on the official Haskell user guide available at `https://www.haskell.org/ghc/docs/7.4.1/html/users_guide/runtime-control.html`.

Evaluating a procedure in parallel

In this recipe, we will conduct two time-consuming tasks in parallel. We will use the `rpar` function provided by the `parallel` package from hackage. The `rpar` function annotates its argument to be evaluated in parallel. Then, we call `runEval` to actually perform the computation.

Getting ready

Install the `parallel` package using cabal as follows:

```
$ cabal install parallel
```

How to do it...

1. Import the parallel package as follows:

   ```
   import Control.Parallel.Strategies (runEval, rpar)
   ```

2. Evaluate two tasks in parallel, and wait for both tasks to finish before returning as seen in the following code snippet:

   ```
   main = do
     print $ runEval $ do
       a <- rpar task1
       b <- rpar task2
       return (a, b)
   ```

3. A time-consuming task can be created as follows:

   ```
   task1 = 8^8^9 :: Integer
   ```

4. Another time-consuming task can be created as follows:

   ```
   task2 = 8^8^8 :: Integer
   ```

5. Compile the code with the `threaded` and `rtsopts` flags enabled, as follows:

   ```
   $ ghc -O2 --make Main.hs -threaded –rtsopts
   ```

6. Run it by specifying the number of cores:

   ```
   $ ./Main +RTS -N2
   ```

 The time-consuming calculations (`task1` and `task2`) in this recipe require a huge amount of memory and may exceed the limitations of the machine in use. Adjust the tasks to be more manageable, such as 4^8^9 or 4^8^8. In this recipe, specifically, the overhead cost of parallelizing these simple mathematical calculations may be greater than the benefits.

How it works...

Time-consuming functions are annotated with `rpar`, which suggests that the computation should occur in parallel. Once `runEval` is applied, the sparked code runs in parallel. Future parts of the code can continue with the execution until the output of these parallel-running threads are needed.

In our recipe, we run `task1` and `task2` in parallel. We immediately return the result to be used in future parts of the code, and the code only waits for the tasks to complete once necessary. The computation is being processed in the background until it is needed later.

See also

To explore examples of using a sequence in a parallel design, refer to the *Controlling parallel algorithms in sequence* recipe.

Controlling parallel algorithms in sequence

In this recipe, we will conduct two time-consuming tasks in parallel. We will use the `rpar` function and the `rseq` function provided by the `parallel` package from hackage. The `rpar` function annotates its argument to be evaluated in parallel. The other function, `rseq`, forces sequential evaluations in what is called the **weak head normal form**.

Getting ready

Install the `parallel` package using cabal as follows:

```
$ cabal install parallel
```

How to do it...

1. Import the parallel package as follows:

   ```
   import Control.Parallel
   import Control.Parallel.Strategies
   Evaluate two tasks in parallel, and wait for both tasks to finish
   before returning.
   main = do
     print $ runEval $ do
       a <- rpar task1
       b <- rpar task2
       rseq a
       rseq b
       return (a, b)
   ```

2. Perform a time-consuming task as follows:

   ```
   task1 = 8^8^9 :: Integer
   ```

3. Perform another time-consuming task as follows:

   ```
   task2 = 8^8^8 :: Integer
   ```

4. Compile the code with the `threaded` and `rtsopts` flags enabled as follows:

   ```
   $ ghc -O2 --make Main.hs -threaded –rtsopts
   ```

5. Run it by specifying the number of cores as follows:

   ```
   $ ./Main +RTS -N2
   ```

How it works...

Time-consuming functions are annotated with `rpar` or `rseq`, which describe whether a computation should happen in parallel or in a sequence. If a function is sparked to be run in parallel, then future parts of the code can be made to run until that value is needed. In that case, the code blocks until the parallel operation is complete. If a function is required to be in sequence, the code will wait until the function has computed a result, and only then will it move on.

In our recipe, we run `task1` and `task2` in parallel. We then run `rseq` on the values to demonstrate the concept of sequencing. The first time we call `rseq`, we are forcing the code to wait until `task1`, which is represented by the variable `a`, is complete. Depending on the parallel design of the algorithm, it may not be necessary to sequence it at all. We also force `task2`, which is represented by the variable `b`, to wait until the value is calculated just to demonstrate how sequencing works.

See also

To see an example of only parallel design without sequencing, refer to the *Evaluating a procedure in parallel* recipe.

Forking I/O actions for concurrency

A quick and easy way to launch an I/O type function in the background is by calling the `forkIO` function provided by the `Control.Concurrent` package. In this recipe, we will demonstrate simple input/output concurrently in Haskell. We will get the number of seconds to wait from the user input, and in the background, it will sleep and print a message once the thread wakes up.

How to do it...

1. Import the built-in concurrency package as follows:

   ```
   import Control.Concurrent (forkIO, threadDelay)
   ```

2. Ask the user the number of seconds the program has to sleep for. Then, sleep for that many seconds by calling our `sleep` function defined in the following code snippet. Finally, recursively call `main` again to demonstrate that the user can continue to input while a thread is running in the background:

   ```
   main = do
     putStr "Enter number of seconds to sleep: "
     time <- fmap (read :: String -> Int) getLine
     forkIO $ sleep time
     main
   ```

3. Define a function that takes in the number of seconds to sleep, and apply
   `threadDelay :: Int -> IO ()` to that value as follows:

```
sleep :: Int -> IO ()
sleep t = do
  let micro = t * 1000000
  threadDelay micro
  putStrLn $ "[Just woke up after "
               ++ show t ++ " seconds]"
```

4. When we run the program, we can quickly input multiple numbers before receiving an output as follows:

```
$ ghci Main.hs


Prelude> main


Prelude> Enter number of seconds to sleep: 3


Prelude> Enter number of seconds to sleep: 2


Prelude> Enter number of seconds to sleep: [Just woke up after 2
seconds]


[Just woke up after 3 seconds]
```

 The `print` and `putrStrLn` functions are not atomic, so you may also get interleaved output.

See also

To send data to a forked action, refer to the *Communicating with a forked I/O action* recipe.

Communicating with a forked I/O action

A quick and easy way to launch an I/O type function in the background is by calling the `forkIO` function provided by the `Control.Concurrent` package. In this recipe, we will be communicating with forked I/O actions by sending messages using a variable type called `MVar`.

Getting ready

Install the `HTTP` package from cabal as follows:

```
$ cabal install HTTP
```

How to do it...

1. Import the relevant packages as follows:

    ```
    import Network.HTTP
    import Control.Concurrent
    ```

2. Create a new variable that will be used by the fork process. The `newEmptyMVar` function is of the `IO (MVar a)` type, so we will extract the expression out and label it `m` as follows:

    ```
    main = do
      m <- newEmptyMVar
      forkIO $ process m
    ```

3. After running the fork, send it some data by calling `putMVar :: MVar a -> a -> IO ()`, as shown in the following lines of code. The variable will hold the given value, and the forked process waiting on that data will resume:

    ```
    putStrLn "sending first website..."
    putMVar m "http://www.haskell.com"
    ```

4. We can reuse the expression and send it more data as follows:

    ```
    putStrLn "sending second website..."
    putMVar m "http://www.gnu.org"
    ```

5. To make sure `main` does not terminate before the forked process is finished, we just force `main` to wait for 10 seconds by calling the `threadDelay` function. This is for demonstration purposes only, and a complete solution should terminate `main` immediately once the fork is complete, as presented in the following code snippet:

    ```
    threadDelay $ 10 * 1000000
    ```

6. Define the code that will be forked to run in parallel as follows:

    ```
    process m = do
      putStrLn "waiting..."
      v <- takeMVar m
      resp <- get v
      putStrLn $ "response from " ++ show v ++ " is " ++ resp
      process m
    ```

7. Create a function to perform an HTTP GET request on a URL as follows:

    ```
    get :: String -> IO String
    get url = do
    ```

```
resp <- simpleHTTP (getRequest url)
body <- getResponseBody resp
return $ take 10 body
```

8. The output of the program will then be as follows:

    $ runhaskell Main.hs

    ```
    sending first website...
    sending second website...
    waiting...
    waiting...
    response from "http://www.haskell.com" is

    <!doctype html>
    <html class="no-js" lang="en">
    <head id="ctl00_Head1"><meta http-equiv="X-UA-C

    response from "http://www.gnu.org" is

    <!DOCTYPE html PUBLIC "-//W3C//DTD XHTML 1.0 Strict//EN"
        "http://www.w3.org/TR/xhtml1/DTD/xhtml1
    waiting...
    ```

See also

To see a simpler example of using `forkIO`, refer to the *Forking I/O actions for concurrency* recipe.

Killing forked threads

When we create a new thread, we can keep track of its corresponding thread ID to kill it later manually.

In this recipe, we will be creating a command-line interface for forking new processes to download a huge file. A download will be initiated with the d command followed by a number. So, running d 1 will launch a thread to download item #1.

We will learn how to kill threads while they are still running. Our command to kill threads will look like k 1 in order to kill the downloaded item #1.

How to do it...

In a new file, which we call `Main.hs`, insert the following code:

1. Import the required packages as follows:

   ```
   import Control.Concurrent
   import qualified Data.Map as M
   ```

2. Let `main` call the helper `download` function:

   ```
   main = download (M.empty :: M.Map Int [ThreadId])
   ```

3. Define a function to take the user queries and appropriately respond as follows:

   ```
   download m = do
      input <- (getLine >>= return . words)
      respond m input >>= download
   ```

4. Respond to a download request:

   ```
   respond m ["d", nstr] = do
     putStrLn "Starting download..."
     let n = read nstr :: Int
     threadId <- forkIO $ massiveDownload n
     return $ M.insertWith (++) n [threadId] m
   ```

5. Respond to a kill request:

   ```
   respond m ["k", nstr] = do
      let n = read nstr :: Int
      case (M.lookup n m) of
        Just threads -> do
          putStrLn "Killing download(s)..."
          mapM_ killThread threads
          download $ M.delete n m
        Nothing -> do
          putStrLn "No such download"
          download m
   ```

6. Respond to an invalid request:

   ```
   respond m _ = do
     putStrLn
         "Type `d #` to start a download or `k #` to kill it."
      return m
   ```

7. Pretend to download a huge file as follows:

   ```
   massiveDownload n = do
      threadDelay $ 10 * 1000000
      putStrLn $ "[Download " ++ (show n) ++" complete!]"
   ```

8. Run the code and evoke a couple of downloads and kill commands as follows:

```
$ runhaskell Main.hs
d 1
Starting download...
d 2
Starting download...
d 3
Starting download...
k 1
Killing download(s)...
[Download 2 complete!]
[Download 3 complete!]
```

How it works...

The program keeps track of a mapping from the download number to thread IDs. Whenever a new download is initiated, we insert the corresponding thread ID to the map. To kill a thread, we call `killThread` on the respective thread ID.

Parallelizing pure functions using the Par monad

The Par monad from the `Control.Monad.Par` package is used to speed up pure functions using parallel threads. Information flow is guided by variables called `IVar`. We can `put` values to `IVar` in parallel or `get` values from it.

Getting ready

Install the Par monad on cabal as follows:

```
$ cabal install monad-par
```

How to do it...

1. Import the Par monad as follows:

   ```
   import Control.Monad.Par
   ```

2. Run a computation in parallel, and perform some interesting function such as counting the number of digits and printing it out.

   ```
   main = print $ length $ show $ runPar mypar
   ```

3. Define an I/O type action as follows:

```
mypar = do
  v1 <- new :: Par (IVar Integer)
  v2 <- new :: Par (IVar Integer)
  fork $ put v1 task1
  fork $ put v2 task2
  v1' <- get v1
  v2' <- get v2
  return (v1' + v2')
```

4. Perform a time-consuming task as follows:

```
task1 = 8^8^8
```

5. Perform another time-consuming task as follows:

```
task2 = 8^8^7
```

6. Compile the code with the `threaded` and `rtsopts` flags enabled, using the following command:

```
$ ghc -O2 --make Main.hs -threaded –rtsopts
```

7. Run it by specifying the number of cores as follows:

```
$ ./Main +RTS -N2
```

```
15151337
```

There's more...

The natural nonparallelized version of the code certainly looks cleaner. In the following example, we see the same principle at work mathematically as the previous example but without the use of monads. However, we no longer have the power of concurrency:

```
import Control.Monad.Par

main = print $ length $ show $ task1 + task2

task1 = 8^8^8
task2 = 8^8^8
```

See also

For dealing with computations that use I/O, refer to the *Forking I/O actions for concurrency* recipe.

Mapping over a list in parallel

In this recipe, we will be applying the map function in parallel. Given a list of values, we will be using multiple threads to apply a function over each value.

How to do it...

1. Import the parallel strategies as follows:

   ```
   import Control.Parallel.Strategies
   ```

2. Map over a list using the `rdeepseq` strategy using the following code snippet:

   ```
   main = do
     let results =
               (parMap rdeepseq (^10) [10^10..10^10+10000]) :: [Int]
       print results
   ```

3. The first few characters of the printed output are shown here after compiling and running the code as follows:

4. Compile the code with the `threaded` and `rtsopts` flags enabled as follows:

   ```
   $ ghc -O2 --make Main.hs -threaded -rtsopts
   ```

5. Run the code by specifying the number of cores as follows:

   ```
   $ ./Main +RTS -N2
   ```

   ```
   [0,3644720378636855297,1420199564594381824,-9091195533231350103,-
   3969065814844243968,5699158338132413177,5185631055696798720,-
   1664423011715345679,-5301432476323807232,-
   6822228826283293807,-3978116359327587328,-
   2988467747382449959,669511447655481344,2530383018990005705,-
   7998143102955305984,  ...
   ```

How it works...

The `parMap` function has the type `Strategy b -> (a -> b) -> [a] -> [b]`. It looks exactly like the type signature of the map function, except that it takes in something called Strategy. A **Strategy** decouples the method of parallelism from the implementation of code. An example of a Strategy is `rdeepseq`, which fully evaluates its argument. For example, Haskell is lazy evaluated, so the code `length [5^5^5, 6^6^6]` will not evaluate the value of 5^5^5 or 6^6^6. We can use the `rdeepseq` example to better control what computations should be evaluated when run in parallel.

In contrast, a slow and simple version of the code is shown as follows:

```
main = do
  print $ map (^10) [10^10..10^10+10000]
```

Try timing the runtime to see the significant differences in using multiple threads.

There's more...

There are many Strategies depending on how the parallelism should be evoked, which are as follows:

- `r0` is the simplest Strategy that simply does not evaluate the expression
- `dot` is used to compose two Strategies together for finer control in more complicated expressions
- `rseq` will immediately evaluate the expression
- `rpar` will annotate the expression to be evaluated in parallel

See also

- If dealing with tuples, refer to the *Accessing tuple elements in parallel* recipe
- For more details on timing code, refer to the *Benchmarking runtime performance in Haskell* recipe or the *Benchmarking runtime performance in the terminal* recipe

Accessing tuple elements in parallel

In this recipe, we will cover how to access elements of a tuple in parallel.

How to do it...

1. Import the built-in package as follows:

   ```
   import Control.Parallel.Strategies
   ```

2. Evaluate the expression in a tuple in parallel. We perform this task twice with different strategies to demonstrate how strategies are easily swapped to change the parallel nature of the code as follows:

   ```
   main = do
     let (a, b) = withStrategy (parTuple2 rseq rseq) (task1, task2)
     print $ seq (a+b) "done 1"
     let (a, bs) = withStrategy (parTuple2 rseq rdeepseq) (task1, tasks)
     print $ seq (a + sum bs) "done 2"
   ```

3. Define time-consuming tasks as follows:

```
task1 = 8^8^8 :: Integer
task2 = 8^8^8 :: Integer
tasks = [10^10..10^10+10000] :: [Integer]
```

4. Compile the code with the `threaded` and `rtsopts` flags enabled, as follows:

```
$ ghc -O2 --make Main.hs -threaded -rtsopts
```

5. Run it by specifying the number of cores as follows:

```
$ ./Main +RTS -N2
```

There's more...

When dealing with tuples of more than two elements, other helper methods exist such as `parTuple3`, `parTuple4`, `parTuple5`, `parTuple6`, `parTuple7`, `parTuple8`, and `parTuple9`.

See also

If dealing with lists, refer to the *Mapping over a list in parallel* recipe.

Implementing MapReduce to count word frequencies

MapReduce is a framework for efficient parallel algorithms that take advantage of divide and conquer. If a task can be split into smaller tasks, and the results of each individual task can be combined to form the final answer, then MapReduce is likely the best framework for this job.

In the following figure, we can see that a large list is split up, and the mapper functions work in parallel on each split. After all the mapping is complete, the second phase of the framework kicks in, reducing the various calculations into one final answer.

In this recipe, we will be counting word frequencies in a large corpus of text. Given many files of words, we will apply the MapReduce framework to find the word frequencies in parallel.

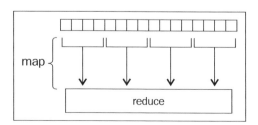

Getting ready

Install the `parallel` package using cabal as follows:

```
$ cabal install parallel
```

Create multiple files with words. In this recipe, we download a huge text file and split it up using the UNIX `split` command as follows:

```
$ wget norvig.com/big.txt
```

```
$ split -d big.txt words
```

```
$ ls words*
```

```
words00
```

```
words01
```

```
words02
```

```
words03
```

...

How to do it...

1. Import the relevant packages as follows:

    ```
    import Data.List (sort, group, sortBy, groupBy, isPrefixOf)
    import Control.Parallel
    import Control.Parallel.Strategies
    import Data.Char (isAlpha, isSpace, toLower)
    import Data.Map (Map, insertWith, empty, toList)
    import System.Directory
    import qualified Data.Map as M
    ```

2. Define the MapReduce logic. The mapping functions should all occur before the reducing logic as follows:

    ```
    mapReduce :: Strategy b -> (a -> b) ->
    Strategy b -> ([b] -> b) -> [a] -> b
    mapReduce mStrategy m rStrategy r input =
      mOutput `pseq` rOutput
      where mOutput = parMap mStrategy m input
            rOutput = r mOutput `using` rStrategy
    ```

3. Define the `mapper` function to count the frequency of words as follows:

```
mapper :: String -> [(String,Int)]
mapper str = freqCount $ getWords str
```

4. Count the number of times a word occurs in a string as follows:

```
freqCount :: [String] -> [(String, Int)]
freqCount xs =
    map (\x -> (head x, length x)) . group . sort $ xs
```

5. Get the words out of an arbitrary corpus of characters as follows:

```
getWords :: String -> [String]
getWords str = words $ filter
                        (\x -> isAlpha x || isSpace x) lower
   where lower = map toLower str
```

6. Reduce the list of word frequencies into one final answer as follows:

```
reducer :: [[(String,Int)]] -> [(String,Int)]
reducer ls = toList $
            foldl (\m (k, v) -> insertWith (+) k v m)
                  (empty :: Map String Int)
                  (concat ls)
```

7. Set up the MapReduce problem and run it:

```
main = do
        files <- getCurrentDirectory >>= getDirectoryContents
        let myFiles = filter ("words `isPrefixOf`) files
            rawFileData <- mapM readFile myFiles
        let freqMap = mapReduce (rpar `dot` rdeepseq)
                                mapper rseq reducer fawFileData
        putStrLn $ "Found " ++ (show.length) freqMap ++ " words!"
        queryInput freqMap
```

8. Ask to use input, and then display the frequency of each word entered:

```
queryInput freqMap = do
  putStrLn "Enter a sentence: "
  sentence <- readLine
  let freqs = map (`lookup` freqMap) (words sentence)
  print $ zip (words sentence) freqs
  queryInput freqMap
```

9. Compile the code with the `threaded` and `rtsopts` flags enabled, as follows:

```
$ ghc -O2 --make Main.hs -threaded -rtsopts
```

10. Run it by specifying the number of cores as follows:

```
$ ./Main +RTS -N2
Found 35537 words!
Enter a sentence:
no one who is young is ever going to be old
[ ("no",Just 2328)
, ("one",Just 3215)
, ("who",Just 2994)
, ("is",Just 9731)
, ("young",Just 624)
, ("is",Just 9731)
, ("ever",Just 254)
, ("going",Just 369)
, ("to",Just 28614)
, ("be",Just 6148)
, ("old",Just 1138) ]
```

Manipulating images in parallel using Repa

Repa is a powerful library for manipulating high-dimensional arrays in parallel. We will use it to read and edit the pixels of an image.

Getting ready

Install **Developer's Image Library** (**DevIL**), a cross-platform image manipulation toolkit. It can be downloaded from `http://openil.sourceforge.net/download.php` or through `apt-get` on Debian systems as follows:

```
$ sudo apt-get install libdevil-dev
```

Install the Repa package from cabal for the DevIL toolkit as follows:

```
$ cabal install repa-devil
```

Create two images named `image1.png` and `image2.png` that have the same dimensions, which are shown as follows:

Here comes the second image:

How to do it...

1. Import the following libraries as follows:

```
import System.Environment (getArgs)
import Data.Word (Word8)
import qualified Data.Array.Repa as R
import Data.Array.Repa hiding ((++))
import Data.Array.Repa.IO.DevIL (runIL, readImage,
    writeImage, IL, Image(RGB))
import Data.Array.Repa.Repr.ForeignPtr (F)
```

2. Read the images, process them, and produce an output image as follows:

```
main = do
  let image1 = "image1.png"
  let image2 = "image2.png"
  runIL $ do
    (RGB a) <- readImage image1
    (RGB b) <- readImage image2
    imageOut <- (computeP $ intersect a b)
                              :: IL (Array F DIM3 Word8)
    writeImage ("output.png") (RGB imageOut)
```

3. Create the helper function to process the images as follows:

```
intersect :: Array F DIM3 Word8 ->
             Array F DIM3 Word8 ->
             Array D DIM3 Word8
intersect a b = R.zipWith (\w1 w2 -> merge w1 w2) a b
  where merge w1 w2 = if w1 == w2 then 0 else 255
```

4. Compile the code with the `threaded` and `rtsopts` flags enabled, as follows:

```
$ ghc -O2 --make Main.hs -threaded -rtsopts
```

5. Run it by specifying the number of cores, as follows:

```
$ ./Main +RTS -N2
```

The output is as follows:

How it works...

The images are read as three-dimensional Repa arrays of pixels, where each pixel is represented by a Word8. The first two dimensions index the images by width and height, and the last dimension selects the color channel (red, green, blue, or alpha).

We run the `zipWith` function provided by Repa to combine two images into one with our intersect/merge rule. In order to actually run this process efficiently in parallel, we must call the `computeP` function.

Benchmarking runtime performance in Haskell

Benchmarking runtime is the process of timing how long it takes for the code to run. We can understand whether our parallel or concurrent code is in fact faster than the naive implementation by proper benchmarking. This recipe will demonstrate how to time code runtime in Haskell.

How to do it...

1. Import the necessary libraries as follows:

```
import System.CPUTime (getCPUTime)
import Control.Monad (replicateM_)
import Control.Parallel.Strategies (NFData, rdeepseq)
import Control.Exception (evaluate)
```

2. Create a function to print out the duration of a pure task. Evaluate the pure expression a very large number of times (10^6), and then calculate the average CPU time it takes to run one pure task. The getCPUTime function returns the number of picoseconds since the start of the program's execution, as shown in the following code snippet:

```
time :: (Num t, NFData t) => t -> IO ()
time y = do
  let trials = 10^6
  start <- getCPUTime
  replicateM_ trials $ do
      x <- evaluate $ 1 + y
      rdeepseq x `seq` return ()
  end    <- getCPUTime
  let diff = (fromIntegral (end - start)) / (10^12)
  putStrLn $ "avg seconds: " ++
    (show (diff / fromIntegral trials))
  return ()
```

3. Test out the timing function as follows:

```
main = do
    putStrLn "Starting pure..."
    time (3+7 :: Int)
    putStrLn "...Finished pure"
```

4. The measurements for conducting a pure task are printed out. Actual measurements will differ depending on the state of the machine.

```
Starting pure…
Avg seconds: 3.2895e-7
…Finished pure
```

See also

The *Benchmarking runtime performance in the terminal* recipe for producing benchmark results outside the Haskell environment.

Using the criterion package to measure performance

For more reliable performance measures, the `criterion` package comes in handy. The package description points out a major flaw in using simple procedures to time pure code.

> _"Because GHC optimizes aggressively when compiling with -O, it is potentially easy to write innocent-looking benchmark code that will only be evaluated once, for which all but the first iteration of the timing loop will be timing the cost of doing nothing."_

Getting ready

Create a `small.txt` file with a few words. Create a file, `big.txt`, filled with text as follows:

```
$ wget norvig.com/big.txt
```

Install the `criterion` library as follows:

```
$ cabal install criterion
```

How to do it...

1. Import the package as follows:

   ```
   import Criterion.Main
   ```

2. Define the I/O function we wish to time as follows:

   ```
   splitUp filename = readFile filename >>= return . words
   ```

3. Benchmark the desired function as follows:

   ```
   main = defaultMain
     [ bgroup "splitUp"
       [ bench "big" $ nfIO $ splitUp "big.txt"
       , bench "small" $ nfIO $ splitUp "small.txt" ] ]
   ```

4. Run the code as follows:

   ```
   $ ghc -O --make Main.hs


   $ ./Main


   warming up
   estimating clock resolution...
   ```

```
mean is 1.082787 us (640001 iterations)
found 42320 outliers among 639999 samples (6.6%)
  1860 (0.3%) low severe
  40460 (6.3%) high severe
estimating cost of a clock call...
mean is 33.40185 ns (10 iterations)
found 2 outliers among 10 samples (20.0%)
  1 (10.0%) high mild
  1 (10.0%) high severe

benchmarking splitUp/big
collecting 100 samples, 1 iterations each, in estimated 65.46450 s
mean: 656.1964 ms, lb 655.5417 ms, ub 657.1513 ms, ci 0.950
std dev: 4.018375 ms, lb 3.073741 ms, ub 5.746751 ms, ci 0.950

benchmarking splitUp/small
mean: 15.33773 us, lb 15.16429 us, ub 15.56298 us, ci 0.950
std dev: 1.010893 us, lb 823.5281 ns, ub 1.277931 us, ci 0.950
found 8 outliers among 100 samples (8.0%)
  5 (5.0%) high mild
  3 (3.0%) high severe
variance introduced by outliers: 61.572%
variance is severely inflated by outliers
```

How it works...

By calling this library's `defaultMain` function in `main`, we can leverage some very powerful benchmarking features. For instance, try running the following command to see a plethora of features supported by criterion:

```
$ ./Main -h
```

Benchmarking runtime performance in the terminal

Benchmarking runtime is the process of timing how long it takes the code to run. This skill is invaluable since it helps compare performance. By externally measuring the runtime as opposed to instrumenting it within the code, we can easily proceed without understanding the inner working of the code. If we're on a Unix-like system such as Linux or OS X, we can use the `time` command, and on Windows systems, we can use `Measure-Command` with PowerShell.

Getting ready

Make sure our machine is either Unix-like (such as Linux or OS X) or Windows. Otherwise, we must search online for a way to time execution.

How to do it...

1. On Unix-like systems, there is a built-in `time` command. When running any piece of code from the terminal, we can prefix it with `time` as follows:

```
$ time runhaskell Main.hs

real 0m0.663s

user 0m0.612s

sys 0m0.057s
```

   The argument to this command is run, and the system resource usage is immediately summarized. The actual accuracy of the results depends on the machine.

2. On Windows, we can use the `Measure-Command` feature in PowerShell. Open PowerShell, go to the correct directory, and execute the following command:

```
> Measure-Command { start-process runhaskell Main.hs –Wait }
```

3. You will see a result with the following format:

```
Days             : 0

Hours            : 0

Minutes          : 0

Seconds          : 1

Milliseconds     : 10
```

```
Ticks             : 10106611
TotalDays         : 1.16974664351852E-05
TotalHours        : 0.000280739194444444
TotalMinutes      : 0.0168443516666667
TotalSeconds      : 1.0106611
TotalMilliseconds : 1010.6611
```

See also

To time execution within the Haskell code itself, refer to the *Benchmarking runtime performance in Haskell* recipe.

10
Real-time Data

This chapter will cover the following recipes:

- ▸ Streaming Twitter for real-time sentiment analysis
- ▸ Reading IRC chat room messages
- ▸ Responding to IRC messages
- ▸ Polling a web server for the latest updates
- ▸ Detecting real-time file directory changes
- ▸ Communicating in real time through sockets
- ▸ Detecting faces and eyes through a camera stream
- ▸ Streaming camera frames for template matching

Introduction

It's fairly easy to first collect data and then analyze it later. However, doing both steps together may be necessary for some tasks. The gratifying nature of analyzing data the moment it is received is the core subject of this chapter. We will cover how to manage real-time data input from Twitter tweets, Internet Relay Chat (IRC), web servers, file-change notifications, sockets, and webcams.

The first three recipes will focus on dealing with real-time data from Twitter. These topics will include streaming posts by users as well as posts related to keywords.

Next, we will use two separate libraries to interact with IRC servers. The first recipe will demonstrate how to join an IRC chat room and start listening for messages, and the next recipe will show us how to listen for direct messages on an IRC server.

If real-time data is not supported, a common fallback is to query for that data often. This process is calling **polling**, and we will learn a quick way to poll a web server in one of the recipes.

We will also detect changes in a file directory when a file is modified, deleted, or created. Imagine implementing Dropbox, OneDrive, or Google Drive in Haskell.

Finally, we will create a simple server-client interaction with sockets and play around with real-time webcam streams.

Streaming Twitter for real-time sentiment analysis

Twitter is flooded with content that arrives every second. A great way to start investigating real-time data is by examining tweets.

This recipe will show how to write code that reacts to tweets relating to a specific search query. We use an external web-endpoint to determine whether the sentiment is positive, neutral, or negative.

Getting ready

Install the `twitter-conduit` package:

```
$ cabal install twitter-conduit
```

For parsing JSON, let's use `yocto`:

```
$ cabal install yocto
```

How to do it...

Follow these steps to set up the Twitter credentials and begin coding:

1. Create a new Twitter app by navigating to `https://apps.twitter.com`.

2. Find the OAuth Consumer Key and OAuth Consumer Secret from this Twitter Application Management page. Set the environmental variables on our system for OAUTH_CONSUMER_KEY and OAUTH_CONSUMER_SECRET respectively. Most Unix-based systems with sh-compatible shells support the `export` command:

    ```
    $ export OAUTH_CONSUMER_KEY="Your OAuth Consumer Key"
    ```

    ```
    $ export OAUTH_CONSUMER_SECRET="Your OAuth Consumer Secret"
    ```

3. Moreover, find the OAuth Access Token and OAuth Access Secret through the same Twitter Application Management page and set the environmental variables accordingly:

    ```
    $ export OAUTH_ACCESS_TOKEN="Your OAuth Access Token"
    ```

    ```
    $ export OAUTH_ACCESS_SECRET="Your OAuth Access Secret"
    ```

> We put our keys, tokens, and secret pins in the environmental variables instead of simply hardcoding them into the program because these variables are as important as passwords. Just like passwords should never be publicly visible, we try our best to keep these tokens and keys out of direct reach from the source code.

4. Download the `Common.hs` file from the sample directory of the `twitter-conduit` package, which is located at `https://github.com/himura/twitter-conduit/tree/master/sample`. Study the `userstream.hs` sample file.

5. First, we import all the relevant libraries:

```
{-# LANGUAGE OverloadedStrings #-}

import qualified Data.Conduit as C
import qualified Data.Conduit.List as CL
import qualified Data.Text.IO as T
import qualified Data.Text as T

import Control.Monad.IO.Class (liftIO)
import Network.HTTP (getResponseBody, getRequest, simpleHTTP,
urlEncode)
import Text.JSON.Yocto
import Web.Twitter.Conduit (stream, statusesFilterByTrack)
import Common
import Control.Lens ((^!), (^.), act)
import Data.Map ((!))
import Data.List (isInfixOf, or)
import Web.Twitter.Types
```

6. In `main`, run our real-time sentiment analyzer for a search query:

```
main :: IO ()

main = do
  let query = "haskell"
  T.putStrLn $ T.concat [ "Streaming Tweets that match \""
                        , query, "\"..."]
  analyze query
```

7. Tap into the Twitter real-time stream with our Twitter API credentials by using the `runTwitterFromEnv'` function provided by the `Common` module. We will use some crazy syntax such as `$$+-` or `^!`. Please do not be intimidated by them. They're mainly used for succinctness. Every time an event is triggered, such as a new tweet or a new follow, we will call our `process` function on it:

```
analyze :: T.Text -> IO ()

analyze query = runTwitterFromEnv' $ do
  src <- stream $ statusesFilterByTrack query
  src C.$$+- CL.mapM_ (^! act (liftIO . process))
```

8. Once we have our event-triggered input, we will run `process` to obtain an output, such as discovering the sentiment of a text. In this example, we append the sentiment output to a comma-separated file:

```
process :: StreamingAPI -> IO ()

process (SStatus s) = do
```

```
let theUser = userScreenName $ statusUser s
let theTweet = statusText s
T.putStrLn $ T.concat [theUser, ": ", theTweet]
val <- sentiment $ T.unpack theTweet
let record = (T.unpack theUser) ++ "," ++
             (show.fromRational) val ++ "\n"
appendFile "output.csv" record
print val
```

9. If the event-triggered input is not a tweet but instead a friendship event or something else, do nothing:

```
process s = return ()
```

10. Define a helper function to clean up the input by removing all @user mentions, #hashtags, or http://websites:

```
clean :: String -> String

clean str = unwords $ filter
               (\w -> not (or
                      [ isInfixOf "@" w
                      , isInfixOf "#" w
                      , isInfixOf "http://" w ]))
               (words str)
```

11. Use an external API to run the sentiment analysis on a body of text. In this example, we use the Sentiment140 API because of its ease and simplicity. Please see http://help.sentiment140.com/api for more information. To prevent getting rate-limited, also supply the appid parameter with an e-mail address or obtain a commercial license:

```
sentiment :: String -> IO Rational
sentiment str = do
  let baseURL = "http://www.sentiment140.com/api/classify?text="
  resp <- simpleHTTP $ getRequest $
          baseURL ++ (urlEncode.clean) str
  body <- getResponseBody resp
  let p = polarity (decode body) / 4.0
  return p
```

12. Extract the sentiment value from the JSON response from our API:

```
polarity :: Value -> Rational

polarity (Object m) = polarity' $ m ! "results"
  where polarity' (Object m) = fromNumber $ m ! "polarity"
        fromNumber (Number n) = n
polarity _ = -1
```

13. Run the code to see tweets displayed right as they are posted publicly by anyone worldwide. The sentiment value will be a rational number between 0 and 1, where 0 is a negative sentiment and 1 is a positive sentiment:

```
$ runhaskell Main.hs
Streaming Tweets that match "x-men"…
```

Have a look at the following output:

```
            : X-men time. I've been waiting for so long.
1 % 2
            : @                ok, quero muito assistir x-men tbm kkk
1 % 2
            : X-men days of future past is a great movie and I recommend everyone
go see it
1 % 1
            : "@            I Wanna See The New X-Men Movie"
1 % 2
            : I NEED TO GO SEE X-MEN TODAY.
1 % 2
            : X-men 3D 😎
1 % 2
            : X-Men Days of Future Past felt like it was about 45 mins long. Barely
 anything happened...did I see the wrong movie??
0 % 1
            : I wanna see X-Men
1 % 2
            : The only good thing to come from this day is seeing X-Men
1 % 2
            : X-MEN WAS AMAZING I GOT A POSTER
1 % 1
```

We can also analyze the data in bulk from the output.csv file. Here's a visual representation of the sentiments:

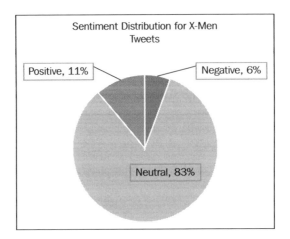

How it works...

The Twitter-conduit package uses the conduit design pattern from the original package placed at `https://hackage.haskell.org/package/conduit`. The conduit documentation states:

> *Conduit is a solution to the streaming data problem, allowing for production, transformation, and consumption of streams of data in constant memory. It is an alternative to lazy I/O which guarantees deterministic resource handling, and fits in the same general solution space as enumerator/iteratee and pipes.*

To interact with Twitter's Application Programming Interface (API), it is necessary to obtain the access and application tokens and keys. We store these values in our environment variables and let the Haskell code retrieve it from there.

The `Common.hs` file takes care of monotonous authentication code, which should be left untouched.

The function that reacts to each Twitter event is `process`. We can modify `process` to accompany our specific needs. More specifically, we can modify the sentiment function to use a different `sentiment` analysis service.

There's more...

Our code listens to any tweets that match our query. This Twitter-conduit library also supports two other real-time streams: `statusesFilterByFollow` and `userstream`. The former retrieves all tweets from a list of prescribed users. The latter retrieves all tweets from the users that the account follows.

For example, modify our code by replacing the `statusesFilterByTrack` query with the UIDs of some Twitter users:

```
analyze:: IO ()
analyze = runTwitterFromEnv' $ do
  src <- statusesFilterByFollow [ 103285804, 450331119
                                , 64895420]
  src C.$$+- CL.mapM_ (^! act (liftIO . process))
```

Moreover, to only retrieve tweets from the users that we are following, we can instead modify our code by replacing the `statusesFilterByTrack` query with `userstream`:

```
analyze :: IO ()
analyze = runTwitterFromEnv' $ do
  src <- stream userstream
  src C.$$+- CL.mapM_ (^! act (liftIO . process))
```

Many more examples can be found through `https://github.com/himura/twitter-conduit/tree/master/sample`.

Reading IRC chat room messages

The Internet Relay Chat (IRC) is one of the oldest and most vibrant group chat room services out there. The Haskell community has a substantially welcoming presence on the Freenode IRC server (`irc.freenode.org`) in the #haskell channel.

In this recipe, we will build an IRC bot that joins a room and listens to text conversations. Our program will emulate an IRC client and connect to one of the many existing IRC servers. This recipe requires no external libraries at all.

Getting ready

Make sure an Internet connection is enabled.

To test out the IRC bot, it helps to install an IRC client. For instance, one of the top IRC clients is **Hexchat**, which can be downloaded from `http://hexchat.github.io`. For a terminal-based IRC client, **Irssi** is a favorite: `http://www.irssi.org`.

Review the *Roll your own IRC bot* article on the Haskell wiki: `http://www.haskell.org/haskellwiki/Roll_your_own_IRC_bot`. This recipe is heavily based on the code presented on the wiki.

How to do it...

In a new file called `Main.hs`, insert the following code:

1. Import the relevant packages:

```
import Network
import Control.Monad (forever)
import System.IO
import Text.Printf
```

2. Specify the IRC server specifics:

```
server = "irc.freenode.org"
port   = 6667
chan   = "#haskelldata"
nick   = "awesome-bot"
```

3. Connect to the server and listen to all text being passed in a chat room:

```
main = do
    h <- connectTo server (PortNumber (fromIntegral port))
```

```
    hSetBuffering h NoBuffering
    write h "NICK" nick
    write h "USER" (nick++" 0 * :tutorial bot")
    write h "JOIN" chan
    listen h

write :: Handle -> String -> String -> IO ()
write h s t = do
  hPrintf h "%s %s\r\n" s t
  printf    "> %s %s\n" s t
```

4. Define our listener. For this recipe, we will just echo all events to the console:

```
listen :: Handle -> IO ()
listen h = forever $ do
  s <- hGetLine h
  putStrLn s
```

See also

To see another way to interact with IRC, see the next recipe, *Responding to IRC messages*.

Responding to IRC messages

Another way to interact with IRC in Haskell is by using the `Network.SimpleIRC` package. This package encapsulates much of the low-level networking and also provides useful IRC interfaces.

In this recipe, we will respond to messages in a channel. If any user types in the trigger phrase, in our case "host?", then we will reply to that user with their host address.

Getting ready

Install the `Network.SimpleIRC` package:

```
$ cabal install simpleirc
```

To test out the IRC bot, it is helpful to install an IRC client. A decent IRC client is Hexchat, which can be downloaded from `http://hexchat.github.io`. For a terminal-based IRC client, Irssi is one of the best: `http://www.irssi.org`.

How to do it...

Create a new file, which we call `Main.hs`, and do the following:

1. Import the relevant libraries:

   ```
   {-# LANGUAGE OverloadedStrings #-}

   import Network.SimpleIRC
   import Data.Maybe
   import qualified Data.ByteString.Char8 as B
   ```

2. Create an event handler when a message is received. If the message is "host?", then reply to the user with information about their host:

   ```
   onMessage :: EventFunc
   onMessage s m = do
     case msg of
       "host?" ->  sendMsg s chan $ botMsg
       otherwise -> return ()
     where chan = fromJust $ mChan m
           msg = mMsg m
           host = case mHost m of
             Just h -> h
             Nothing -> "unknown"
           nick = case mNick m of
             Just n -> n
             Nothing -> "unknown user"
           botMsg = B.concat [ "Hi ", nick, "
                              , your host is ", host]
   ```

3. Define on which events to listen:

   ```
   events = [(Privmsg onMessage)]
   ```

4. Set up the IRC server configuration. Connect to any list of channels and bind our event:

   ```
   freenode =
     (mkDefaultConfig "irc.freenode.net" "awesome-bot")
     { cChannels = ["#haskelldata"]
     , cEvents   = events
     }
   ```

5. Connect to the server. Don't run in a new thread, but print debug messages, as specified by the corresponding Boolean parameters:

   ```
   main = connect freenode False True
   ```

6. Run the code, and open an IRC client to test it out:

```
[22:59:32] <binroot> hi
[22:59:34] <binroot> host?
[22:59:34] <awesome-bot> Hi binroot, your host is pool-███ ██ ██ ███.washdc.fios.verizon.net
```

See also

To connect to an IRC server without using an external library, see the previous recipe, *Reading IRC chat room messages*.

Polling a web server for latest updates

Some websites change dramatically very often. For instance, Google News and Reddit are usually loaded with recent postings the moment we refresh the page. To maintain the latest data at all times, it might be best to run an HTTP request often.

In this recipe, we poll new Reddit posts every 10 seconds as summarized in the following diagram:

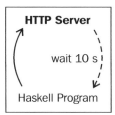

How to do it...

In a new file called `Main.hs`, perform the following steps:

1. Import the relevant libraries:

```
import Network.HTTP
import Control.Concurrent (threadDelay)
import qualified Data.Text as T
```

2. Define the URL to poll:

```
url = "http://www.reddit.com/r/pics/new.json"
```

3. Define the function to obtain the latest data from an HTTP GET request:

```
latest :: IO String

latest = simpleHTTP (getRequest url) >>= getResponseBody
```

4. Polling is simply the act of recursively conducting a task after waiting for a specified amount of time. In this case, we will wait 10 seconds before asking for the latest web data:

```
poll :: IO a

poll = do
   body <- latest
   print $ doWork body
   threadDelay (10 * 10^6)
   poll
```

5. Run the polling:

```
main :: IO a
main = do
   putStrLn $ "Polling " ++ url ++ " …"
   poll
```

6. After each web request, analyze the data. In this recipe, count the number of times Imgur shows up:

```
doWork str = length $ T.breakOnAll
                (T.pack "imgur.com/") (T.pack str)
```

Detecting real-time file directory changes

In this recipe, we will instantly detect when a new file is created, modified, or deleted. Similar to the popular file synchronization software Dropbox, we will be able to do interesting actions every time such an event occurs.

Getting ready

Install the `fsnotify` package:

```
$ cabal install fsnotify
```

How to do it...

In a new file called `Main.hs`, perform these steps:

1. Import the relevant libraries:

```
{-# LANGUAGE OverloadedStrings #-}
import Filesystem.Path.CurrentOS
import System.FSNotify
import Filesystem
import Filesystem.Path (filename)
```

2. Run the file watcher on the current directory:

```
main :: IO ()

main = do
  wd <- getWorkingDirectory
  print wd

  man <- startManager
  watchTree man wd (const True) doWork
  putStrLn "press return to stop"

  getLine
  putStrLn "watching stopped, press return to exit"

  stopManager man
  getLine
  return ()
```

3. Handle each of the file change events. In this recipe, we just print out the action to the console:

```
doWork :: Event -> IO ()

doWork (Added filepath time) =
  putStrLn $ (show $ filename filepath) ++ " added"
doWork (Modified filepath time) =
  putStrLn $ (show $ filename filepath) ++ " modified"
doWork (Removed filepath time) =
  putStrLn $ (show $ filename filepath) ++ " removed"
```

4. Run the code and start modifying some files in the same directory. For example, create a new file, edit it, and then remove it:

```
$ runhaskell Main.hs


press return to stop
FilePath "hello.txt" added
FilePath "hello.txt" modified
FilePath "hello.txt" removed
```

How it works...

The `fsnotify` library binds to the event-notification services specific to a platform-specific filesystem. On Unix-based systems, this is usually `inotify` (http://dell9.ma.utexas.edu/cgi-bin/man-cgi?inotify).

Communicating in real time through sockets

Sockets provide a convenient way of communicating between programs in real time. Think of them as a chat client.

In this recipe, we will pass messages from one program to another and obtain responses.

How to do it...

Insert the following code in a new file called `Main.hs`:

1. Create the server code:

```
import Network ( listenOn, withSocketsDo, accept
              , PortID(..), Socket )
import System.Environment (getArgs)
import System.IO ( hSetBuffering, hGetLine, hPutStrLn
                 , BufferMode(..), Handle )
import Control.Concurrent (forkIO)
```

2. Create a socket connection to listen on, and attach our handler, `sockHandler`, on it:

```
main :: IO ()

main = withSocketsDo $ do
    let port = PortNumber 9001
    sock <- listenOn port
    putStrLn $ "Listening..."
    sockHandler sock
```

3. Define the handler to process each message received:

```
sockHandler :: Socket -> IO ()

sockHandler sock = do
    (h, _, _) <- accept sock
    putStrLn "Connected!"
    hSetBuffering h LineBuffering
    forkIO $ process h
    forkIO $ respond h
    sockHandler sock
```

4. Define how to process messages sent by the client:

```
process :: Handle -> IO ()
process h = do
    line <- hGetLine h
    print line
    process h
```

5. Send messages to the client through user input:

```
respond h = withSocketsDo $ do
   txt <- getLine
   hPutStrLn h txt
   respond h
```

6. Now, create the client code in a new file, `client.hs`. First, import the libraries:

```
import Network (connectTo, withSocketsDo, PortID(..))
import System.Environment (getArgs)
import System.IO ( hSetBuffering, hPutStrLn
                  , hGetLine, BufferMode(..) )
```

7. Connect the client to the corresponding port and set up the responder and listener threads:

```
main = withSocketsDo $ do
   let port = PortNumber 9001
   h <- connectTo "localhost" port
   putStrLn $ "Connected!"
   hSetBuffering h LineBuffering
   forkIO $ respond h
   forkIO $ process h
   loop
```

8. Get user input and send it as a message:

```
respond h = do
   txt <- getLine
   hPutStrLn h txt
   respond h
```

9. Listen to incoming messages from the server:

```
process h = do
   line <- hGetLine h
   print line
   process h
```

10. Test out the code by first running the server:

```
$ runhaskell Main.hs
```

11. Next, on a separate terminal, run the client:

```
$ runhaskell client.hs
```

12. We can now send messages between the two by typing and hitting *Enter*:

```
Hello?
```

```
"yup, I can hear you!"
```

How it works...

The `hGetLine` function is blocking the code execution, which means that code execution halts at that point until a message is received. This allows us to wait for messages to conduct real-time reactions.

We first specify a port on the computer, which is simply a number that is not yet reserved by other programs. The server sets up the socket, and the client connects to it without needing to set it up. The messages passed between the two happen in real time.

A visualization of the server-client model is demonstrated in the following diagram:

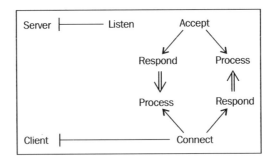

Detecting faces and eyes through a camera stream

The camera is another source for real-time data. As frames come and go, we can perform powerful analysis using the OpenCV library.

In this recipe, we conduct facial detection through a live camera stream.

Getting ready

Install the OpenCV, SDL, and FTGL libraries for image manipulation and computer vision:

```
sudo apt-get install libopencv-dev libsdl1.2-dev ftgl-dev
```

Install an OpenCV library using cabal:

```
cabal install cv-combinators
```

How to do it...

Create a new source file, `Main.hs`, and follow these steps:

1. Import the relevant libraries:

```
import AI.CV.ImageProcessors
import qualified AI.CV.OpenCV.CV as CV
import qualified Control.Processor as Processor
import Control.Processor ((--<))
import AI.CV.OpenCV.Types (PImage)
import AI.CV.OpenCV.CxCore (CvRect(..), CvSize(..))
import Prelude hiding (id)
import Control.Arrow ((&&&), (***))
import Control.Category ((>>>), id)
```

2. Define the source of the camera stream. We will be using the built-in webcam. To instead use a video, we can replace `camera 0` with `videoFile "./myVideo.mpeg"`:

```
captureDev :: ImageSource
captureDev = camera 0
```

3. Shrink the size of the stream for faster performance:

```
resizer :: ImageProcessor
resizer = resize 320 240 CV.CV_INTER_LINEAR
```

4. Detect the faces in an image using the training dataset provided by OpenCV:

```
faceDetect :: Processor.IOProcessor PImage [CvRect]

faceDetect = haarDetect
  "/usr/share/opencv/haarcascades/haarcascade_frontalface
  _alt.xml" 1.1 3 CV.cvHaarFlagNone (CvSize 20 20)
```

5. Detect the eyes in the image using the training data set provided by OpenCV:

```
eyeDetect :: Processor.IOProcessor PImage [CvRect]
eyeDetect = haarDetect "/usr/share/opencv/haarcascades/
  haarcascade_eye.xml" 1.1 3 CV.cvHaarFlagNone
  (CvSize 20 20)
```

6. Draw rectangles around faces and eyes:

```
faceRects = (id &&& faceDetect) >>> drawRects

eyeRects = (id &&& eyeDetect) >>> drawRects
```

7. Capture the camera's stream, detect the faces and eyes, draw rectangles, and display them in two different windows:

```
start = captureDev >>> resizer --< (faceRects *** eyeRects)
            >>> (window 0 *** window 1)
```

8. Perform the real-time camera streaming and stop once a key is pressed:

```
main :: IO ()
main = runTillKeyPressed start
```

9. Run the code and look at the webcam to detect faces and eyes as shown in the screenshot that follows this command:

```
$ runhaskell Main.hs
```

How it works...

To detect faces, eyes, or other objects, we use the `haarDetect` function, which performs a classifier trained from many positive and negative test cases. These test cases are provided by OpenCV and are typically located in `/usr/share/opencv/haarcascades/` on Unix-based systems.

The cv-combinator library provides a convenient abstraction to OpenCV's low-level manipulations. To run any useful code, we must define a source, a process, and a final destination (also referred to as a *sink*). In our case, the source was the machine's built-in camera. We first resize the image to something more manageable (`resizer`), split the stream into two in parallel (`--<`), draw boxes around faces in one while drawing boxes around eyes in the other, and finally output the streams to two separate windows. For more documentation of the cv-combinators package, see `https://hackage.haskell.org/package/cv-combinators`.

Streaming camera frames for template matching

Template matching is a machine-learning technique to find areas of an image that match a given template image. We will apply template matching to every frame of a real-time video stream to locate an image.

Getting ready

Install the OpenCV and c2hs toolkits:

```
$ sudo apt-get install c2hs libopencv-dev
```

Install the CV library from cabal. Be sure to include the `-fopencv24` or `-fopencv23` parameter depending on which version of OpenCV is installed:

```
$ cabal install CV -fopencv24
```

Also, create a small template image. In this recipe, we use an image of Lena, which is usually used in many image-processing experiments. We name this image file `lena.png`:

How to do it...

In a new file, `Main.hs`, start with these steps:

1. Import the relevant libraries:

    ```
    {-#LANGUAGE ScopedTypeVariables#-}
    module Main where
    import CV.Image (loadImage, rgbToGray, getSize)
    import CV.Video (captureFromCam, streamFromVideo)
    import Utils.Stream (runStream_, takeWhileS, sideEffect)
    import CV.HighGUI (showImage, waitKey)
    import CV.TemplateMatching ( simpleTemplateMatch
                               , MatchType(..) )
    import CV.ImageOp ((<#))
    import CV.Drawing (circleOp, ShapeStyle(..))
    ```

2. Load the template image and start the template matching on a camera stream:

    ```
    main = do
      Just t <- loadImage "lena.jpg"
      Just c <- captureFromCam 0
      runStream_ . sideEffect (process t) .
        takeWhileS (\_ -> True) $ streamFromVideo c
    ```

3. Perform an action on each frame of the camera stream. Specifically, use template matching to locate the template and draw a circle around it:

    ```
    process t img = do
      let gray = rgbToGray img
      let ((mx, my), _) =
        simpleTemplateMatch CCOEFF_NORMED gray t
      let circleSize = (fst (getSize t)) `div` 2
      let circleCenter = (mx + circleSize, my + circleSize)
      showImage "test" (img <# circleOp (0,0,0)
        circleCenter circleSize (Stroked 3))
      waitKey 100
      return ()
    ```

4. Run the code using the following command and show an image of the template. A black circle will be drawn around the found image:

```
$ runhaskell Main.hs
```

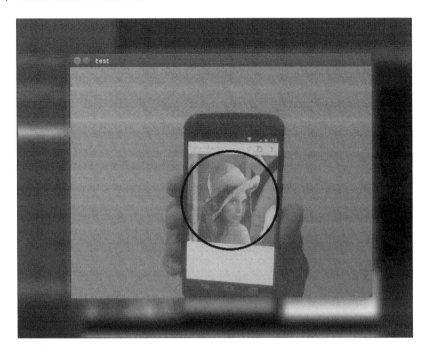

There's more...

More OpenCV examples can be found at `https://github.com/aleator/CV/tree/master/examples`.

11
Visualizing Data

In this chapter, we will cover the following visualization techniques:

- ▶ Plotting a line chart using Google's Chart API
- ▶ Plotting a pie chart using Google's Chart API
- ▶ Plotting bar graphs using Google's Chart API
- ▶ Displaying a line graph using gnuplot
- ▶ Displaying a scatter plot of two-dimensional points
- ▶ Interacting with points in three-dimensional space
- ▶ Visualizing a graph network
- ▶ Customizing the looks of a graph network diagram
- ▶ Rendering a bar graph in JavaScript using D3.js
- ▶ Rendering a scatter plot in JavaScript using D3.js
- ▶ Diagramming a path from a list of vectors

Introduction

Visualization is important in all steps of data analysis. Whether we are just getting acquainted with the data or have completed our analysis, it is always useful to have an intuitive understanding through a graphical aid. Fortunately, Haskell comes with a plethora of libraries to facilitate this endeavor.

In this chapter, we will cover recipes to produce line, pie, bar, and scatter plots using various APIs. Going beyond typical data visualization, we will also learn to draw network diagrams. Moreover, in the last recipe, we will describe navigation directions by drawing vectors on a blank canvas.

Plotting a line chart using Google's Chart API

We will use the convenient Google Chart API (`https://developers.google.com/chart`) to render a line chart. This API produces a URL that points to a PNG image of the graph. This lightweight URL can be easier to handle than the actual image itself.

Our data will come from a text file that contains a list of numbers separated by lines. The code will generate a URL to present this data.

Getting ready

Install the `GoogleChart` package as follows:

```
$ cabal install hs-gchart
```

Create a file called `input.txt` with numbers inserted line by line as follows:

```
$ cat input.txt
2
5
3
7
4
1
19
18
17
14
15
16
```

How to do it...

1. Import the Google Chart API library as follows:

   ```
   import Graphics.Google.Chart
   ```

2. Gather the input from the text file and parse it as a list of integers:

   ```
   main = do
     rawInput <- readFile "input.txt"
     let nums = map (read :: String -> Int) (lines rawInput)
   ```

3. Create a chart URL out of the image by setting the attributes appropriately, as shown in the following code snippet:

   ```
   putStrLn $ chartURL $
     setSize 500 200 $
     setTitle "Example of Plotting a Chart in Haskell" $
     setData (encodeDataSimple [nums]) $
     setLegend ["Stock Price"] $
     newLineChart
   ```

4. Running the program will output a Google Chart URL as follows:

   ```
   $ runhaskell Main.hs

   http://chart.apis.google.com/chart?chs=500x200&chtt=Example+of+Plo
   tting+a+Chart+in+Haskell&chd=s:CFDHEBTSROPQ&chdl=Stock+Price&cht=
   lc
   ```

Ensure an Internet connection exists and navigate to that URL to view the chart, as shown in the following screenshot:

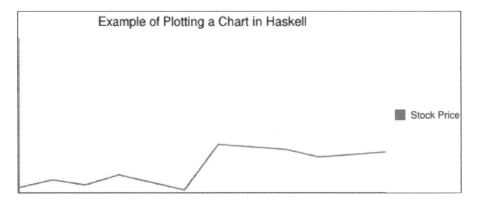

How it works...

Google encodes all graph data within the URL. The more complicated our graph, the longer the Google Chart URL. In this recipe, we use the `encodeDataSimple` function that creates a relatively shorter URL, but only accepts integers between 0 and 61 inclusive.

There's more...

To visualize a more detailed graph that allows data to have decimal places, we can use the `encodeDataText :: RealFrac a => [[a]] -> ChartData` function instead. This function allows for decimal numbers between 0 and 100 inclusive.

To represent larger ranges of integers in a graph, we should use the `encodeDataExtended` function, which supports integers between 0 and 4095 inclusive.

More information about the Google Charts Haskell package can be found at `https://hackage.haskell.org/package/hs-gchart`.

See also

This recipe required a connection to the Internet to view a graph. If we wish to perform all actions locally, refer to the *Displaying a line graph using gnuplot* recipe. Other Google API recipes can include *Plotting a pie chart using Google's Chart API* and *Plotting bar graphs using Google's Chart API*.

Plotting a pie chart using Google's Chart API

The Google Chart API provides a very elegant-looking pie chart interface. We can generate images of well-designed pie charts by feeding our input and labels properly, as described in this recipe.

Getting ready

Install the GoogleChart package as follows:

```
$ cabal install hs-gchart
```

Create a file called `input.txt` with numbers inserted line by line as follows:

```
$ cat input.txt
2
5
3
7
4
1
19
18
17
14
15
16
```

How to do it...

1. Import the Google Chart API library as follows:

    ```
    import Graphics.Google.Chart
    ```

2. Gather the input from the text file and parse it as a list of integers, as shown in the following code snippet:

    ```
    main = do
      rawInput <- readFile "input.txt"
      let nums = map (read :: String -> Int) (lines rawInput)
    ```

3. Print out the Google Chart URL from the pie chart attributes shown in the following code:

```
putStrLn $ chartURL $
  setSize 500 400 $
  setTitle "Example of Plotting a Pie Chart in Haskell" $
  setData (encodeDataSimple [nums]) $
  setLabels (lines rawInput) $
  newPieChart Pie2D
```

4. Running the program will output a Google Chart URL as follows:

$ runhaskell Main.hs

**http://chart.apis.google.com/chart?chs=500x400&chtt=Example+of+Plo
tting+a+Pie+Chart+in+Haskell&chd=s:CFDHEBTSROPQ&chl=2|5|3|7|4|1|19
|18|17|14|15|16&cht=p**

Ensure an Internet connection exists and navigate to that URL to view the chart shown in the following image:

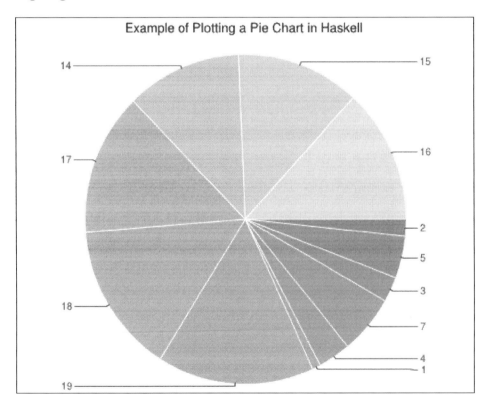

How it works...

Google encodes all graph data within the URL. The more complicated the graph, the longer the Google Chart URL. In this recipe, we use the `encodeDataSimple` function, which creates a relatively shorter URL, but only accepts integers between 0 and 61 inclusive. The legends of the pie chart are specified by the `setLabels :: [String] -> PieChart -> PieChart` function in the same order as the data.

There's more...

To visualize a more detailed graph that allows data to have decimal places, we can use the `encodeDataText :: RealFrac a => [[a]] -> ChartData` function instead. This function allows decimal numbers between 0 and 100 inclusive.

To represent larger ranges of integers in a graph, we should use the `encodeDataExtended` function, which supports integers between 0 and 4095 inclusive.

More information about the Google Charts Haskell package can be found at `https://hackage.haskell.org/package/hs-gchart`.

See also

- *Plotting a line chart using Google's Chart API*
- *Plotting bar graphs using Google's Chart API*

Plotting bar graphs using Google's Chart API

The Google Chart API also has great support for bar graphs. In this recipe, we will produce a bar graph of two sets of inputs in the same diagram to show the usefulness of this API.

Getting ready

Install the `GoogleChart` package as follows:

```
$ cabal install hs-gchart
```

Create two files called `input1.txt` and `input2.txt` with numbers inserted line by line as follows:

```
$ cat input1.txt
```

2

5

3

```
7
4
1
19
18
17
14
15
16


$ cat input2.txt
4
2
6
7
8
2
18
17
16
17
15
14
```

How to do it...

1. Import the Google Chart API library as follows:

   ```
   import Graphics.Google.Chart
   ```

2. Gather the two input values from both the text files and parse them as two separate lists of integers, as shown in the following code snippet:

   ```
   main = do
     rawInput1 <- readFile "input1.txt"
     rawInput2 <- readFile "input2.txt"
     let nums1 = map (read :: String -> Int) (lines rawInput1)
     let nums2 = map (read :: String -> Int) (lines rawInput2)
   ```

3. Set up the bar chart too and print out the Google Chart URL as follows:

```
putStrLn $ chartURL $
  setSize 500 400 $
  setTitle "Example of Plotting a Bar Chart in Haskell" $
  setDataColors ["00ff00", "ff0000"] $
  setLegend ["A", "B"] $
  setData (encodeDataSimple [nums1, nums2]) $
  newBarChart Horizontal Grouped
```

4. Running the program will output a Google Chart URL as follows:

```
$ runhaskell Main.hs
```

```
http://chart.apis.google.com/chart?chs=500x400&chtt=Example+of+Plo
tting+a+Bar+Chart+in+Haskell&chco=00ff00,ff0000&chdl=A|B&chd=s:CFD
HEBTSROPQ,ECGHICSRQRPO&cht=bhg
```

Ensure an Internet connection exists and navigate to that URL to view the following chart:

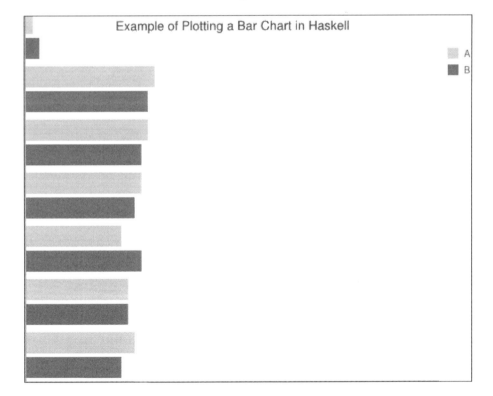

How it works...

Google encodes all graph data within the URL. The more complicated the graph, the longer the Google Chart URL. In this recipe, we use the `encodeDataSimple` function, which creates a relatively shorter URL, but only accepts integers between 0 and 61 inclusive.

There's more...

To visualize a more detailed graph that allows data to have decimal places, we can use the `encodeDataText :: RealFrac a => [[a]] -> ChartData` function instead. This function allows decimal numbers between 0 and 100 inclusive.

To represent larger ranges of integers in a graph, we should use the `encodeDataExtended` function, which supports integers between 0 and 4095 inclusive.

More information about the Google Charts Haskell package can be found at `https://hackage.haskell.org/package/hs-gchart`.

See also

To use other Google Chart tools, refer to the *Plotting a pie chart using Google's Chart API* and *Plotting a line chart using Google's Chart API* recipes.

Displaying a line graph using gnuplot

An Internet connection is typically unnecessary for plotting a graph. So, in this recipe, we will demonstrate how to make a line graph locally.

Getting ready

The library used in this recipe uses gnuplot to render the graph. We should first install gnuplot.

On Debian-based systems such as Ubuntu, we can install it using `apt-get` as follows:

```
$ sudo apt-get install gnuplot-x11
```

The official place to download gnuplot is on its main website available at `http://www.gnuplot.info`.

After gnuplot is set up, install the `EasyPlot` Haskell library using cabal as follows:

```
$ cabal install easyplot
```

How to do it...

1. Import the `EasyPlot` library as follows:

    ```
    import Graphics.EasyPlot
    ```

2. Define a list of numbers to plot as follows:

    ```
    main = do
      let values = [4,5,16,15,14,13,13,17]
    ```

3. Plot the chart on the `X11` window as shown in the following code snippet. The `X11` X Window System terminal is used by many Linux-based machines. If running on Windows, we should instead use the `Windows` terminal. On Mac OS X, we should replace `X11` with `Aqua`:

    ```
    plot X11 $
      Data2D [ Title "Line Graph"
             , Style Linespoints
             , Color Blue]
          [] (zip [1..] values)
    ```

Running the code produces a `plot1.dat` datafile as well as a visual graph from the selected terminal, as shown in the following screenshot:

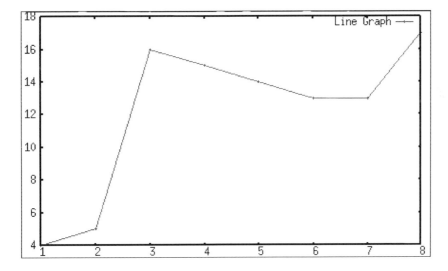

How it works...

The `EasyPlot` library translates all user-specified code into a language understood by gnuplot to graph the data.

See also

To use the Google Chart API instead of easy plot, refer to the *Plotting a line chart using Google's Chart API* recipe.

Displaying a scatter plot of two-dimensional points

This recipe covers a quick and easy way to visualize a list of 2D points as scattered dots within an image.

Getting ready

The library used in this recipe uses gnuplot to render the graph. We should first install gnuplot.

On Debian-based systems such as Ubuntu, we can install it using `apt-get` as follows:

```
$ sudo apt-get install gnuplot-x11
```

The official place to download gnuplot is from its main website, `http://www.gnuplot.info`.

After gnuplot is set up, install the `easyplot` Haskell library using cabal as follows:

```
$ cabal install easyplot
```

Also, install a helper CSV package as follows:

```
$ cabal install csv
```

Also, create two comma-separated files, `input1.csv` and `input2.csv`, which represent two separate sets of points as follows:

```
$ cat input1.csv
1,2
3,2
2,3
2,2
3,1
2,2
2,1


$ cat input2.csv
```

```
7,4
8,4
6,4
7,5
7,3
6,4
7,6
```

How to do it...

1. Import the relevant packages as follows:

   ```
   import Graphics.EasyPlot

   import Text.CSV
   ```

2. Define a helper function to convert a CSV record into a tuple of numbers as follows:

   ```
   convertRawCSV :: [[String]] -> [(Double, Double)]
   convertRawCSV csv = [ (read x, read y) | [x, y] <- csv ]
   ```

3. Read the two CSV files as follows:

   ```
   main = do
     csv1Raw <- parseCSVFromFile "input1.csv"
     csv2Raw <- parseCSVFromFile "input2.csv"

     let csv1 = case csv1Raw of
           Left err -> []
           Right csv -> convertRawCSV csv

     let csv2 = case csv2Raw of
           Left err -> []
           Right csv -> convertRawCSV csv
   ```

4. Plot both the datasets alongside each other on the same graph with different colors. Use the X11 terminal for the X Window System used by many Linux-based machines, as shown in the following lines of code. If running on Windows, the terminal to use is Windows. On Mac OS X, we should replace X11 with Aqua:

   ```
   plot X11 $ [ Data2D [Color Red] [] csv1
   , Data2D [Color Blue] [] csv2 ]
   ```

5. Run the program to display the graph shown in the following screenshot:

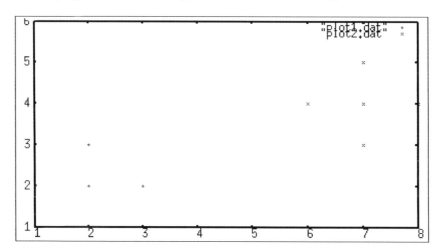

How it works...

The `EasyPlot` library translates all user-specified code into language understood by gnuplot to graph the data. The last argument to plot can take in a list of many datasets to graph.

See also

To visualize 3D points, refer to the *Interacting with points in a three-dimensional space* recipe.

Interacting with points in a three-dimensional space

When visualizing points in 3D space, it is often very useful to rotate, zoom, and pan the representation interactively. This recipe demonstrates how to plot data in 3D and interact with it in real time.

Getting ready

The library used in this recipe uses gnuplot to render the graph. We should first install gnuplot.

On Debian-based systems such as Ubuntu, we can install it using `apt-get` as follows:

```
$ sudo apt-get install gnuplot-x11
```

The official place to download gnuplot is from its main website available at `http://www.gnuplot.info`.

After gnuplot is set up, install the `easyplot` Haskell library using Cabal as follows:

`$ cabal install easyplot`

Also, install a helper CSV package as follows:

`$ cabal install csv`

Also, create two comma-separated files, `input1.csv` and `input2.csv`, which represent two separate sets of points as follows:

`$ cat input1.csv`

```
1,1,1
1,2,1
0,1,1
1,1,0
2,1,0
2,1,1
1,0,1
```

`$ cat input2.csv`

```
4,3,2
3,3,2
3,2,3
4,4,3
5,4,2
4,2,3
3,4,3
```

How to do it...

1. Import the relevant packages as follows:

    ```
    import Graphics.EasyPlot

    import Text.CSV
    ```

2. Define a helper function to convert a CSV record into a tuple of numbers as follows:

    ```
    convertRawCSV :: [[String]] -> [(Double, Double, Double)]

    convertRawCSV csv = [ (read x, read y, read z)
                        | [x, y, z] <- csv ]
    ```

3. Read the two CSV files as follows:

```
main = do
  csv1Raw <- parseCSVFromFile "input1.csv"
  csv2Raw <- parseCSVFromFile "input2.csv"

  let csv1 = case csv1Raw of
        Left err -> []
        Right csv -> convertRawCSV csv

  let csv2 = case csv2Raw of
        Left err -> []
        Right csv -> convertRawCSV csv
```

4. Plot the data using the `plot'` function, which leaves gnuplot running to allow for an `Interactive` option. Use the `X11` terminal for the X Window System used by many Linux-based machines, as shown in the following lines of code. If running on Windows, the terminal to use is `Windows`. On Mac OS X, we should replace `X11` with `Aqua`:

```
plot' [Interactive] X11 $
  [ Data3D [Color Red] [] csv1
  , Data3D [Color Blue] [] csv2]
```

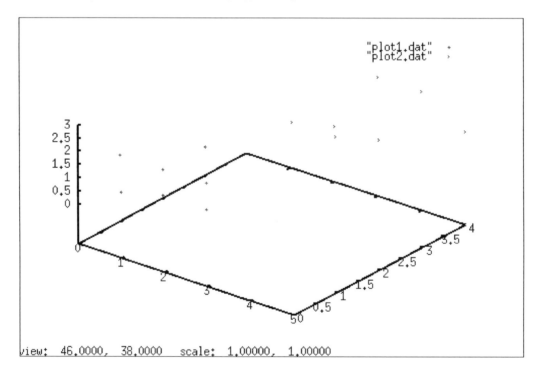

How it works...

The `EasyPlot` library translates all user-specified code into a language understood by gnuplot to graph the data. The last argument to plot can take in a list of many datasets to graph. By using the `plot'` function, we leave gnuplot running so that we can interact with the graph by rotating, zooming, and panning the three-dimensional visual.

See also

To visualize 2D points, refer to the *Displaying a scatter plot of two-dimensional points* recipe.

Visualizing a graph network

Graphical networks of edges and nodes can be difficult to debug or comprehend, and thus, visualization helps tremendously. In this recipe, we will convert a graph data structure into an image of nodes and edges.

Getting ready

To use Graphviz, the graph visualization library, we must first install it on the machine. The official website of Graphviz contains the download and installation instructions (http://www.graphviz.org). On Debian-based operating systems, Graphviz can be installed using `apt-get` as follows:

```
$ sudo apt-get install graphviz-dev graphviz
```

Next, we need to install the Graphviz Haskell bindings from Cabal as follows:

```
$ cabal install graphviz
```

How to do it...

1. Import the relevant libraries as follows:

   ```
   import Data.Text.Lazy (Text, empty, unpack)
   import Data.Graph.Inductive (Gr, mkGraph)
   import Data.GraphViz (GraphvizParams, nonClusteredParams,
   graphToDot)
   import Data.GraphViz.Printing (toDot, renderDot)
   ```

2. Create a graph defined by identifying the pairs of nodes that form edges using the following lines of code:

   ```
   myGraph :: Gr Text Text
   myGraph = mkGraph [ (1, empty)
                     , (2, empty)
   ```

```
                        ,  (3, empty) ]
            [ (1, 2,  empty)
            ,  (1, 3,  empty) ]
```

3. Set the graph to use the default parameters as follows:

    ```
    myParams :: GraphvizParams n Text Text ()  Text
    myParams = nonClusteredParams
    ```

4. Print out the dot representation of the graph to the terminal as follows:

    ```
    main :: IO ()
    main = putStr $ unpack $ renderDot $ toDot $
            graphToDot myParams myGraph
    ```

5. Run the code to obtain a dot representation of the graph, which can be saved in a separate file as follows:

    ```
    $ runhaskell Main.hs > graph.dot
    ```

6. Run the `dot` command provided by Graphviz on this file to render an image as follows:

    ```
    $ dot -Tpng graph.dot > graph.png
    ```

7. We can now view the resulting `graph.png` file shown in the following screenshot:

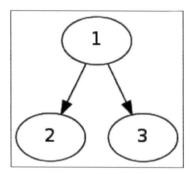

How it works...

The `graphToDot` function converts a graph into the DOT language for describing graphs. This is a text serialization for a graph, which can be read by the Graphviz `dot` command and converted into a viewable image.

There's more...

In this recipe, we used the `dot` command. The Graphviz website also describes other commands that convert DOT language text into viewable images:

dot - "hierarchical" or layered drawings of directed graphs. This is the default tool to use if edges have directionality.

neato - "spring model" layouts. This is the default tool to use if the graph is not too large (about 100 nodes) and you don't know anything else about it. Neato attempts to minimize a global energy function, which is equivalent to statistical multidimensional scaling.

fdp - "spring model" layouts similar to those of neato, but does this by reducing forces rather than working with energy.

sfdp - multiscale version of fdp for the layout of large graphs.

twopi - radial layouts, after Graham Wills 97. Nodes are placed on concentric circles depending their distance from a given root node.

circo - circular layout, after Six and Tollis 99, Kauffman and Wiese 02. This is suitable for certain diagrams of multiple cyclic structures, such as certain telecommunications networks.

See also

To further change the look and feel of a graph, refer to the *Customizing the looks of a graph network diagram* recipe.

Customizing the looks of a graph network diagram

To better present the data, we will cover how to customize the design of a graphical network diagram.

Getting ready

To use Graphviz, the graph visualization library, we must first install it on the machine. The official website of Graphviz contains the download and installation instructions available at `http://www.graphviz.org`. On Debian-based operating systems, Graphviz can be installed using `apt-get` as follows:

```
$ sudo apt-get install graphviz-dev graphviz
```

Next, we need to install the Graphviz Haskell bindings from Cabal as follows:

```
$ cabal install graphviz
```

How to do it...

1. Import the relevant functions and libraries to customize a Graphviz graph as follows:

```
import Data.Text.Lazy (Text, pack, unpack)
import Data.Graph.Inductive (Gr, mkGraph)
import Data.GraphViz (
  GraphvizParams(..),
  GlobalAttributes(
    GraphAttrs,
    NodeAttrs,
    EdgeAttrs
    ),
  X11Color(Blue, Orange, White),
  nonClusteredParams,
  globalAttributes,
  fmtNode,
  fmtEdge,
  graphToDot
  )
import Data.GraphViz.Printing (toDot, renderDot)
import Data.GraphViz.Attributes.Complete
```

2. Define our custom graph by first specifying all the nodes, and then specifying which pairs of nodes form edges, as shown in the following code snippet:

```
myGraph :: Gr Text Text
myGraph = mkGraph [ (1, pack "Haskell")
                  , (2, pack "Data Analysis")
                  , (3, pack "Haskell Data Analysis")
                  , (4, pack "Profit!")]
          [ (1, 3, pack "learn")
          , (2, 3, pack "learn")
          , (3, 4, pack "???")]
```

3. Define our own custom graph parameters as follows:

```
myParams :: GraphvizParams n Text Text () Text
myParams = nonClusteredParams {
```

4. Let the graphing engine know that we want the edges to be directed arrows as follows:

```
isDirected       = True
```

5. Set our own global attributes for a graph, node, and edge appearance as follows:

```
, globalAttributes = [myGraphAttrs, myNodeAttrs,
  myEdgeAttrs]
```

6. Format nodes in our own way as follows:

```
, fmtNode           = myFN
```

7. Format edges in our own way as follows:

```
, fmtEdge           = myFE
}
```

8. Define the customizations as shown in the following code snippet:

```
where myGraphAttrs =
              GraphAttrs [ RankDir FromLeft
                         , BgColor [toWColor Blue] ]
          myNodeAttrs =
              NodeAttrs [ Shape BoxShape
                        , FillColor [toWColor Orange]
                        , Style [SItem Filled []] ]
          myEdgeAttrs =
              EdgeAttrs [ Weight (Int 10)
                        , Color [toWColor White]
                        , FontColor (toColor White) ]
          myFN (n,l) = [(Label . StrLabel) l]
          myFE (f,t,l) = [(Label . StrLabel) l]
```

9. Print the DOT language representation of the graph to the terminal.

```
main :: IO ()
main = putStr $ unpack $ renderDot $ toDot $ graphToDot myParams
myGraph
```

10. Run the code to obtain a dot representation of the graph, which can be saved in a separate file as follows:

```
$ runhaskell Main.hs > graph.dot
```

11. Run the dot command provided by Graphviz on this file to render an image as follows:

```
$ dot -Tpng graph.dot > graph.png
```

We can now view the resulting `graph.png` file, as shown in the following screenshot:

How it works...

The `graphToDot` function converts a graph into the DOT language to describe graphs. This is a text serialization for a graph that can be read by the Graphviz `dot` command and converted into a viewable image.

There's more...

Every possible customization option for the graph, nodes, and edges can be found on the `Data.GraphViz.Attributes.Complete` package documentation available at http://hackage.haskell.org/package/graphviz-2999.12.0.4/docs/Data-GraphViz-Attributes-Complete.html.

Rendering a bar graph in JavaScript using D3.js

We will use the portable JavaScript library called `D3.js` to draw a bar graph. This allows us to easily create a web page that contains a graph from the Haskell code.

Getting ready

An Internet connection is necessary for the setup.

Install the `d3js` Haskell library as follows:

```
$ cabal install d3js
```

Create a website template to hold the generated JavaScript code as follows:

```
$ cat index.html
```

The JavaScript code will be as follows:

```
<html>
  <head>
    <title>Chart</title>
  </head>
  <body>
    <div id='myChart'></div>
    <script charset='utf-8' src='http://d3js.org/d3.v3.min.js'></
script>
    <script charset='utf-8' src='generated.js'></script>
  </body>
</html>
```

How to do it...

1. Import the relevant packages as follows:

   ```
   import qualified Data.Text as T
   import qualified Data.Text.IO as TIO
   import D3JS
   ```

2. Create a bar chart using the `bars` function. Feed the specified values and number of bars to draw, as shown in the following code snippet:

   ```
   myChart nums numBars = do
     let dim = (300, 300)
     elem <- box (T.pack "#myChart") dim
     bars numBars 300 (Data1D nums) elem
     addFrame (300, 300) (250, 250) elem
   ```

3. Define the values and number of bars to draw as follows:

   ```
   main = do
     let nums = [10, 40, 100, 50, 55, 156, 80, 74, 40, 10]
     let numBars = 5
   ```

4. Use the `reify` function to generate the JavaScript D3.js text out of the data. Write the JavaScript to a file named `generated.js` as follows:

   ```
   let js = reify $ myChart nums numBars
   TIO.writeFile "generated.js" js
   ```

5. With both the `index.html` file and the `generated.js` file existing alongside each other, we can open the `index.html` web page using a browser that supports JavaScript, and see the resulting graph shown as follows:

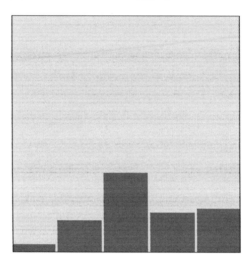

How it works...

The `D3.js` library is a JavaScript library used for creating elegant visuals and graphs. We use our browser to run the JavaScript code, and it also acts as our graph-rendering engine.

See also

For another use of `D3.js`, refer to the *Rendering a scatter plot in JavaScript using D3.js* recipe.

Rendering a scatter plot in JavaScript using D3.js

We will use the portable JavaScript library called `D3.js` to draw a scatter plot. This allows us to easily create a web page that contains a graph from the Haskell code.

Getting ready

An Internet connection is necessary to perform this setup.

Install the `d3js` Haskell library as follows:

```
$ cabal install d3js
```

Create a website template to hold the generated JavaScript code as follows:

```
$ cat index.html
```

The JavaScript code will be as follows:

```
<html>
  <head>
    <title>Chart</title>
  </head>
  <body>
    <div id='myChart'></div>
    <script charset='utf-8' src='http://d3js.org/d3.v3.min.js'></
script>
    <script charset='utf-8' src='generated.js'></script>
  </body>
</html>
```

How to do it...

1. Import the relevant libraries as follows:

   ```
   import D3JS
   import qualified Data.Text as T
   import qualified Data.Text.IO as TIO
   ```

2. Define the scatter plot and feed in the list of points as follows:

   ```
   myPlot points = do
     let dim = (300, 300)
     elem <- box (T.pack "#myChart") dim
     scatter (Data2D points) elem
     addFrame (300, 300) (250, 250) elem
   ```

3. Define a list of points to plot as follows:

   ```
   main = do
     let points = [(1,2), (5,10), (139,138), (140,150)]
   ```

4. Use the `reify` function to generate the JavaScript `D3.js` text out of the data. Write the JavaScript to a file named `generated.js` as follows:

   ```
   let js = reify $ myPlot points
   TIO.writeFile "generated.js" js
   ```

5. With both the `index.html` and `generated.js` files existing alongside each other, we can open the `index.html` web page using a browser that supports JavaScript, and see the resulting graph shown as follows:

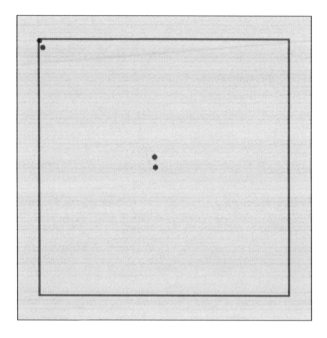

How it works...

The `graphToDot` function converts a graph into the DOT language to describe graphs. This is a text serialization for a graph, which can be read by the Graphviz `dot` command and be converted into a viewable image.

See also

For another use of `D3.js`, refer to the *Rendering a bar graph in JavaScript using D3.js* recipe.

Diagramming a path from a list of vectors

In this recipe, we will use the `diagrams` package to draw a path from driving directions. We simply categorize all possible travel headings into eight cardinal directions with an associated distance. We use directions provided by Google Maps in the following screenshot and reconstruct the directions from a text file:

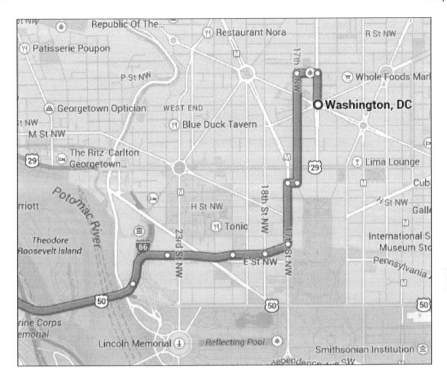

Getting ready

Install the `diagrams` library as follows:

```
$ cabal install diagrams
```

Create a text file called `input.txt` that contains one of the eight cardinal directions followed by the distance, with each step separated by a new line:

```
$ cat input.txt
```

```
N 0.2

W 0.1

S 0.6

W 0.05

S 0.3

SW 0.1

SW 0.2

SW 0.3

S 0.3
```

How to do it...

1. Import the relevant libraries as follows:

```
{-# LANGUAGE NoMonomorphismRestriction #-}
import Diagrams.Prelude
import Diagrams.Backend.SVG.CmdLine (mainWith, B)
```

2. Draw a line-connected path from a list of vectors as follows:

```
drawPath :: [(Double, Double)] -> Diagram B R2
drawPath vectors = fromOffsets . map r2 $ vectors
```

3. Read a list of directions, represent it as a list of vectors, and draw the path as follows:

```
main = do
  rawInput <- readFile "input.txt"
  let vs = [ makeVector dir (read dist)
           | [dir, dist] <- map words (lines rawInput)]
  print vs
  mainWith $ drawPath vs
```

4. Define a helper function to create a vector out of a direction and its corresponding distance as follows:

```
makeVector :: String -> Double -> (Double, Double)
makeVector "N" dist = (0, dist)
makeVector "NE" dist = (dist / sqrt 2, dist / sqrt 2)
makeVector "E" dist = (dist, 0)
makeVector "SE" dist = (dist / sqrt 2, -dist / sqrt 2)
makeVector "S" dist = (0, -dist)
makeVector "SW" dist = (-dist / sqrt 2, -dist / sqrt 2)
makeVector "W" dist = (-dist, 0)
makeVector "NW" dist = (-dist / sqrt 2, dist / sqrt 2)
makeVector _ _ = (0, 0)
```

5. Compile the code and run it as follows:

```
$ ghc --make Main.hs
$ ./Main -o output.svg -w 400
```

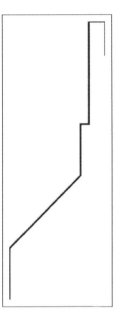

How it works...

The `mainWith` functions takes in a `Diagram` type and generates the corresponding image file when invoked in the terminal. We obtain the `Diagram` from our `drawPath` function, which glues together vectors by their offsets.

12
Exporting and Presenting

In this chapter, will cover how to export results and nicely present them through the following recipes:

- ► Exporting data to a CSV file
- ► Exporting data as JSON
- ► Using SQLite to store data
- ► Saving data to a MongoDB database
- ► Presenting results in an HTML web page
- ► Creating a LaTeX table to display results
- ► Personalizing messages using a text template
- ► Exporting matrix values to a file

Introduction

After gathering, cleaning, representing, and analyzing, the last important step in data analysis is to export and present the data in a usable format. The recipes in this chapter will cover how to save a data structure on disk for later use by other programs. Moreover, we will show how to present the data elegantly with Haskell.

Exporting data to a CSV file

Sometimes, it's more convenient to view data using a spreadsheet program such as LibreOffice, Microsoft Office Excel, or Apple Numbers. A standard way to export and import simple spreadsheet tables is through **Comma Separated Values** (**CSVs**).

In this recipe, we will use the `cassava` package to easily encode a CSV file out of a data structure.

Getting ready

Install the Cassava CSV package from cabal, using the following command line:

```
$ cabal install cassava
```

How to do it...

1. Import the relevant packages using the following code:
    ```
    import Data.Csv
    import qualified Data.ByteString.Lazy as BSL
    ```

2. Define an association list of data that will be exported as CSV. For this recipe, we will pair letters and numbers together, as shown in the following code:

```
myData :: [(Char, Int)]
myData = zip ['A'..'Z'] [1..]
```

3. Run the encode function to convert the data structure into a lazy ByteString CSV representation, as shown in the following code:

```
main = BSL.writeFile "letters.csv" $ encode myData
```

How it works...

A CSV file is simply a list of records. The encode function in the Cassava library takes a list of items that implement the ToRecord typeclass.

In this recipe, we can see that tuples of size 2 such as ('A', 1) are valid arguments to the encode function. By default, tuples of size 2 to 7 are supported along with lists of arbitrary sizes. Each element of the tuple or list must implement the ToField typeclass, which most built-in primitive data types support by default. More details on the package can be found at https://hackage.haskell.org/package/cassava.

There's more...

In order to easily convert a data type into CSV, we can implement the ToRecord typeclass.

For example, the Cassava documentation shows the following example of converting a Person data type into a CSV record:

```
data Person = Person { name :: Text, age :: Int }

instance ToRecord Person where
    toRecord (Person name age) = record [
        toField name, toField age]
```

See also

For JSON instead, refer to the following *Exporting data as JSON* recipe.

Exporting data as JSON

A convenient way to store data that may not adhere to a strict schema is through JSON. To accomplish this, we will use a painless JSON library called **Yocto**. It sacrifices performance for readability and small size.

In this recipe, we will export a list of points as JSON.

Getting ready

Install the Yocto JSON encoder and decoder from cabal using the following command:

```
$ cabal install yocto
```

How to do it...

Start by creating a new file, which we call `Main.hs` and perform the following steps:

1. Import the relevant data structures, as shown in the following code:

    ```
    import Text.JSON.Yocto
    import qualified Data.Map as M
    ```

2. Define a data structure for 2D points:

    ```
    data Point = Point Rational Rational
    ```

3. Convert a `Point` data type into a JSON object, as shown in the following code:

    ```
    pointObject (Point x y) =
       Object $ M.fromList [ ("x", Number x)
                           , ("y", Number y)]
    ```

4. Create the points and construct a JSON array out of them:

    ```
    main = do
       let points = [ Point 1 1
                    , Point 3 5
                    , Point (-3) 2]
       let pointsArray = Array $ map pointObject points
    ```

5. Write the JSON array to a file, as shown in the following code:

    ```
       writeFile "points.json" $ encode pointsArray
    ```

6. When running the code, we will find the `points.json` file created, as seen in the following code:

    ```
    $ runhaskell Main.hs
    $ cat points.json
    [{"x":1,"y":1}, {"x":3,"y":5}, {"x":-3,"y":2}]
    ```

There's more...

For a more efficient JSON encoder, see the Aeson package located at
`http://hackage.haskell.org/package/aeson`.

See also

To export data to CSV, refer to the previous recipe titled *Exporting data to a CSV file.*

Using SQLite to store data

SQLite is one of the most popular databases for compactly storing structured data. We will use the SQL binding for Haskell to store a list of strings.

Getting Ready

We must first install the SQLite3 database on our system. On Debian-based systems, we can issue the following installation command:

```
$ sudo apt-get install sqlite3
```

Install the SQLite package from cabal, as shown in the following command:

```
$ cabal install sqlite-simple
```

Create an initial database called test.db that sets up the schema. In this recipe, we will only be storing integers with strings as follows:

```
$ sqlite3 test.db "CREATE TABLE test (id INTEGER PRIMARY KEY, str text);"
```

How to do it...

1. Import the relevant libraries, as shown in the following code:

   ```
   {-# LANGUAGE OverloadedStrings #-}
   import Control.Applicative
   import Database.SQLite.Simple
   import Database.SQLite.Simple.FromRow
   ```

2. Create a FromRow typeclass implementation for TestField, the data type we will be storing, as shown in the following code:

   ```
   data TestField = TestField Int String deriving (Show)
   instance FromRow TestField where
      fromRow = TestField <$> field <*> field
   ```

3. Create a helper function to retrieve everything form the database just for debugging purposes, as shown in the following code:

   ```
   getDB :: Connection -> IO [TestField]

   getDB conn = query_ conn "SELECT * from test"
   ```

4. Create a helper function to insert a string into the database, as shown in the following code:

```
insertToDB :: Connection -> String -> IO ()
insertToDB conn item =
  execute conn
  "INSERT INTO test (str) VALUES (?)"
  (Only item)
```

5. Connect to the database, as shown in the following code:

```
main :: IO ()

main = withConnection "test.db" dbActions
```

6. Set up the string data we want to insert, as shown in the following code:

```
dbActions :: Connection -> IO ()

dbActions conn = do
  let dataItems = ["A", "B", "C"]
```

7. Insert each of the elements to the database, as shown in the following code:

```
  mapM_ (insertToDB conn) dataItems
```

8. Print out the database, using the following code:

```
  r <- getDB conn
  mapM_ print r
```

9. We can verify that the database contains the newly inserted data by evoking the following command:

```
$ sqlite3 test.db "SELECT * FROM test"


1|A
2|C
3|D
```

See also

For another type of database, refer to the following *Saving data to a MongoDB database* recipe.

Saving data to a MongoDB database

MongoDB can very naturally store unstructured data using the JSON syntax. In this recipe, we will store a list of people to MongoDB.

Getting ready

We must first install MongoDB on our machine. The installation files can be downloaded from `http://www.mongodb.org`.

We need to make a directory for the database using the following command:

```
$ mkdir ~/db
```

Finally, start the MongoDB daemon on that directory using the following command:

```
$ mongod -dbpath ~/db
```

Install the MongoDB package from cabal using the following command:

```
$ cabal install mongoDB
```

How to do it...

Create a new file called `Main.hs` and perform the following steps:

1. Import the libraries as follows:

   ```
   {-# LANGUAGE OverloadedStrings, ExtendedDefaultRules #-}
   import Database.MongoDB
   import Control.Monad.Trans (liftIO)
   ```

2. Define a data type for the names of people as follows:

   ```
   data Person = Person { first :: String
                        , last :: String }
   ```

3. Set up a couple of data items we wish to store as follows:

   ```
   myData :: [Person]
   myData = [ Person "Mercury" "Merci"
            , Person "Sylvester" "Smith"]
   ```

4. Connect to the MongoDB instance and store all the data as follows:

   ```
   main = do
       pipe <- runIOE $ connect (host "127.0.0.1")
       e <- access pipe master "test" (store myData)
       close pipe
       print e
   ```

5. Convert the `Person` data type into the proper MongoDB type as follows:

```
store vals = insertMany "people" mongoList
  where mongoList = map
                    (\(Person f l) ->
                      ["first" =: f, "last" =: l])
                    vals
```

6. We must ensure that a MongoDB daemon is running. If not, we can create a process that listens to the directory of our choice using the following command:

```
$ mongod --dbpath ~/db
```

7. After running the code, we can double-check if the operation was successful by navigating to MongoDB using the following commands:

```
$ runhaskell Main.hs
```

```
$ mongo
```

```
>  db.people.find()
```

```
{ "_id" : ObjectId("536d2b13f8712126e6000000"), "first" :
  "Mercury", "last" : "Merci" }
```

```
{ "_id" : ObjectId("536d2b13f8712126e6000001"), "first" :
  "Sylvester", "last" : "Smith" }
```

See also

For SQL usage, refer to the previous *Using SQLite to store data* recipe.

Presenting results in an HTML web page

Sharing data online is one of the quickest ways to reach a broad audience. However, typing data into HTML directly can be time consuming. This recipe will generate a web page using the Blaze Haskell library to present data results. For more documentation and tutorials, visit the project webpage at `http://jaspervdj.be/blaze/`.

Getting ready

Install the Blaze package from cabal using the following command:

```
$ cabal install blaze-html
```

How to do it...

In a new file called `Main.hs`, perform the following steps:

1. Import all the necessary libraries as follows:

    ```
    {-# LANGUAGE OverloadedStrings #-}

    import Control.Monad (forM_)
    import Text.Blaze.Html5
    import qualified Text.Blaze.Html5 as H
    import Text.Blaze.Html.Renderer.Utf8 (renderHtml)
    import qualified Data.ByteString.Lazy as BSL
    ```

2. Convert the list of string into an HTML unordered list as shown in the following code snippet:

    ```
    dataInList :: Html -> [String] -> Html
    dataInList label items = docTypeHtml $ do
      H.head $ do
        H.title "Generating HTML from data"
      body $ do
        p label
        ul $ mapM_ (li . toHtml) items
    ```

3. Create a list of strings to render as an HTML web page as follows:

    ```
    main = do
      let movies = [ "2001: A Space Odyssey"
                   , "Watchmen"
                   , "GoldenEye" ]
      let html = renderHtml $ dataInList "list of movies" movies
      BSL.writeFile "index.html" $ html
    ```

4. Run the code to generate the HTML file to open using a browser as follows:

    $ runhaskell Main.hs

    The output will be as follows:

    list of movies

    - 2001: A Space Odyssey
    - Watchmen
    - GoldenEye

See also

To present data as a LaTeX document and consequently as a PDF, refer to the following *Creating a LaTeX table to display results* recipe.

Creating a LaTeX table to display results

This recipe will create a table in LaTeX programmatically to facilitate document creation. We can create a PDF out of the LaTeX code and share it as we please.

Getting Ready

Install `HaTeX`, the Haskell LaTeX library, from cabal:

```
$ cabal install LaTeX
```

How to do it...

Create a file named `Main.hs` and follow these steps:

1. Import the libraries as follows:

   ```
   {-# LANGUAGE OverloadedStrings #-}
   import Text.LaTeX
   import Text.LaTeX.Base.Class
   import Text.LaTeX.Base.Syntax
   import qualified Data.Map as M
   ```

2. Save a LaTeX file with our specifications as follows:

   ```
   main :: IO ()
   main = execLaTeXT myDoc >>= renderFile "output.tex"
   ```

3. Define the document, which is split up into a preamble and a body, as follows:

   ```
   myDoc :: Monad m => LaTeXT_ m

   myDoc = do
     thePreamble
     document theBody
   ```

4. The preamble contains author data, title, and formatting options, among other things, as presented in the following code:

```
thePreamble :: Monad m => LaTeXT_ m

thePreamble = do
  documentclass [] article
  author "Dr. Databender"
  title "Data Analyst"
```

5. Define the list of data we would like to convert into a LaTeX table as follows:

```
myData :: [(Int,Int)]

myData = [ (1, 50)
         , (2, 100)
         , (3, 150)]
```

6. Define the body as follows:

```
theBody :: Monad m => LaTeXT_ m

theBody = do
```

7. Set up the title and section, and construct the table as shown in the following code snippet:

```
  maketitle
  section "Fancy Data Table"
  bigskip
  center $ underline $ textbf "Table of Points"
  center $ tabular Nothing [RightColumn, VerticalLine,
    LeftColumn] $ do
    textbf "Time" & textbf "Cost"
    lnbk
    hline
    mapM_ (\(t, c) -> do texy t & texy c; lnbk) myData
```

8. After running the code using the following commands, we can obtain the PDF and view it:

$ runhaskell Main.hs

$ pdflatex output.tex

The output will be as follows:

Data Analyst

Dr. Databender

May 10, 2014

1   Fancy Data Table

Table of Points

Time	Cost
1	50
2	100
3	150

See also

To construct a web page instead, refer to the previous recipe titled *Presenting results in an HTML web page*.

Personalizing messages using a text template

Sometimes we have a large list of usernames and relating data and we wish to individually send each person a message. This recipe will create a text template that will be filled out from the data.

Getting ready

Install the `template` library using cabal:

```
$ cabal install template
```

How to do it...

Perform the following steps in a new file called `Main.hs`:

1. Import the libraries as follows:

```
{-# LANGUAGE OverloadedStrings #-}
```

```
import qualified Data.ByteString.Lazy as S
```

```
import qualified Data.Text as T
import qualified Data.Text.IO as TIO
import qualified Data.Text.Lazy.Encoding as E
import qualified Data.ByteString as BS
import Data.Text.Lazy (toStrict)
import Data.Text.Template
```

2. Define the data we are dealing with as follows:

```
myData = [ [ ("name", "Databender"), ("title", "Dr.") ],
           [ ("name", "Paragon"), ("title", "Master") ],
           [ ("name", "Marisa"), ("title", "Madam") ] ]
```

3. Define the template for the data as follows:

```
myTemplate = template "Hello $title $name!"
```

4. Create a helper function to convert data items to a template as follows:

```
context :: [(T.Text, T.Text)] -> Context
context assocs x = maybe err id . lookup x $ assocs
   where err = error $ "Could not find key: " ++ T.unpack x
```

5. Match each data item to the template and print everything out to a text file, as shown in the following code snippet:

```
main :: IO ()
main = do
  let res = map (\d -> toStrict (
                   render myTemplate (context d) )) myData
    TIO.writeFile "messages.txt" $ T.unlines res
```

6. Run the code to see the resulting file:

```
$ runhaskell Main.hs


$ cat messages.txt


Hello Dr. Databender!
Hello Master Paragon!
Hello Madam Marisa!
```

Exporting matrix values to a file

In data analysis and machine learning, matrices are a popular data structure that often need to be exported and imported into the program. In this recipe, we will export a sample matrix using the Repa I/O library.

Getting ready

Install the `repa-io` library using cabal as follows:

```
$ cabal install repa-io
```

How to do it...

Create a new file, which we name `Main.hs`, and insert the code explained in the following steps:

1. Import the relevant libraries as follows:

   ```
   import Data.Array.Repa.IO.Matrix
   import Data.Array.Repa
   ```

2. Define a 4 x 3 matrix as follows:

   ```
   x :: Array U DIM2 Int
   x = fromListUnboxed (Z :. (4::Int) :. (3::Int))
     [ 1, 2, 9, 10
     , 4, 3, 8, 11
     , 5, 6, 7, 12 ]
   ```

3. Write the matrix to a file as follows:

   ```
   main = writeMatrixToTextFile "output.dat" x
   ```

How it works...

The matrix is represented simply as a list of its elements in row-major order. The first two lines of the file define the type of data and the dimensions.

There's more...

To read a matrix back from this file, we can use the `readMatrixFromTextFile` function to retrieve the two-dimensional matrix. More documentation about this package is available at `https://hackage.haskell.org/package/repa-io`.

Index

Thank you for buying
Haskell Data Analysis Cookbook

About Packt Publishing

Packt, pronounced 'packed', published its first book "*Mastering phpMyAdmin for Effective MySQL Management*" in April 2004 and subsequently continued to specialize in publishing highly focused books on specific technologies and solutions.

Our books and publications share the experiences of your fellow IT professionals in adapting and customizing today's systems, applications, and frameworks. Our solution based books give you the knowledge and power to customize the software and technologies you're using to get the job done. Packt books are more specific and less general than the IT books you have seen in the past. Our unique business model allows us to bring you more focused information, giving you more of what you need to know, and less of what you don't.

Packt is a modern, yet unique publishing company, which focuses on producing quality, cutting-edge books for communities of developers, administrators, and newbies alike. For more information, please visit our website: www.packtpub.com.

About Packt Open Source

In 2010, Packt launched two new brands, Packt Open Source and Packt Enterprise, in order to continue its focus on specialization. This book is part of the Packt Open Source brand, home to books published on software built around Open Source licenses, and offering information to anybody from advanced developers to budding web designers. The Open Source brand also runs Packt's Open Source Royalty Scheme, by which Packt gives a royalty to each Open Source project about whose software a book is sold.

Writing for Packt

We welcome all inquiries from people who are interested in authoring. Book proposals should be sent to author@packtpub.com. If your book idea is still at an early stage and you would like to discuss it first before writing a formal book proposal, contact us; one of our commissioning editors will get in touch with you.

We're not just looking for published authors; if you have strong technical skills but no writing experience, our experienced editors can help you develop a writing career, or simply get some additional reward for your expertise.

Haskell Financial Data Modeling and Predictive Analytics

ISBN: 978-1-78216-943-7   Paperback: 112 pages

Get an in-depth analysis of financial time series from the perspective of a functional programmer

1. Understand the foundations of financial stochastic processes.

2. Build robust models quickly and efficiently.

3. Tackle the complexity of parallel programming.

Clojure Data Analysis Cookbook

ISBN: 978-1-78216-264-3   Paperback: 342 pages

Over 110 recipes to help you dive into the world of practical data analysis using Clojure

1. Get a handle on the torrent of data the modern Internet has created.

2. Recipes for every stage from collection to analysis.

3. A practical approach to analyzing data to help you make informed decisions.

Please check **www.PacktPub.com** for information on our titles

Made in the USA
Lexington, KY
19 July 2014